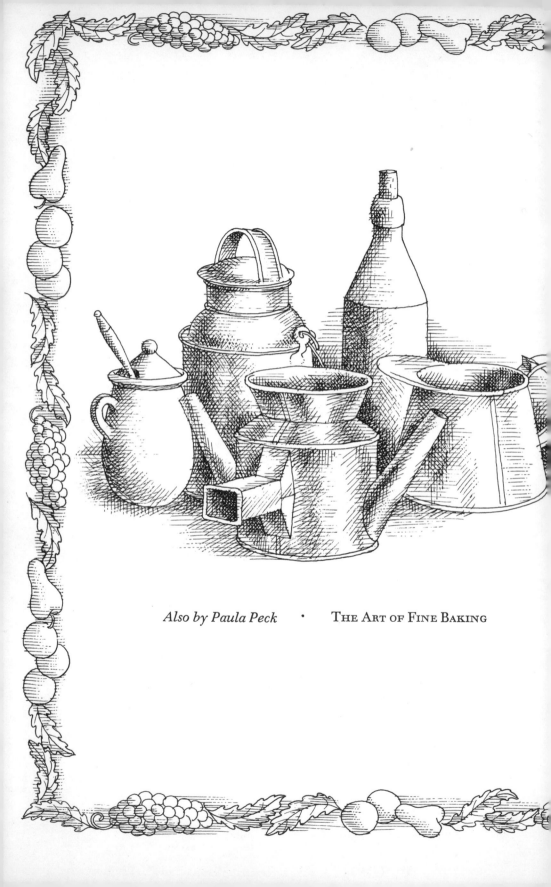

Also by Paula Peck • The Art of Fine Baking

Paula Peck's

ART OF GOOD COOKING

Illustrations by Mel Klapholz

Simon and Schuster • New York

PUBLISHED BY SIMON AND SCHUSTER
ROCKEFELLER CENTER, 630 FIFTH AVENUE
NEW YORK, NEW YORK 10020

DESIGNED BY EVE METZ
MANUFACTURED IN THE UNITED STATES OF AMERICA

For my Family
and for Ann

Contents

Paula Peck's

ART OF GOOD COOKING

Introduction

WHY WRITE STILL ANOTHER COOKBOOK, I asked myself, when there are so many available? I must confess one motive was selfish—I wanted to have between two covers my own favorite recipes—collected, or created, or adapted over the years. But more important, I finally concluded that I had material sufficiently original to warrant a book such as this one.

The encouraging and cordial letters I have received since my earlier book, *The Art of Fine Baking*, was published have made me realize there is an interest in my unconventional approach to cooking. My belief is that tradition should not hamper us if we find a better way of doing things. Thus I have discovered many an unorthodox cooking procedure through experiment.

Perhaps I should be grateful that I had no formal training in cooking as I was growing up. My mother is a good plain cook, but I had no interest in cooking until, when I was twenty years old, I went to a Quaker work camp in a Mexican village. At the work camp, each member of the group had to take a turn in the kitchen at least one day a week, cooking for as many as twenty. We also were required to plan the menu and do the marketing on cooking day. We had a strict budget. Despite the fact that we had no running water in the kitchen, that fruits and vegetables had to be scrubbed and specially treated, that the meats available were very limited, I found myself enjoying the marketing and the cooking. We had one cookbook, but it didn't occur to me to use it. I resorted to my imagination instead.

I was a failure in one respect: I always had great difficulty staying within the limits of the budget—a problem I still have today. However, members of the group enjoyed the meals I cooked, and I thoroughly enjoyed cooking.

Soon after I returned home from Mexico I married a man who was especially fond of foreign food. He had been eating in restaurants of various nationalities for most of his adult life. It was not easy to persuade him to eat a meal at home, even once or twice a week. This was a problem for me because the cooking bug had bitten me and I wanted to spend long periods in the kitchen. I also wanted someone to eat what I had concocted.

The problem resolved itself when we had a baby and were no longer able to eat out regularly. To make it easier for my husband, I tried to reproduce at home the dishes which he enjoyed eating in foreign restaurants. His appreciation gave me encouragement. I began to read and to collect cookbooks. I started a recipe file of my own.

Luckily, I had some firsthand assistance. A weekly visitor to our home, Angèle, was a close friend of my husband. She had learned to cook from her husband, Lucien Pascal, an expert French chef who had worked at Delmonico's and several other top French restaurants in New York. I also had the fortune to have as my next-door neighbor (and babysitter), Mrs. Sokolowski, an excellent baker and cook, who had once managed a fine hotel in Poland. With my husband's encouragement, I enrolled in a cooking course given by James Beard. At the end of the course, he asked me to work as his assistant, and eventually I taught the baking classes at his school. In this capacity I learned much, because a teacher is her own best pupil.

I have a philosophy about the kitchen. A kitchen is beautiful when the utensils and tools show. I like to see an old pitcher filled with wooden spoons of every variety standing near my stove. I always keep a handsome basket of onions conveniently placed near the sink and wooden chopping block. I do not favor the slick kind of kitchen where there is no trace of the culinary processes. I buy garlic by the string, as it is sold in the garlic market of Marseille, and hang it from the wall where it can be not only useful but ornamental.

One of the pleasures of cooking is collecting imaginative equipment. For example, some of the apple peelers which were produced about the time of the Civil War are still excellent mechanical devices for peeling apples. Old cherry pitters, nutmeg graters, cabbage shredders and the like also are intriguing and useful.

All kitchen equipment should be solid, and heavy-duty. Flimsy pots and pans are impractical. Even steel pots with copper bottoms are unserviceable because they heat too fast. Black iron skillets are best for sautéing and frying. For stewing and simmering, enameled iron or heavy cast aluminum is best. Saucepans and stewing pots should have heavy, tightly fitting lids. Knives should be sharp, and made of carbon, not stainless, steel. They should be kept in a knife rack which protects the blades.

Generally, stirring in pots should be done with wooden spoons. However, when a liquid is blended into a flour-fat mixture, it is best to use a wire whisk, one made, preferably, of fine wire. This avoids a lumpy sauce. So, such whisks are indispensable for creating sauces.

Regarding a stove, the best is the type made primarily for restaurants. There are several brands. They all are good and relatively inexpensive, compared to stoves designed for the home. Some people object to restaurant-type stoves because they are either black enamel or stainless steel, because the parts are heavy and because the stove is not so easily taken apart for cleaning as stoves made for home use.

As to the finish, I admit that a stainless steel stove presents a slight problem in maintenance. However, the black stove is, in my opinion, quite handsome: I have lived with one for a number of years. It has a shelf on top which can be used for raising yeast dough, or for heating plates for dinner. It is such an excellent stove that I don't mind the little extra effort involved in taking care of it.

If you are serious about cooking, you need a large, thick, wooden block for chopping vegetables, parsley and meats. The sort used by butchers is ideal; certainly it should not be a mere 12- or 14-inch block of wood.

Cabinets are a must, of course. However, they should be the background and not the entire kitchen. Don't be timid about displaying foods—a bowl of lemons or eggs, for example. Cabinets are useful because not everything used in the kitchen is pretty or interesting. But take advantage of the utensils and foods which are decorative and don't hide them in cupboards. Use your cupboards for storing staples that do not need refrigeration, as well as for ordinary pots and pans. Because I like to prepare and refrigerate a number of foods of long-range usefulness—such as homemade concentrate of beef and chicken—I find an extra refrigerator indispensable. I also have a 20-cubic-foot freezer, which I use for storing baked goods, nuts, small cuts of meat such as minute steaks, scaloppine of veal, meat bones for stock, and the like.

What about long-range shopping? To me the question is more—what to buy where? I do not do one big weekly shopping at a supermarket. Meat is the most important item on my shopping list, and I find the quality of the meat and poultry at my butcher's much superior to the pre-cut, packaged varieties obtainable elsewhere. It seems to me very worthwhile to spend additional money to get well treated, top quality meats, cut to order in exactly the amounts I require. Similarly, I buy fresh fish—never frozen—from the best fish store I know. Fresh fruits and vegetables are equally worth seeking out in shops that specialize in quality produce. For spices, herbs and special ingredients for foreign dishes, I enjoy the trips I make to the special sources listed on pages 15-16 and other little shops in foreign neighborhoods, which unfortunately do not ship.

We who live in big cities are lucky in the variety of unusual foods and ingredients we can find when we look for them. But the basic philosophy of seeking out quality and the unusual can be applied wherever you may live. Special ingredients can be ordered by mail, as can almost every type of food in these days of rapid transportation. The important thing is to be adventurous and to care about your ingredients. No magic wand of cooking techniques or exotic sauces can transform a poor cut of meat into something more than passable, if that. So if you are a serious cook, work with the best. It is the basis of the art of good cooking.

Shopping Sources

The companies listed here will ship mail orders to any part of the country. The author will be glad to receive information, in care of the publishers, about other mail order sources for unusual equipment or foods not easily available.

Equipment

The following shops specialize in fine kitchen utensils of every kind. Many items are imported: heavy enameled pots, beautiful terrines, fine knives, wire whisks, etc.

Bazar Français, *666 Avenue of the Americas, New York City.* Catalogue available.

The Bridge Company, *498 Third Avenue, New York City.* No catalogue.

La Cuisinière, *903 Madison Avenue, New York City.* Limited catalogue available.

Williams-Sonoma, *576 Sutton Street, San Francisco, California.* Limited catalogue available.

Ingredients

Casa Moneo, *218 West 14th Street, New York City.* No catalogue but price list to be available. All sorts of foods for Spanish and Mexican cookery: large cans of anchovies, chorizo, excellent chili powder, whole dried chilies, fine coffees, imported canned goods from Mexico and Spain.

Japanese Foodland, Inc., *2620 Broadway, New York City.* Price list available. Japanese and some Chinese specialties: abalone, wasabi powder, pickled and fresh ginger. Excellent Japanese soy sauce.

KASSOS BROTHERS, *570 Ninth Avenue, New York City.* No catalogue. Greek and Middle Eastern specialties: many varieties of olives, Feta cheese, excellent pickling spices, Greek pastas, many kinds of olive oil, salted anchovies, tarama, pine nuts, etc.

LEKVAR BY THE BARREL (formerly H. Roth and Son), *1577 First Avenue, New York City.* Catalogue available. All sorts of Hungarian and some German specialties: excellent Hungarian paprika; many baking specialties, including unusual utensils imported from Europe; spices, etc.

MANGANARO FOODS INC., *488 Ninth Avenue, New York City.* Catalogue available. All sorts of Italian specialty foods, salted capers.

TRINACRIA IMPORTING COMPANY, *415 Third Avenue, New York City.* No catalogue. A most unusual shop which specializes in all sorts of Italian and Near and Middle Eastern foods, nuts, as well as all of the spices and ingredients needed for cooking East Indian and many other nationality foods. Many beautiful kitchen utensils, as well as foods.

MARYLAND GOURMET MART, INC., *414 Amsterdam Avenue, New York City.* Catalogue available. A very special type of butcher who will ship to any place in the United States. The veal is superb, so is the beef and aged mutton. Actually, all the meats are excellent. In conjunction with the butcher shop is a gourmet shop which stocks many imported specialties, as well as spices, from all over the world.

SEARS ROEBUCK. Large pressure-canners, canning supplies. Catalogue available (see your classified telephone directory).

SOME PERSONAL VIEWS ON INGREDIENTS

Herbs

HERBS IN COOKING

To retain the full flavor of herbs in a cooked dish, add fresh herbs ½ hour before completion of cooking, dried herbs during the last 10 minutes. Even garlic should be added only in the last ½ hour of cooking. The only exceptions to this rule are chili powder and paprika, which do not lose their flavors in long cooking.

PARSLEY

Parsley is the "common" herb—and truly indispensable in cooking. There are two varieties. One is curly-leaved and very decorative. The other has a flat leaf, has more flavor and resembles cilantro—in appearance only. The flat-leaved variety is known as Italian parsley and usually can be obtained from Italian greengrocers.

Never try to substitute dried parsley for fresh: the dry simply has no flavor.

Recipes hardly ever call for a sprinkling or even a tablespoonful of parsley. Become accustomed to using parsley by the handful.

CILANTRO

Cilantro, an herb with a Spanish name (pronounced see-lan-tro), is also known as Chinese parsley. It is really the leaves of the herb coriander. It can be grown from seed, or purchased in either Chinese or Latin American markets. It is very pungent and there is no substitute for it. Coriander seeds themselves have an entirely different flavor than the plant.

Spices

CURRY POWDER

This volume certainly is not being subsidized by any food company. However, curry powders vary a great deal—some of them are even bitter. I venture to recommend the one made by Crosse and Blackwell.

GINGER

Dry ginger in small cans has practically no relation to the fresh ginger root which can be purchased in Oriental food stores. If you are not located near such a store, you might order pickled ginger (it is a purpley red) which comes in jars and keeps in the refrigerator indefinitely. It has a true fresh ginger flavor.

To use fresh or pickled ginger, grate it on a fine grater (also available in Oriental food stores at nominal prices).

Use the little cans of dry, powdered ginger in cakes and cookies, but never in Oriental dishes.

PAPRIKA

Full-flavored paprika does not come in tiny cans but is sold in bulk. It may be ordered by mail (see Shopping Sources).

Paprika comes in 3 strengths—hot, medium and sweet. Once you have tasted real paprika of any strength, you will never again be tempted to use that tiny can of paprika for anything except color.

PEPPERCORNS

There are black and white peppercorns. The white ones are milder because the outer black shell has been removed. The advantage in using white peppercorns is that they do not leave tiny black particles on the food you are seasoning. I prefer the black ones, and use a good-size pepper mill—actually a coffee grinder—for grinding pepper in good quantity. Pepper should be liberally sprinkled on steak, salad, chops and the like. You will find your own uses.

HORSERADISH

Using the horseradish which can be bought in jars, already prepared, is scarcely better than using no horseradish at all. If possible, buy a whole horseradish root in a Jewish or eastern European food store, or grow some roots yourself.

The traditional way to prepare fresh horseradish is to scrape the skin off the outside, then grate the cleaned root by hand. The grating process creates weepy eyes and runny noses because the fresh root is so strong.

If you own an electric grinder, the diced root may be ground up. Also, if you own a blender, the diced root may be whirled to shreds, using white vinegar for liquid. Use only enough vinegar so that the root is ground up; do not make it too liquid.

If the root has been grated or ground, it should be seasoned with a little white vinegar, salt and sugar. Horseradish made in the blender needs only the salt and sugar. The finished product should be somewhat dry rather than liquid.

Store horseradish in a tightly closed jar, in the refrigerator. The prepared horseradish will keep its strength for about 2 weeks. See also the following reference to wasabi (Japanese horseradish).

WASABI

Wasabi is a light green, powdered, Japanese horseradish. It is inexpensive and can be ordered from a Japanese store (see Shopping Sources). The wasabi powder is mixed with water to make a paste.

Wasabi is extremely strong and pungent. It is an excellent reinforcement for the prepared horseradish which comes in jars and has little taste. Drain bottled horseradish of its liquid and add a bit of wasabi paste to the horseradish. You will be surprised at the improvement. The only drawback is that wasabi turns white horseradish very slightly green. (I don't mind this, however.)

SOY SAUCE

Any soy sauce is better than no soy sauce. However, I feel much inclined to suggest the soy sauce made in Japan by a company called Kikkoman. It is never too salty or overpowering, as are many of the soy sauces produced in this country.

VINEGAR

Vinegar for vinaigrette sauce or for any salad dressing should always be a fine, mild, wine vinegar. You can make your own if you can find a source of vinegar "mother." This is a bacterial culture to which wine (white or red) is added. Just a tiny bit of mother is needed.

When the mother is stored—in a covered crock, preferably—it grows and begins to look like a piece of liver. It is important to add wine from time to time, otherwise the vinegar may get too strong.

To use, strain from the crock into a smaller crock or jar.

There are other vinegars, cider, malt, and such. These are used primarily in pickle-making and preserving.

Vegetables — as flavoring and for salads

DUXELLES

Duxelles is a concentrate of mushrooms which keeps for several weeks in the refrigerator. Spoons of it may be added to sauces, scrambled eggs, or to anything you wish to have a strong mushroom flavor. It can be made from whole mushrooms or only from stems and bits. You will be wise to make a fairly large quantity at one time and store it in the refrigerator. My method for making duxelles differs from the usual. The advantage is that it takes a much shorter time, and also uses less butter.

- 2 *pounds mushrooms, finely chopped*
- 1/8 *pound sweet butter* (1/4 *cup*)
- 1 *teaspoon salt*
- 1 *teaspoon monosodium glutamate*
- 1/2 *teaspoon coarsely ground black pepper*
- 2 *tablespoons cognac*
- *rounds of brown or parchment paper to fit the top of a pint jar*

Place mushrooms in a heavy skillet with no liquid or fat. Cover skillet and place over medium heat. After a few minutes, the liquid from the mushrooms will begin to evaporate. Leave covered until the mushrooms almost begin to stick to the pan. Remove lid. Stir and add butter. Continue to cook about 10 more minutes. Season with salt, monosodium glutamate, and pepper. Stir well. Pack into a clean pint jar.

Immerse round of paper into the cognac so that paper is saturated on both sides. Place paper on top of mushrooms. Screw lid on tightly, and refrigerate.

Onions, Shallots, Garlic

SAUTEING ONIONS

When I was a child I lived in quite a heterogeneous neighborhood. One of my best friends was (and still is) a Polish girl, Helen Rudski, now Krawiec. Her mother is a wonderful cook, but most of her recipes cannot be included in this book because of lack of space and also because they would require endless testing—Mrs. Rudski cooks by the handful and pinch. One of her best dishes is piroghi. She fills squares of noodle dough with a combination of mashed potatoes and farmer cheese, seals the edges and cooks the piroghi in boiling salted water. Before serving, Mrs. Rudski spoons over each piroghi a sautéed onion mixture which I was never able to duplicate until I watched her one day. Her method of sautéing onions is so unique that I want to include it here.

MRS. RUDSKI'S SAUTEED ONIONS

Chop onions fine. Place in a heavy skillet with no liquid or fat. Cover skillet. Place over medium heat. After a few minutes the liquid from the onions will evaporate, leaving the onions quite dry in the skillet. Add a good chunk of butter, possibly ¼ pound for 3 large Spanish onions, and continue to sauté onions, uncovered, until they are a golden brown. This method results in onions with a strangely sweet flavor. They may be used in a variety of ways, especially with steak and other dishes calling for sautéed onions. I have adapted this method to cooking mushrooms in the preceding recipe for Duxelles.

SMALL WHITE ONIONS

Small white onions are delicious in many types of stews and sautéed dishes. There are usually many to peel, and here is an easy way to process them:

Pour boiling water over the onions and let stand about 5 minutes. Pour off water and simply slip the skins off the onions.

To prevent the onions from popping out at one end during the cooking make a small cross with a knife at the root end of each onion.

SHALLOTS

Shallots are the most delicate member of the onion family. They should be peeled, minced and sautéed in butter until they are soft. Then a liquid is usually added to them to make a sauce.

Shallots are generally small, and sometimes 2 or 3 are attached to each other at the root end. Their skins are a rusty brown color. Chopped scallions make a fairly acceptable substitute, but if you wish to obtain shallots and cannot find them in your neighborhood you can order them by mail (see Shopping Sources). Store in your refrigerator.

GARLIC

As you will notice in reading the recipes in this book, I think most highly of garlic. A little bit, a clove or 2, goes a long way, but strangely enough, a large amount blends with the other flavors and does not give a very garlicky flavor.

I keep a heavy copper mallet with which to pound garlic to a pulp. You may also mince it finely.

To peel garlic easily, pound the unpeeled cloves with a mallet. The outer skin may be removed easily.

THE TOSSED GREEN SALAD

To make it all wrong, take some iceberg lettuce—the heart, never the outer green leaves. Pour over it a concoction which is an orangey color (popularly known as "French" dressing), toss briefly, and you will have what is known as a tossed green salad. Sometimes the dressing is not orange, but a creamy white. However, the color doesn't make it taste much better.

To make a truly delicious tossed green salad, start with as great a variety of salad greens as you can find: Boston lettuce, Bibb lettuce (very expensive), chicory, escarole, field salad, romaine, very young dandelion greens, arugula, spinach leaves, watercress, etc. Wash all the greens well and break them into bite-size pieces. If you live in a house where the kitchen opens upon a bit of open space, put all your greens into a French salad basket and swing it out of doors until no more drops of water fly about. Otherwise, dry the greens as well as you can. Then wrap the greens in several layers of paper towels, which will absorb the remaining water, and place the package in the refrigerator for several hours. If you wish, this may be done two or three days ahead of time, the greens wrapped (after first wrapping in paper towels) in a damp kitchen towel, and placed in the vegetable crisper of your refrigerator. The greens will remain crisp and delicious.

Vinaigrette Sauce (see page 57) is the true French dressing. For some tastes, including that of my own family, a bit more olive oil is needed. Adjust this as your taste dictates.

When I expect company and don't want to be bothered by a lot of last-minute fuss, I place a good amount of dressing into the bottom of my salad bowl several hours before dinner. I then place the assorted greens very lightly on top, cover again with a damp cloth or paper towel and place in the refrigerator until it is time to toss and serve the salad. Naturally, all sorts of ingredients may be added to a salad of this kind—a bit of crumbled Roquefort cheese, some sliced tomato, onion rings, etc. However, I prefer my salad as I have first described it.

There are other miscellaneous points which should be made in relation to salad. Contrary to popular opinion, I believe that, aside from aesthetics, a wooden bowl should not be used unless it is washed in soapy water, rinsed and dried thoroughly after each use. When the oils and seasonings of a dressing penetrate wood, something quite unappetizing results. There are many handsome glass and ceramic bowls which are very suitable for salad.

Another point I should perhaps clarify is my attitude toward iceberg lettuce. In the spring and early summer the outer leaves are quite a lovely green, and very palatable. Any other softer, greener salad green is far better during most of the year.

CUCUMBERS

The pulpy, seeded center of the cucumber is often better discarded because it is watery and tends to dilute whatever dressing or sauce is mixed with it.

If the cucumber is to be peeled, peel it before removing the center. Cut the cucumber in half, lengthwise. With a small spoon, scrape out the pulpy center and seeds.

TOMATOES, HOW TO PEEL

Three methods may be employed to peel tomatoes.

They may be placed in boiling water briefly until the skin is loose and can be peeled off easily.

The other method—better for Mexican dishes because it results in a slightly charred flavor—is to place the tomatoes right over an open flame on top of the stove. The skin will blister and char and can then be peeled off easily.

To skin tomatoes over electric burners, spear them with a fork, and hold them close to the heat. Turn occasionally until the skin is wrinkled and can be removed easily. Tomatoes skinned this way may not acquire the charred flavor that an open gas flame affords.

Liquids for Cooking

Never use water for cooking if you can possibly obtain either stock or wine. The only possible exception to this rule might be in the cooking of a very hearty, rich soup which contains enough ingredients to give plenty of flavor. Even when preparing soup, try to use at least part stock to begin with. (See page 50 for Concentrate of Chicken or Beef; see also basic stocks in soup chapter.)

Fats for Cooking

Many recipes call for some sort of fat. The one *not* to use, ever, ever, is homogenized shortening. Its flavor is always detectable and never pleasant.

Either sweet butter or olive oil is acceptable—the choice depends on the dish being prepared—and the results are always excellent. Lard or vegetable oil (such as peanut or corn oil) is best for deep-fat frying. Vegetable (salad) oils for the most part have no unpleasant taste; the worst that can happen is that they will impart no particular flavor at all. Sometimes a combination of half olive and half vegetable oils is very good.

For sautéing, clarified butter and olive oil are both very good. Chicken fat is also useful in certain dishes. Clarified butter can be made in quantity and stored over a long period in the refrigerator.

Only sweet butter is used for baking.

BUTTER, SALT AND SWEET

Sweet butter is always preferable because it gives a special flavor which cannot be duplicated. However, if you plan to use sweet butter (or salt butter, for that matter) for sautéing meat or chops, add a little salad (vegetable) oil or olive oil to the butter. No more than a tablespoon or 2 will be needed to ¼ pound butter to prevent the butter from burning.

CLARIFIED BUTTER

Clarified butter is a pure fat, from which all the milk solids and water have been removed. It is used primarily for sautéing meats. (During the sautéing process regular butter can burn and cause an unpleasant taste.)

To make clarified butter, place any quantity of sweet or salt butter into a deep saucepan. Melt it over low heat and continue to cook the butter until the foam disappears from the top and there is a light brown sediment in the bottom of the pan.

A large amount of butter, such as 10 pounds, may take over 2 hours to clarify. The liquid butter should not brown, but should remain golden.

When the butter looks perfectly clear, remove it from the heat. Skim any brown crust from the top. Let butter cool. Then pour it through a cheesecloth-lined strainer into containers, leaving the sediment in the bottom of the pot. Stored in the refrigerator, clarified butter keeps almost indefinitely.

If pure clarified butter is used for sautéing, it is not necessary to add any other oil (olive or salad) to prevent the butter from burning.

CHICKEN FAT

To render chicken fat, cut it into small dice; then place in a heavy saucepan over low heat. When bits of fat look gray rather than yellow, add 1 small minced onion for each pound of fat. Continue to cook over low heat until onion and bits of fat are brown. Strain into a clean jar. This keeps indefinitely in the refrigerator.

Use in mashed potatoes and sautéed onions, and in chopped liver, of course. A little rendered chicken fat is delicious in cooked sauerkraut.

Never discard the brown bits (grieben) which remain after the chicken fat has been rendered. They keep indefinitely in the refrigerator, and are wonderful in chopped liver. Or when they are reheated till crisp and hot, they make a marvelous tidbit with cocktails.

PRESERVED CREAM

Here is a method of keeping heavy cream for 6 to 8 weeks in the refrigerator. The cream is very thick and is excellent for thickening sauces, with or without egg yolks. Even after it develops a slight mold, this can be scraped off and the cream underneath can still be used.

To make preserved cream, place at least a pint of heavy cream into a very deep saucepan. Boil the cream over high heat until it is reduced to less than half its original quantity, but do not boil it so long that it turns yellow (from the butterfat content).

Pour into a clean jar and refrigerate. When perfectly cool, cover the cream tightly. Use by the tablespoonful, primarily to thicken reduced sauces for chicken or fish.

HOMEMADE SOUR CREAM

This is a delicacy rarely encountered, yet it is very easy to make and is a thoroughly delightful topping for fruit or pastry desserts. Homemade sour cream can be kept in the refrigerator 4 to 6 weeks. It will get thicker as it stands, and will taste even better.

2 *cups heavy cream*
5 *teaspoons buttermilk*

Combine cream and buttermilk in a screw-top jar. Shake the jar for a minute.

Let stand at room temperature 48 hours. If room is especially cool (on a winter's day), let stand an extra 12 to 24 hours. The mixture will thicken.

Refrigerate at least 24 hours—preferably longer—before using.

WHIPPED CREAM

This method permits you to prepare whipped cream and to have it especially stiff for decorating.

1 *cup heavy cream*
2 *tablespoons granulated sugar*
1 *teaspoon vanilla*

Be sure cream is very cold and preferably at least a day old. Whip with a rotary beater or mixer, adding sugar before the cream begins to thicken. Whip till cream holds peaks but be careful not to overbeat. Fold in vanilla.

Line a strainer with a piece of kitchen toweling or a triple layer of cheesecloth. Pour whipped cream into the lined strainer. Place strainer into a bowl in which the strainer is suspended but does not touch the bottom of the bowl. Cover contents of strainer by draping the excess cloth over the top, and place bowl containing strainer in refrigerator. Cream will keep up to 2 days and will become stiffer and stiffer as it stands and eliminates excess water.

CROUTONS

Croutons are small bits of butter-toasted bread. They are delicious, and useful either with soups or over vegetables.

To make them, cut off the crusts of several slices of white bread (count on about 1 slice of bread per person). Cut the decrusted bread into tiny cubes about the size of peas.

Melt a good amount of butter in a skillet and toss in the bread cubes. Sauté, over medium heat, turning frequently until the bread cubes are golden brown and crisp. Do not add them to soup or vegetables until serving time, as they will lose their crispness.

GARLIC-SEASONED CROUTONS

Garlic croutons are made by adding a small amount of very finely minced garlic to the pan just as the croutons are finished. Stir to distribute the garlic flavor evenly.

TORTILLAS

Tortillas are made of ground corn and look like very flat pancakes. Freshly made tortillas are a delicacy rarely encountered outside Mexico—it is very difficult to produce them at home. In Mexico, the tortilla dough is usually patted out by hand to make thin pancakes, a procedure which takes much practice.

Fortunately, tortillas may be purchased in cans, and these are very adequate for use in making such things as tacos, tostadas or enchiladas, but not for eating by themselves.

Canned tortillas can be delicious when they are fried in hot lard till they are crisp and golden, but not brown. The lard should be an inch or 2 deep.

Fried tortillas may be garnished simply with canned green chili and jack cheese, and placed in the oven until the cheese has melted. Or they may be spread with Refried Beans, sprinkled with chopped, raw onion and Parmesan cheese, and served with any Mexican dish.

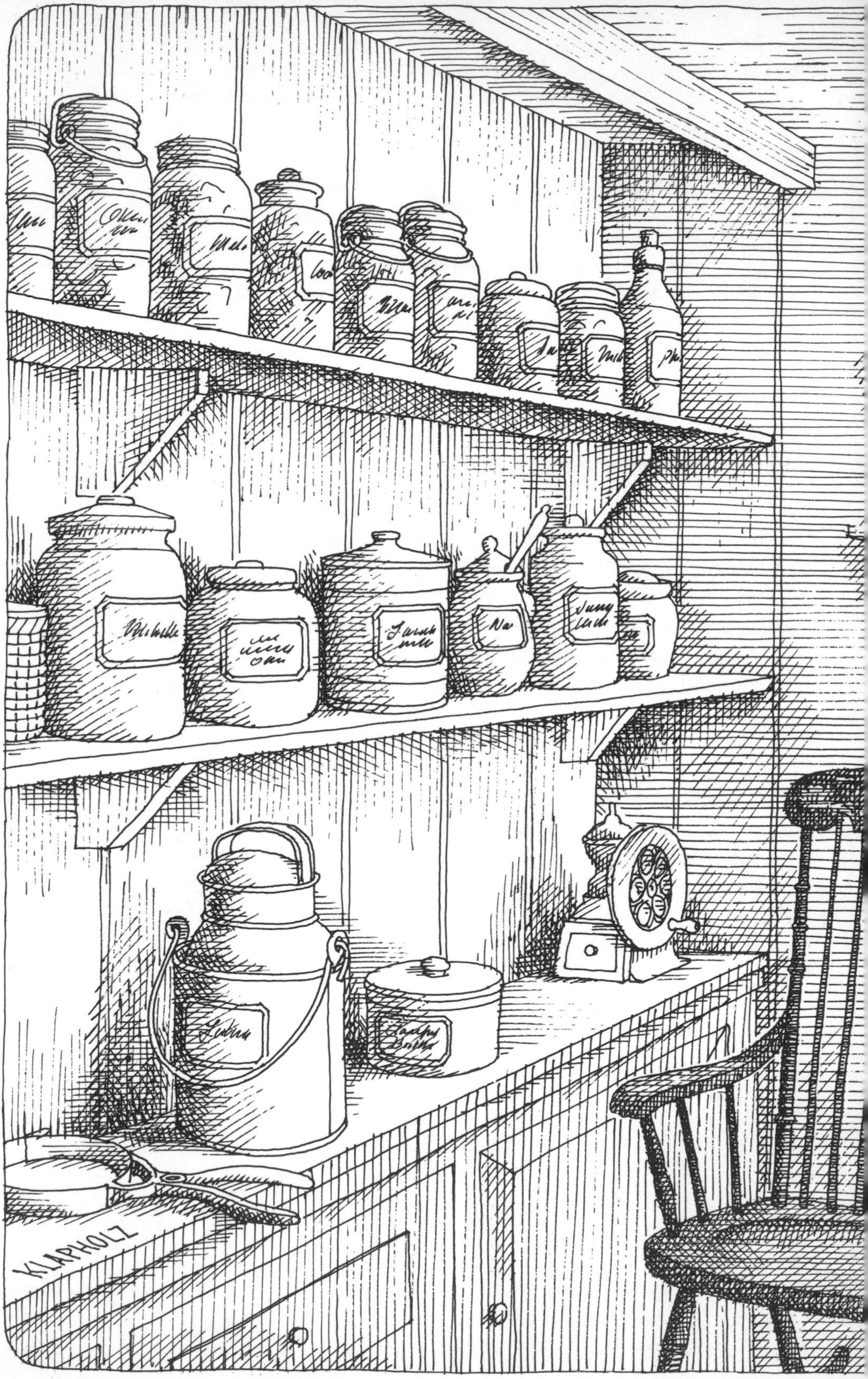
KLAPHOLZ

1. HOMEMADE FOODS IN RESERVE

MANY A HOSTESS'S REPUTATION is based on the fact that she is never caught unprepared by by unexpected guests.

The freezer is certainly helpful, but there are occasions when there isn't enough time to thaw foods. At such moments, a jar of excellent spicy, oil-covered olives sitting on the pantry shelf or a can of home-roasted, seasoned nuts or a hard Italian salami in the refrigerator is very useful.

Homemade pickled herring, home-canned pâté, vinaigrette sauce all keep perfectly in the refrigerator for long periods of time and can be easily and quickly served.

Along with these standbys, there are other items, such as salsa fria, which can make a feast out of a broiled hamburger. Some are lesser known than others; but they have one thing in common: they all keep almost indefinitely in the refrigerator or at room temperature.

In addition to those things which you make yourself, it is a good idea to keep a shelf in the pantry for bought items which can be turned into a quick snack or first course. There is on the market, for example, an excellent canned prosciutto ham. Canned kidney beans or white beans, tuna fish, anchovies, tongue which comes in a jar and, of course, olive oil and good wine vinegar give the cook great scope in preparing either a family snack or a company treat.

Naturally, there should always be on hand a good supply of either commercially or home-canned chicken or beef stock for braising vegetables or creating more hearty soups or sauces. Commercially canned beef gravy is also a very useful product to keep available.

Home Canning

Just as frozen foods don't take the place of fresh produce, they also don't take the place of home-canned foods. Admittedly, the freezer is indispensable in many areas: for example, frozen baked goods are particularly successful, as are small cuts of meat which can be thawed quickly at the last minute. Home-frozen peaches and berries are memorable, especially when they are turned into smooth sherbets with a flick of the blender.

However, canning is a thing unto itself. What can be better in mid-winter than opening a jar of home-canned split pea or cabbage soup, heating and eating?

One of the most useful home-canned foods is pâté. Canned pâté keeps almost indefinitely. There are just a few precautions necessary for success with this venture. First, never use liver in a home-canned pâté. The liver acquires a boiled taste which is not at all agreeable. Also, since pâté is not cooked again after the can is opened, I have always taken the precaution of keeping the processed cans in the refrigerator.

Pâté can be kept, sealed in its own fat, in the refrigerator for several weeks. But after that period, no matter how well-sealed the pâté, it loses flavor.

To can pâté at home, some equipment is needed: a large pressure-canner—the largest you can find, which will be about 21 quarts—tin cans, and a tin-can sealer. These items can be obtained from the mail order firms that serve rural communities primarily (see Shopping Sources).

HOME-CANNED PATE

3 *pounds boneless veal*
5 *pounds boneless pork*
2½ *pounds fresh pork fat*
1½ *pounds ham*
1½ *pounds smoked beef tongue*
1 *cup cognac*
4 *tablespoons salt*
2 *tablespoons monosodium glutamate*
2 *tablespoons pepper*
1½ *teaspoons allspice*
1 *teaspoon cloves*
1 *teaspoon cinnamon*
10 *cloves garlic, minced*

Grind 1 pound veal and 1 pound pork through fine blade of meat grinder. Coarsely dice remaining meat and pork fat, or put through the coarse blade of the meat grinder.

Add cognac and all seasonings to coarsely diced meats. Mix well. Work in finely ground meats, mixing well. Your hands are the best tools for this.

Pack into No. 2 cans, leaving a ¼-inch space at tops. Wipe off rims of cans. Place all cans on a baking sheet in a 350 degree oven. Heat in oven till contents of cans are hot and there is barely any pinkness in center.

Seal cans, according to directions which come with tin-can sealer. Place cans into the pressure-canner. Seal canner and exhaust canner for 7 to 10 minutes. (Follow directions that come with canner. Directions given for liverwurst or headcheese may be applied to pâté.) After canner has been exhausted, bring pressure to 10 pounds and maintain for 65 minutes. Cool cans as quickly as possible. Store in refrigerator.

To serve, open cans at both ends. Push pâté out. Scrape off the layer of fat at one end. There will also be a delicious jelly. Serve it with the pâté.

Yield: approximately 11 No. 2 cans of pâté.

PICKLED HERRING IN MILCH SAUCE

6 *firm schmaltz herrings*
3/4 *cup white vinegar*
2 1/4 *cups water*
1 *tablespoon pickling spices*
2/3 *cup sugar*
1 *tablespoon salt*
3 *large Spanish onions*
milch of 6 *to* 8 *herrings* (*see note at end of recipe*)

Soak schmaltz herrings overnight in a large bowl of ice water in the refrigerator.

Combine the vinegar, water and pickling spices in an enameled saucepan. Bring to a rolling boil. Stir in sugar. Add salt (which is said to give more firmness to the herrings). Let pickling mixture stand overnight at room temperature.

The next morning, make a thick layer of newspaper on which to work. With a pair of scissors, cut off fins of herring. Split open stomachs with scissors and remove and reserve any milch. With a sharp knife, make an incision down the backs, cutting to the bone. Filet backs, cutting to the bone. Filet the herring, starting from the tail. This is a comparatively easy job because it involves pulling the meat away from the backbone rather than using a knife. Do not be concerned about the small bones that remain in the herring. These seem to dissolve or disappear after a few days in the pickling mixture. After the herrings have been fileted, pull off the skins, starting from the tails. Rinse and dry herring on paper towels.

Peel the onions and cut into medium slices. Separate into rings.

Whirl the milch in an electric blender, or force through a food mill or sieve. Pour off the vinegar mixture from spices, discarding spices. Stir vinegar into puréed milch.

Make alternate layers of herring slices and plenty of onions in a 2- to 3-quart crock. When crock is almost full, pour over the vinegar-milch mixture to cover. Cover crock and chill in refrigerator at least 5 days—or up to 4 months. The pickled flavor will get stronger as the herring stands.

Note: When you purchase the fish, ask if the herring have milch

(*continued on the next page*)

in them. If there is no milch, or very little (as is often the case with schmaltz herring), perhaps the store will sell or give you some separately.

Fileting and skinning herrings is a smelly job. To remove odor from hands after you are finished, wash well with soap, then rub in a bit of ordinary cooking oil. Follow with a bit of cologne.

CREAMED PICKLED HERRING

Pour the pickled herring into a colander or strainer to drain off all of the pickling mixture. Do keep onions, by all means. For each 6 pickled herrings to be creamed, use about 1 quart sour cream that is at least 3 or 4 days old (it should be very thick). Pour off any liquid from the top. Combine herring, onions and sour cream gently in a bowl and stir together. Garnish with fresh, chopped dill.

ROLLMOPS

6 *firm schmaltz herrings, soaked, fileted and skinned as described for Pickled Herring in Milch Sauce*
3 *tablespoons hot mustard (English or Düsseldorf)*
24 *small slices onion*
½ *carrot, scraped and cut into 24 matchsticks*
½ *sour pickle, cut into 24 matchsticks*
24 *toothpicks*
2 *large Spanish onions*
pickling mixture with milch, as described for Pickled Herring in Milch Sauce

Cut each herring filet in half, lengthwise. Spread halved herring filets with hot mustard. On the narrow end of each filet place a piece of onion, carrot and pickle. Roll up filets, jelly-roll style. Skewer with toothpicks.

Peel and slice Spanish onions. In a crock, make alternate layers of rollmops and onions until all are used. Pour pickling mixture over to cover. Cover crock and place in refrigerator for at least a week before using.

ITALIAN PICKLES FOR ANTIPASTO

Take a good variety of vegetables: green peppers, cauliflower, tiny onions, hearts of artichokes, string beans, celery, carrots, zucchini. Cut into bite-size pieces, using a serrated vegetable cutter if you have one. Combine all except artichoke hearts in a large saucepan. Cover with water and bring just to a rolling boil. Drain well. Cook the hearts of artichoke separately until they are just tender. Drain and add to the vegetables. Add some Marinated Capers (recipe below), a good quantity of Oil-kept Olives (see page 45), several whole cloves of garlic, some whole peppercorns, and 2 or 3 bay leaves. Mix well. Pack tightly into jars. Pour boiling wine vinegar over all, being sure the vinegar completely covers the vegetables. Cover the jars tightly and store in refrigerator at least 5 days before using. Keeps for several months.

MARINATED CAPERS

Obtain some salted capers—at least a pound or 2. They may be bought either loose or in jars at Italian grocery stores (see Shopping Sources). Pack them tightly into jars. Place a whole clove of garlic in each jar, as well as some fresh or dried dill. Pour enough good wine vinegar into each jar to cover the capers completely. If wine vinegar is not available, use a good quality dry red wine. These capers are completely unlike the ones commercially bottled in brine, and they are a wonderful addition to any salad, first-course plate or recipe calling for capers.

GREEN TOMATO PRESERVES

6 *pounds green tomatoes, sliced*
1 *pound fresh ginger, peeled and sliced thinly*
1 *small bottle or package slaked lime (calcium hydroxide U.S.P.) purchased at drugstore and diluted according to directions given on bottle*
4 *cups sugar*
5 *cups cider vinegar*
1 *tablespoon cloves*
1 *tablespoon allspice*
2 *sticks of cinnamon*

Place sliced green tomatoes and sliced ginger into a bowl, and cover with lime solution. Let stand for 24 hours. Rinse in ice water, then drain well.

In a deep pot, combine sugar, vinegar, and spices. Bring to a boil, and cook till a medium syrup forms. Add tomatoes and ginger. Cook over medium heat until tomatoes and ginger look clear. Remove from heat. Pack into jars, adding syrup to cover. Cover tightly and store at room temperature.

BREAD AND BUTTER PICKLES

These are fine as part of a mixed hors d'oeuvre platter, or as a relish for meat.

24 *medium-size cucumbers, thinly sliced*
3/4 *cup coarse salt (approximately)*
4 *onions, thinly sliced*
1 *cup olive oil*
lump alum—as many pieces as you have jars (available in drugstores)
as many whole cloves of garlic as you have jars

2 *quarts cider vinegar*
½ *cup white mustard seeds*
¼ *cup black mustard seeds*
1 *tablespoon pickling spices*
2 *tablespoons celery seeds*
3 *quart jars or* 6 *pint jars*

In a large bowl, make alternate layers of sliced cucumbers, salt and sliced onions. Let stand in refrigerator 5 hours. Rinse in ice water and drain well, pressing out as much liquid as possible. Return vegetables to bowl and add olive oil. Toss vegetables in oil. Put a piece of lump alum into each jar. Pack vegetables tightly into jars, and add a clove of garlic to each jar.

Pour cider vinegar into an enameled pot. Add mustard seeds, pickling spices and celery seeds; bring to a rolling boil. Pour boiling mixture into each jar to cover vegetables. Cover tightly and let stand at least a week before using. These pickles don't need refrigeration, but it's a good idea to keep at least 1 jar in the refrigerator because pickles always taste better when they are cold.
Yield: 3 quarts pickles.

CONSERVE OF RADISH AND CHICKEN FAT

This is an old recipe of Jewish origin. The conserve will keep in the refrigerator for a long time and is delicious served with any pâté, ham, pot roast or liverwurst.

black or white radishes
1 *tablespoon salt for each pint of shredded radish*
rendered chicken fat (⅓ cup for each pint of pressed radishes)
1 *small chopped onion for each pint of shredded radish*
½ *teaspoon black pepper for each pint of radish*

Scrape radishes to remove outer skin. Shred coarsely with coarse side of grater. Sprinkle with salt, and allow to stand in refrigerator, covered, for at least 2 hours. Remove from refrigerator. Place shredded radishes in a colander or strainer. Rinse with ice water and, with your hands, press out as much water as possible from the radishes, so they are quite dry.

Place in a bowl. Add chicken fat, onion and pepper. Mix well. Pack into clean jars, cover tightly, and store in refrigerator.

MIDDLE EAST CHEESE BITS

These cheese bits keep for months in the refrigerator. They make a most satisfying first-course plate served with crisp greens, a slice of salami and a few black olives and capers. Middle East Cheese Bits may be made with yogurt or sour cream, but half and half gives a good flavor.

1 *pint sour cream*
1 *pint yogurt*
1 *tablespoon salt*
1 *teaspoon freshly ground pepper*
2 *teaspoons caraway seeds*
olive oil

Line a strainer with a kitchen towel or with cheesecloth, and place over a bowl. Mix sour cream and yogurt together and pour into strainer. Place in refrigerator for at least 36 hours, or until the mixture is very firm and a good deal of the liquid has drained into bowl.

Discard liquid, and place firm mixture into bowl. Stir in salt, pepper and caraway seeds. Return to cloth-lined strainer to permit further draining for 12 more hours.

Place contents of strainer in a pastry bag fitted with a large, plain round tube. (If this isn't available, the cheese bits can be shaped into rounds with 2 teaspoons.) Cover a cooky sheet with a towel or a triple layer of cheesecloth. With the pastry bag and tube, or with 2 teaspoons, form small balls of the mixture on the cloth. The balls should be no larger than ⅔ inch in diameter. Cover the balls with another cloth and allow to stand at room temperature for at least 24 hours, or till they are firm enough to pick up with the fingers.

Pack into a clean pint-size jar. Add enough good olive oil to completely cover cheese bits; then cover jar tightly and store in the refrigerator till needed.

If you wish to avoid olive oil for caloric or other reasons, the cheese bits may be packed in a clean jar and covered with a strong brine (made by dissolving as much salt as possible in a cup of water). Packed either way, the cheese bits will keep, refrigerated, for several months.

SICILIAN ANCHOVY PEPPERS

This is a very old recipe from a little village in Sicily. It is traditionally made with hot peppers, but small, thin-skinned frying peppers may be substituted.

4 pounds hot finger peppers, or small Italian frying peppers
as many firm anchovies as you have peppers
olive oil

Spread peppers on a large tray which has been lined with a towel. Allow to stand in a well-lighted place—in the sun if possible—for about 6 days, or until peppers are slightly dry, wrinkled and soft. Slit each pepper up 1 side. Remove seeds. Stuff 1 or 2 anchovies into each pepper.

Line a large strainer with a towel or a double layer of cheesecloth. Place all the anchovy-stuffed peppers into the strainer. Put a plate on top and weight it down with something heavy—a stone, or whatever you have. Allow to stand overnight, to drain, over a bowl which will catch the liquid. In the morning the peppers will be pressed and flat. Pack them into jars which have been previously sterilized in boiling water.

Heat olive oil to 300 degrees F. Ladle hot oil over peppers in jars so that oil completely covers peppers. Cover tightly with clean lids. The stuffed peppers will keep indefinitely at room temperature.

ASSORTED FRUITS IN MADEIRA

This can be an assortment of any dried fruits: prunes, apricots, apples, pears, peaches, cherries, raisins, figs, currants, etc. Wash the fruits. Place in a large clean crock, and add enough Madeira to cover. Let stand at least a week. Check crock every 2 or 3 days and add more Madeira as the fruit absorbs the liquid. When the fruit is saturated with Madeira, it is ready to be packed into jars or crocks. Add more Madeira if necessary, to be sure fruit is well covered. The Madeira-soaked fruits may be used as a relish with almost any meat or fowl; or some of it can be chopped and added to a dressing for roast goose. It will keep indefinitely if care is taken that the fruit is always covered with Madeira.

PICKLED SPICED CHERRIES

Pit sour black cherries, and add white vinegar just to cover. Let stand 24 hours, covered. Place cherries in a colander and allow to drain for 3 hours.

Measure cherries. Add an equal quantity (by volume) of sugar, plus 2 or 3 cinnamon sticks and some whole sloves. Let stand one week, stirring once a day. Pack into jars and cover tightly. Serve as a relish for duck, goose or pork.

PICKLED DRIED FIGS

2 *pounds dried figs*
2 *cups cider vinegar*
2 *cups sugar*
2 *tablespoons pickling spices*
4 *tablespoons chopped candied ginger*

Wash fruit, and place in a large bowl. Cover with water and soak overnight.

In the morning, drain fruit. Reserve all remaining water, and place this liquid in a saucepan, adding vinegar, sugar and pickling spices. Stir over low heat till sugar is dissolved. Raise heat and boil for 10 minutes.

Add figs and candied ginger. Simmer until fruit is tender and syrup has thickened.

Pack into small, clean jars, making sure the fruit is completely covered with the syrup. Store at least 1 week before using.

HOME-ROASTED FILBERTS OR PECANS

2 *cups shelled filberts or pecans*
¼ *cup butter, melted*
2 *teaspoons salt, coarse if possible*
1 *teaspoon pepper*

Set oven temperature at 350 degrees.

Toss nuts in melted butter. Place in a shallow pan in preheated oven. Roast nuts about 25 minutes, shaking the pan once or twice until they are evenly browned, but not, of course, burned.

Remove from oven. Drain any excess butter. Sprinkle with salt and pepper, and mix to distribute the seasoning evenly. Serve at room temperature.

These can be made weeks ahead and stored in a tightly covered jar or tin in the freezer or refrigerator. The nuts will keep their crisp, freshly roasted quality.

OIL-KEPT OLIVES

Good olives, plump or shriveled black ones, or firm, salty green ones are a wonderful addition to any party, or to any salad bowl. Unfortunately, people often resort to tasteless, textureless canned or jar-packed olives. This is unnecessary, since olives are good travelers and can be kept indefinitely when packed in jars and covered with olive oil. Olives of all varieties may be ordered by mail (see Shopping Sources). For a real treat, buy a good assortment of olives. Mix in a bowl, then add a spoonful of freshly ground pepper and some pickling spices. Pack tightly into jars—the black mixed with the green. Cover with olive oil, or, if you prefer, a mixture of wine vinegar and olive oil. Cover the jars tightly. These don't need refrigeration.

INDIAN SCRAMBLE

A crispy mixture, good for nibbling with drinks. Moong beans, chickpea flour and roasted chickpeas may be found in Oriental food shops, or ordered by mail (see Shopping Sources).

1 *pound moong beans*
peanut oil for deep fat frying
½ *pound chickpea flour*
1 *teaspoon curry powder*
1 *teaspoon salt*
buttermilk
1 *pound soft, roasted chickpeas (bought already roasted) (optional)*
salt, pepper

Rinse moong beans in plenty of water. Place in a bowl. Cover with warm water and allow to stand overnight. The next day, drain well, and dry beans on paper towels.

Heat oil to 375 degrees. Put about ¾ cup of the moong beans into a strainer with mesh fine enough to keep beans from falling through. Immerse strainer in hot fat, holding the handle. The temperature of the fat will immediately go down. Keep moong beans immersed in fat till temperature rises to 375 degrees again. Then remove strainer with beans and drain them on paper towels. Repeat until all the moong beans have been fried.

Combine chickpea flour, curry powder and salt in a bowl. Add enough buttermilk to make a mixture thick enough to keep its shape

—not soft and runny, but not as heavy as a dough. Lower fat temerature to 350 degrees. Put a little chickpea flour mixture into a potato ricer. Place over hot fat, and press down handle of ricer so that shreds of chickpea flour mixture fall into hot fat. Fry till shreds are crisp. Remove with strainer or slotted spoon and drain on paper towels. Repeat till all of mixture has been fried.

Mix fried moong beans, chickpea flour shreds and roasted chickpeas together. Sprinkle with plenty of salt, freshly ground black pepper and a little curry powder, if desired. Spread evenly in an 11 x 15 jelly-roll pan. Place in a 350 degree oven for 20 minutes. Remove from oven. Cool completely before packing into clean jars. Cover tightly, and keep in refrigerator or freezer. Serve at room temperature or slightly warmed.

Sauces, Gravies and Dressings

HOLLANDAISE SAUCE

My method for making hollandaise sauce is slightly unorthodox; however, it works and it is quick.

½ *cup sweet butter*
1 *tablespoon lemon juice*
4 *large egg yolks*
⅓ *teaspoon monosodium glutamate*
salt, white pepper to taste

Melt butter with lemon juice in a small pan.

Place egg yolks in another fairly small pan. Add monosodium glutamate, salt and pepper.

When the butter and lemon juice are melted and bubbling, beat them into the egg yolks, using a wire whisk. The heat of the butter-lemon juice will cook the yolks and cause the sauce to thicken.

If the sauce should not thicken sufficiently (because the butter mixture is not hot enough), replace the pan over very low heat and stir constantly with a whisk until the desired consistency is reached.

If the sauce should not thicken sufficiently (because the butter mixture is not hot enough), replace the pan over very low heat and stir constantly with a whisk unil the desired consistency is reached.

BEARNAISE SAUCE

1 *teaspoon dried tarragon*
¼ *cup wine vinegar*
½ *cup butter*
4 *large egg yolks*
⅓ *teaspoon monosodium glutamate*
salt and pepper

Place tarragon in a very small saucepan. Add vinegar. Boil over high heat until there is hardly any liquid left in the pan.

Melt butter and add vinegar mixture to it. Bring just to the bubbling point.

Place egg yolks in a small saucepan. Add monosodium glutamate, salt and pepper. Beat butter-vinegar mixture into the yolks. If butter mixture is hot enough, the sauce will thicken instantly; if it is too hot, and the sauce separates, beat in a little boiling water, a few drops at a time, until the sauce is smooth.

Béarnaise sauce goes particularly well with sautéed filet of beef.

WHITE SAUCE

2 *tablespoons flour*
2 *tablespoons butter*
1 *cup cream or milk*
salt, pepper to taste
½ *teaspoon monosodium glutamate*

Melt butter in a heavy saucepan. Remove saucepan from heat and stir in flour with a wooden spoon. Place over low heat and cook, stirring constantly, about 5 minutes. Remove from heat and, using a wire whisk, beat in cream or milk. Replace over heat and stir with whisk till sauce thickens. Season with salt, pepper and monosodium glutamate.

HORSERADISH SAUCE

This sauce goes particularly well with boiled beef, if perchance plain horseradish proves too strong for the eaters.

3 *tablespoons butter*
3 *tablespoons flour*
1 *cup light cream*
½ *cup beef broth*
¼ *cup grated or ground horseradish*
salt and pepper to taste
½ *teaspoon monosodium glutamate*

Melt butter in a saucepan. Remove from heat. Stir in flour. Replace over low heat and stir for 5 minutes. While this roux is cooking, heat cream and broth together until they are boiling. Pour into butter-flour mixture, stirring briskly with a wire whisk to avoid lumps. Bring to a boil, stirring constantly. If sauce is a nice consistency when it begins to boil, remove from heat, stir in horseradish and serve. If sauce is too thin, continue to cook until it is thick enough, but stir in horseradish at the last moment. Season with salt, pepper and monosodium glutamate before serving.

CONCENTRATE OF CHICKEN OR BEEF

This concentrate is an excellent base for homemade soup. Also, a spoonful or 2 makes a delicious dressing for vegetables and keeps the calorie count down. Or you might try adding a spoonful to your vegetables while they are steaming in butter. Any braised meat dish can be vastly improved with a little homemade concentrate.

For practical reasons, it is better to make a great deal at once and it may be necessary for you to find an out-size pot, if you don't already own a large-size canner or pressure-cooker. I use a 10-gallon pot which I fill three quarters full, with either chicken bones (backs, available at chicken-parts shops), chicken carcasses which I've accumulated and frozen, or beef and veal bones which I've cajoled from my butcher over a period of weeks and had waiting in the freezer.

Cover the bones with water. Add a handful of salt and a spoonful or 2 of monosodium glutamate. Start cooking over high heat, uncovered. As liquid begins to simmer, lower heat and simmer at least 12 hours. After 12 hours, liquid should be somewhat reduced. Taste for seasoning. If necessary, add more salt and monosodium glutamate. Add a peeled onion, 3 or 4 stalks of celery, a handful of parsley and a parsnip, if available. Raise heat and permit stock to boil rapidly till vegetables are soft. Cool slightly. Remove bones and vegetables, being sure to press out as much liquid as possible before discarding them. (This is probably the messiest part of the whole job.)

Cool remaining stock. Remove as much fat from top as possible. The easiest way to do this is to refrigerate stock until fat is solid enough to be removed in a single piece, but this may not be practical if you don't have a very large refrigerator. When you have removed as much fat as you can, replace pot on stove over high heat. Boil stock down till it is syrupy enough to coat a metal spoon. Be careful to watch it at this stage because it burns easily when it becomes thick.

Pour into clean glass jars. Cool, uncovered. Cut some rounds of paper to fit the tops of the jars, and soak them in a little cognac. Fit cognac paper into tops of cooled jars. Cover tightly and store in refrigerator.

To make a cup of stock, put 1 tablespoon concentrate into a cup and fill the cup with water. To make it especially flavorful, add a tablespoonful of mixed chopped celery leaves, parsley and scallions. Yield: about 2 pints.

PAN SAUCE FOR SAUTEED MEATS

To make a simple pan sauce for any meat which you have sautéed (a tournedos, for example), first remove meat from pan and keep warm in a low oven. If there is much fat in the pan, pour off most of it. Add a few spoonfuls of chopped shallots or scallions and sauté till soft. Pour in about ⅔ cup red wine for beef (use white wine for veal). Turn the heat to high and let wine reduce in pan. When it is reduced to less than half, season with salt and pepper. If you desire, a spoonful or 2 of beef gravy (canned may be used) or Concentrate of Beef can be stirred into the sauce to give it more body. Add a spoonful of chopped parsley and pour over the meat.

Various additions may be made to the pan sauce—cream may be added, for example, or mushrooms may be sautéed with the shallots, before the wine is added.

UNTHICKENED SAUCE FOR ROAST BEEF, LAMB, VEAL OR PORK

Although there are often variations on the theme, the specific instructions for making a full-bodied sauce for any roast are basic.

Ask your butcher for extra bones of the same type as the meat you are purchasing. While the meat is roasting—or even before you begin the roast itself—cover the bones with liquid in a heavy pot, using half stock and half dry red or white wine if available. Simmer the bones over medium heat for as long as possible, at least as long as the roast is in the oven.

Add a stalk of celery with its leaves, whole onion and a carrot. When you have turned off the heat from the roast (about 15 to 20 minutes before you carve it), remove the bones and vegetables from the pot of simmering liquid and discard them. Skim off any fat. Raise heat under remaining liquid and reduce the liquid to slightly less than half. Season with salt, pepper and a little monosodium glutamate. Add a few drops of commercial gravy coloring.

When the roast itself has been transferred from the roasting pan to a serving board, pour off any fat in the pan. Then rinse out the pan with some of the prepared sauce to capture the flavor of the roast itself. If there are any brown bits or pieces in the pan, scrape them free and add to the sauce. If you have not used wine in making the sauce, add a few spoonfuls of Madeira at the end.

Just before serving the sauce, add a spoonful or 2 of finely chopped parsley, along with 1 scallion, very finely minced. If juices run when the roast itself is carved, add them to the sauce.

Serve sauce hot, but not boiling, with the roast.

GIBLET GRAVY (FOR TURKEY)

Place cleaned giblets (gizzard, heart and neck—not liver) into a saucepan. Add enough stock to come about 2 inches over the giblets. Season with salt and monosodium glutamate. Bring to a boil. Lower heat and cover pot. Simmer giblets about 1½ hours, or until they are tender. Remove pot from stove and allow to cool.

When the pot is cool enough to handle, remove giblets. Cut them into small pieces, removing the meat from the neck bone and discarding the bone. Place giblets into blender jar. Add enough cooking stock to just cover the pieces, and whirl in blender until you have a smooth purée. Set aside until later, and reserve remaining stock in saucepan.

After the turkey has been roasted and removed from pan, pour off any excess grease. Bring remaining stock to a boil; pour into roasting pan and, with a wooden spoon, loosen all the bits of brown pieces sticking to the pan. Pour these pan drippings into the blender jar with the giblets; whirl smooth again.

Transfer the contents of blender jar to saucepan. Stir in 1 cup of heavy cream, and add a little commercial gravy coloring if sauce looks too pale. Bring to a boil. Lower heat and simmer about 5 minutes, stirring once or twice. Remove pan from heat and add ¼ cup Madeira, as well as ½ cup chopped parsley.

BASIC BEEF GRAVY

Basic beef gravy is an essential ingredient of many subtle sauces. The making of it is a long and tedious process, yet well worth the effort, particularly if the sauce itself is frozen in small amounts, perhaps half-pints, or if it is canned (refer to a canning manual for directions as to how to can soups).

I give below a recipe for basic beef gravy. Make it; can it; freeze it; keep it in the refrigerator for a week or two weeks in a tightly closed, very clean jar. If you wish to keep it longer without canning or freezing, pour the sauce into a heavy saucepan every four or five days and reboil it for five minutes. Then rebottle the sauce in a clean jar and keep in the refrigerator until needed, or until four days have again passed.

If all this sounds like too much work and effort, I strongly suggest keeping on hand a supply of commercially canned beef gravy. There are two brands which I know to be good: Franco-American and Howard Johnson.

Since I use beef gravy primarily as a binder or a "sauce body," a very little bit of beef gravy goes a long way. Usually, when wine and spices are used, the flavor of a commercially canned gravy cannot be detected.

For those of you who are ambitious enough to wish to attempt a homemade beef gravy, a recipe follows. It is a simple, basic recipe. If you are canning or freezing, do certainly double or triple the recipe.

7 *pounds veal bones*
2 *large onions, coarsely chopped*
5 *carrots, scrapped and chopped coarsely*
6 *stalks celery, including leaves, coarsely chopped*
1 *teaspoon thyme*
1 *teaspoon coarsely ground pepper*
4 *crumbled bay leaves*
4 *cloves garlic, crushed or finely minced*
salt to taste
1 *teaspoon monosodium glutamate*
½ *cup flour*
3 *quarts water, or preferably stock*
1½ *cups tomato puree*
1 *cup chopped leeks, including the green part*
1 *cup parsley, not chopped*

Set oven at 475 degrees. Combine bones, onion, carrots, celery, leeks, thyme, pepper, bay leaves and garlic in a large, flat roasting pan. Sprinkle well with salt and monosodium glutamate. Place in preheated oven and roast for at least 40 minutes, or until all ingredients are browned. Sprinkle with flour. Toss all together lightly and continue to roast another fifteen minutes.

Transfer all ingredients of roasting pan to a large pot. Add 3 cups of stock or water to roasting pan and cook on top of stove, over medium heat, stirring to scrape up all the brown bits that stick to the pan. Pour liquid from roasting pan into the large pot. Add remaining stock or water, tomato puree and parsley. Bring to a rapid boil. Lower heat and simmer, uncovered for two hours. Skim occasionally, especially to remove fat as it rises to the top.

When gravy coats a spoon and is shiny, cool it until it can be handled easily. Then strain the sauce and discard all of the solid matter. Chill and remove any remaining fat from top.

From here on, can it, freeze it, or simply keep in the refrigerator as described previously.

COURT BOUILLON

1½ *bottles white wine*
2 *cups water*
1 *onion*
1 *bay leaf*
¼ *teaspoon thyme*
8 *peppercorns*
1 *teaspoon monosodium glutamate*
salt

Combine all ingredients in a deep saucepan. Bring to a boil. Lower heat. Simmer at least 15 minutes. Primarily used for poaching fish or seafood, but vegetables may also be cooked in this bouillon.

ASPIC

Aspic is simply well-seasoned clarified soup stock made with plenty of bones and allowed to chill until it forms a jelly. It is used to coat various cold foods, such as chicken breasts, eggs or veal.

If you are working with canned stock, it may be necessary to add some gelatin to make the consommé gel sufficiently. This may even be necessary if you are using homemade stock.To judge, put a few spoonfuls of consommé or soup stock into a metal measuring cup. Place in refrigerator until it is very cold. If it is of aspic quality, it will become firm. If it doesn't become firm at all, or if it forms a very soft jelly, gelatin must be added.

To make a completely liquid consommé into aspic, stir 1 envelope of unflavored gelatin into each 2 cups of cold consommé. Allow to stand for a few minutes. Then place over low heat and bring to the simmering point. Stir until gelatin is completely dissolved. Remove from heat. Cool, then chill till consommé is the consistency of unbeaten egg white, or somewhat syrupy.

Be sure the food you are coating with aspic is well chilled before spooning aspic over it. If you are coating chicken, say, place it on a rack over a pan to catch the excess aspic. When food has been coated with 1 coat of aspic, place it in the refrigerator (along with the bowl of aspic). If the food was well chilled ahead of time it will need only a few minutes to set.

Remove from refrigerator. Decorate as desired (with tarragon leaves, bits of cut-out truffle or black olive, pimento, etc.). Spoon another coat of syrupy aspic over decorations. Place food in refrigerator until ready to serve.

If you are working with a homemade consommé which gels very softly, add ½ envelope of gelatin to each pint of consommé. Proceed exactly according to procedure outlined above.

If you wish to make a fish aspic (for coating fish), use plenty of fish bones, as well as heads, if they are available. Use at least half wine for your cooking liquid. Season to taste with salt, pepper and monosodium glutamate. Clarify as for ordinary stock.

VINAIGRETTE SAUCE

Make this vinaigrette in quantity. Double or triple the recipe if your refrigerator can store that much. It will keep indefinitely. Spoon it over hot cooked vegetables—string beans, carrots, broccoli, diced eggplant—allow to come to room temperature, and you have a company treat. And you will find that thinly sliced leftover meat, such as boiled beef, roast pork or veal, is delicious after it has been marinated an hour or 2 in a few spoonfuls of this vinaigrette. So is thinly sliced cooked sausage—knockwurst or Polish kolbasa.

⅓ *cup finely chopped pimento*
¼ *cup capers*
1 *clove garlic, very finely chopped or crushed*
2 *teaspoons salt*
½ *teaspoon coarsely ground fresh pepper*
½ *teaspoon dried dill weed*
½ *teaspoon dried tarragon*
1 ¾ *cups olive oil*
¾ *cup wine vinegar*

Place all ingredients in a quart Mason jar. Place lid on jar and shake vigorously for 2 or 3 minutes. Store at room temperature. Oil and vinegar will again separate in jar, so be sure to shake well before using.

When using sauce, add to each ¾ cup: 2 tablespoons finely chopped fresh parsley, and, optionally, ½ hard-cooked egg, finely chopped. Chopped sweet or sour gherkins may also be added.

MAYONNAISE

Mayonnaise may be made in a blender, and it is adequate. However, for perfect mayonnaise, the beating process must continue even after the sauce has thickened in the blender.

1 *egg*
2 *tablespoons lemon juice*
1 *teaspoon salt*
1 *teaspoon powdered mustard*
½ *teaspoon white pepper*
2 *cups oil, approximately* (*use all olive oil or half olive oil and half salad oil*)

Place egg in the blender. Add lemon juice, salt, mustard and pepper. Whirl briefly, then add oil in a very fine stream. Do not add oil too quickly or mayonnaise will not thicken. Add as much oil as the sauce will absorb. When the mayonnaise is thick and does not draw in any more oil, transfer it from the blender jar to the bowl of your mixer. Turn mixer on high speed and continue to add oil, in a fine stream, until the mayonnaise is very thick and yellow, and stands in peaks when the beater is withdrawn. If you have no mixer, use a fine wire whisk to beat in the additional oil.

TAPENADE

This is a cold black sauce from the South of France that can be used in varying ways—as a table condiment, with poached fish or hard-cooked eggs, or as a dip for raw vegetables. It is very tangy and pungent, and should be used sparingly.

4 *ounces firm anchovies that have been packed in olive oil*
one 7-ounce can of tuna fish

⅓ cup capers
4 cloves garlic
24 black olives, pitted
juice of 3 lemons
1 teaspoon freshly ground black pepper
⅔ cup olive oil (approximately)
¼ cup cognac
round of paper to fit top of jar

Place first 7 ingredients into jar of blender. Blend, stopping motor occasionally to scrape down sides of jar. Gradually add olive oil, adding enough to make a sauce about as thick as mayonnaise. Pack into pint jar. Pour cognac over round of paper which has been cut to fit top of jar, then place cognac paper on top of tapenade. If there is any cognac left, pour it on top of paper. Cover jar tightly and store in refrigerator. Tapenade will keep almost indefinitely.
Yield: less than 1 pint.

PESTO

This is a thick, green sauce that may be used in a variety of ways. As a first course, it can serve as a dressing for hard-cooked eggs, or for cooked or raw vegetables. It is also delicious with pasta or seafood.

1 cup olive oil (approximately)
8 cloves garlic
2 cups coarsely chopped fresh basil or dill
1 cup parsley
2 teaspoons salt
pepper

Place a quarter of the oil into blender jar. Add garlic and some of the greens. Whirl in blender till smooth. If necessary, add a little more

(continued on the next page)

oil. Then add more greens. Continue this procedure until all the greens have been incorporated into a thick, green sauce. More or less olive oil may be needed. The consistency of the sauce should be almost as thick as mayonnaise.

Season with salt and pepper. Pack into a jar, and pour a little olive oil on top. Cover jar and store in refrigerator. Pesto keeps well for as long as a couple of months.
Yield: 1 pint.

SALSA FRIA (HOT SAUCE)

Salsa fria appears on almost every table in Mexico. It is delicious with all grilled foods or on crisp fried tortillas. To make guacamole, which is almost the national dish of Mexico, chop 1 or 2 ripe avocados coarsely, season with salt and stir in 2 or 3 tablespoons of salsa fria.

- 3 *large tomatoes, or* 1 *No.* 2 *can tomatoes*
- 2 *onions, minced*
- 3 *cloves garlic, minced*
- 4 *tablespoons wine vinegar*
- ½ *teaspoon oregano*
- 1 *green pepper, minced*
- 3 *small hot peppers, minced*
- 1 *teaspoon chopped fresh cilantro (optional)*
- 1 *teaspoon tabasco sauce*

If fresh tomatoes are used, place them directly over a high gas flame till skin chars and blisters. Peel off skin. Cut tomatoes in half, remove stem end, and with your hands, squeeze out juice and seeds.

If canned tomatoes are used, drain them well, then squeeze out excess liquid and seeds.

Chop tomatoes coarsely. Add all remaining ingredients. Put into a clean quart jar and cover tightly. Store in refrigerator. Salsa fria keeps for a month or so.

Among the preceding recipes are two that I try always to make up in large quantities—Vinaigrette Sauce (page 57) and Concentrate of Chicken or Beef (page 50). They keep indefinitely, and they are among the most useful and versatile items to include in your home-made foods in reserve.

2. FIRST COURSES

THE FIRST COURSE OF A MEAL should be attractive to the eye, not too copious in quantity, and certainly as interesting as any other part of the meal. There is a wealth of variety in first courses of all nations.

Since we live in a relatively servantless era, it is generally impractical to serve a hot first course at the dining room table, which must then be cleared to make way for the entrée. Yet I feel that standard-brand crackers, nuts and dips have no place at a dinner party and are dull tidbits, indeed, to offer guests with drinks before sitting down to dinner. A more imaginative approach to dining is to begin with a cold first course in the living room, serving it with cocktails or wines. This arrangement frees the hostess to attend to last-minute details in the kitchen or at the dining table.

Thought should be given as to how you will serve your cold first course. For a small group of 4 to 6, it is practical and appealing to arrange a large platter of pâté, garnished with clear aspic and watercress. Present a bowl of good olives along with a tray of crusty bread. Guests are free to help themselves as they please, and drink as they eat.

For a slightly larger group, it might be more practical to arrange individual first-course plates. This takes a little more of your time, but makes serving easier, particularly if the room or coffee table is small.

If you are having a larger group—over 10, perhaps—you might well set up your first course as a small buffet, on a separate table away from the coffee table, and again invite people to help themselves.

First Course Salads and Antipasti

Many of the marinated vegetables and salads in chapter 9 are appropriate to serve as first courses.

SWISS CHEESE SALAD

½ pound Swiss or Gruyère cheese, cut into ½″ cubes
6 hard-cooked eggs, diced
½ cup sour cream
2 tablespoons mayonnaise
1½ teaspoons mustard
1 tablespoon horseradish
¼ teaspoon powdered cumin
salt and pepper to taste

In a bowl, toss cheese and diced eggs lightly together. In a separate bowl, combine sour cream, mayonnaise, mustard, horseradish and cumin. Season to taste with salt and pepper. Pour over cheese-egg mixture and toss very gently. Serve on crisp salad greens.

Serves 6.

MARINATED ONIONS AND BLUE CHEESE SALAD

1 cup olive oil
6 tablespoons lemon juice
salt and pepper to taste
½ cup crumbled blue cheese
2⅔ cups thinly sliced red onions, separated into rings
½ cup chopped parsley

Combine oil, lemon juice and seasonings. Add cheese. Pour over onions. Cover tightly and chill for at least 2 days. Before serving, mix in chopped parsley. Serve on crisp salad greens with thinly sliced rye bread and butter.

Serves 6.

EGGS IN ASPIC

6 *poached eggs (see directions below)*
2½ *cups well-seasoned, clear Aspic (page* 56)
tiny bits of pimento, black truffles or olives, tarragon leaves, for garnish
3 *thin slices boiled ham*

To poach eggs: Put water into a large skillet to a depth of about 2 inches. Add salt and a teaspoon of vinegar. Bring to a boil. Lower heat till liquid is just simmering. Break eggs, one by one, into a saucer or small cup. Gently slide eggs, individually, into simmering liquid. Poach about 3 minutes, or till eggs are just set. Remove with skimmer and place eggs on a towel which has been rung out in cold water. Allow eggs to stand till they are perfectly cool.

The aspic should be cold and syrupy, about the consistency of unbeaten egg white. Pour about ¼ inch of the aspic into the bottoms of 6 round or oval custard cups—metal is better than glass or ceramic since it conducts cold (or heat) faster. Place the cups in the refrigerator until the aspic sets. When aspic has set, arrange a pretty garnish on top, using pimento, tarragon leaves, or what you have. Dribble a few drops of aspic on top of garnish. Chill to set.

Curl sliced ham around the inside of each cup so that it is standing on end. Trim some of the white from the poached eggs. Place an egg in the center of each cup. Gently add clear aspic to the top of cups. The aspic will find its way around ham and egg and form a coating. Chill several hours, or till firm.

To serve, unmold each cup on a lettuce leaf. First slide a small sharp knife all around sides of each mold, allowing some air to get into mold. Invert a plate holding a lettuce leaf on top of mold. Shake hard, once or twice. The contents of the mold should now be on the plate. If it isn't, dip the bottom of each mold briefly into hot water; then invert again and shake out contents of the mold.

Serves 6.

EGG AND SALMON TARTLETS

1½ cups cooked fresh salmon, flaked
⅔ cup well-seasoned homemade mayonnaise
6 baked Tartlet Shells (page 349)
6 eggs (poached and trimmed as for Eggs in Aspic)
caviar (optional)
black olive slices, cut into pretty shapes

Gently combine cooled, flaked salmon with homemade mayonnaise. Make a layer of salmon mixture in each baked tartlet shell. Place a trimmed poached egg on top of salmon. If caviar is available, surround sides of eggs with caviar. If it isn't, use additional homemade mayonnaise, pressing it through a star tube to make a garnish around egg. Decorate the top of each egg with a decorative cut-out of black olive.

Serves 6.

EGG SALAD

10 hard-cooked eggs
1 green pepper, minced
1 onion, minced
1 cup homemade mayonnaise
salt and pepper to taste

Dice eggs. Add remaining ingredients and toss gently. Serve on crisp greens, or use for stuffing marinated mushrooms, endive leaves, small tomatoes, or any other vegetable which lends itself to stuffing.

Serves 6.

MARINATED HARD-COOKED EGGS AND ONION RINGS

⅔ cup olive oil
4 tablespoons wine vinegar
salt and pepper to taste
10 hard-cooked eggs, sliced
1 cup thinly sliced red or yellow onions, separated into rings
chopped parsley

Combine oil, vinegar, salt and pepper.

Arrange egg slices in a serving dish. Sprinkle top with onion rings. Pour dressing over eggs and onions. Marinate at least 2 hours before serving. Sprinkle with chopped parsley before serving.

Serves 6.

HERRING AND ONIONS

This first course is simplicity itself—yet so delicious! Serve with thinly sliced, buttered pumpernickel.

2 schmaltz herrings, or 4 schmaltz herring filets
1 large red onion, thinly sliced and separated into rings

If you are starting with whole herrings, skin them and remove heads, if any. Then filet. With a sharp knife, make an incision down the entire back of fish. Now cut through the stomach part of fish which has not yet been split. With a scissors, cut off any fins. Starting from tail, with the help of a knife remove fish from bones, doing first one side, then the other. You may actually be able to pull the herring away from the bones with your fingers, once you get it started. After you have removed the 4 filets from the bones, inspect them carefully, and remove with tweezers any small bones which remain behind.

Cut herring filets into small pieces, about 1 inch square. Combine with onion rings and toss gently. Serve quite cold on a crisp bed of salad greens.

TARAMA

This is a rich, delicious concoction of Middle Eastern origin. It can be served as is on a platter of greens with crusty bread or Syrian bread (a flat, sesame-coated bread)—if you can get it. Tarama also makes a delicious stuffing for marinated mushrooms. It holds its shape so well that it can be pressed through a pastry tube into mushrooms. A bit of pitted black olive is a perfect garnish.

½ *cup tarama (salted roe; see Shopping Sources)*, or ⅔ *cup red caviar*
1 *slice onion*
juice of 2 *lemons*
3 *slices white bread, crusts removed, soaked in water till soft, then squeezed dry*
1 *to* 1½ *cups olive oil*
1 *tablespoon chopped parsley*

Place tarama or red caviar in blender. Add onion, lemon juice and bread. Add a quarter of the olive oil and turn on blender. Add more olive oil, very slowly, while the blender is working. Use enough olive oil to make a mixture like a thick mayonnaise. Stir in chopped parsley.

Serves 6.

FRESH STURGEON IN MARINADE

1 *cup white wine*
½ *cup water*
a few peppercorns
salt
1 *small onion*
a few sprigs parsley
1 *celery stalk with leaves*
2 *pounds boneless fresh sturgeon*
⅔ *cup olive oil*
½ *cup chopped parsley*

Combine wine, water, peppercorns, salt, onion, parsley and celery in a saucepan slightly larger than the piece of sturgeon. Bring to a boil. Simmer for 15 minutes. Add sturgeon. Cover and simmer sturgeon for 15 minutes. Remove from broth.

Turn heat under broth up high and reduce till there is no more than ⅓ cup liquid in pot. Strain, and reserve liquid. Slice sturgeon neatly. Mix pot liquid with olive oil. Pour over sturgeon slices which have been arranged in a serving dish. Chill well. Sprinkle with chopped parsley before serving.

Serves 6.

ANCHOVIES

Anchovies make a wonderful first course. I am not speaking of the mushy, salty ones which come in tiny inexpensive cans and practically disintegrate when you try to pick them up. Good anchovies are firm and much akin to good herring. They do not come in those little tiny cans, but in large ones, about 10 times the size (see Shopping Sources). But even after a can has been opened the anchovies keep for many weeks, provided they are covered with olive oil.

Other good anchovies are the salted ones sold in Italian or Greek grocery stores. These need some preparation, however. They must be soaked in fresh cold water for an hour or 2. A little vinegar may be added. Then, under cold running water, the skins should be rubbed off the anchovies and the filets pulled from the center backbone. This job is slightly time-consuming, and the canned ones, provided you find the right kind, are much easier to use.

To serve as a first course, arrange anchovies (4 to 6 per person) slightly overlapping each other on a platter. Sprinkle with a few spoonfuls of olive oil. Just before serving, garnish with onion rings, and hard-cooked eggs which have been finely chopped. Tiny tomatoes go well with this, as does thinly sliced rye bread and butter.

SMOKED SALMON IN SOUR CREAM-HORSERADISH SAUCE

½ *pound smoked salmon, shredded*
½ *cup finely minced shallots, red onion, or scallions*
2 *teaspoons fresh chopped dill*
¾ *cup sour cream*
2 *tablespoons horseradish (approximately)*
1 *tablespoon mayonnaise*
salt and pepper

Add shallots and dill to smoked salmon.

In a separate bowl, combine sour cream, horseradish and mayonnaise. Season with salt and pepper. Taste, and add additional horseradish if necessary.

Add dressing to salmon mixture. Toss gently. Serve in red cabbage leaf cups, using about 2 tablespoons of salmon mixture for each leaf. Garnish with additional chopped dill. Serve with thinly sliced buttered rye or pumpernickel.

Serves 6.

ITALIAN ANTIPASTO, FLORENTINE STYLE

⅔ *cup olive oil*
1 *cup celery, cut into 1" pieces*
1 *cup fennel, diced*
2 *cups chopped onions*
1 *cup cauliflower pieces*
1 *cup small mushrooms*
1 *cup green pepper, cut into 1-inch pieces*
6 *cloves garlic, minced*
½ *cup tomato purée*
1 *cup dry white wine*
½ *pound bay scallops*
½ *pound shelled, cleaned shrimp*
1 *teaspoon dried basil*
1 *cup chopped parsley*
salt and pepper to taste
½ *cup green olives*
½ *cup black olives*
¼ *cup capers*
4 *hard-cooked eggs, quartered*
8 *anchovies*

In a heavy saucepan, heat olive oil till it is almost smoking. Add celery, fennel, onions, cauliflower, mushrooms, green pepper and garlic. Toss and continue to cook for just a few minutes. Add tomato purée and white wine. When mixture begins to simmer and the vegetables are almost soft, add the scallops and shrimp. Simmer till seafood is cooked, no more than 5 to 8 minutes. Add basil, half of parsley and salt and pepper to taste. Add olives and capers. Chill at least 3 hours.

Before serving, sprinkle with remaining parsley and garnish with hard-cooked egg quarters and anchovies.

Serves 8 to 10.

SEAFOOD IN DILL PESTO

½ cup white wine
½ cup water
½ teaspoon monosodium glutamate
6 peppercorns
1 bay leaf
1 small onion
1 teaspoon salt
1 pound shelled, cleaned shrimp
1 pound bay scallops
½ cup olive oil
4 cloves garlic
1½ cups fresh dill weed, or 3 tablespoons dried dill and 1 cup fresh parsley

In a saucepan combine first 7 ingredients. Bring to a boil, and simmer for 5 minutes. Add shrimp and scallops. Simmer only till shrimp turn pink and scallops lose their translucency—no more than 4 or 5 minutes. Remove seafood from liquid and set aside. Turn heat up high and reduce liquid in saucepan till there is no more than ⅓ cup.

While liquid is reducing, pour olive oil into blender. Add garlic and dill (or garlic, dried dill and some fresh parsley). Whirl in blender. Add as much dill (or fresh parsley) as the oil will absorb. When it will not absorb any more, add the reduced liquid. Blend. Pour over reserved seafood and mix. Chill before serving.

Serves 6.

ABALONE, MEXICO CITY

Abalone is a shellfish from the West Coast. When bought fresh, it must be pounded with a heavy object to be tenderized. However, it

(continued on the next page)

may be obtained from Chinese and Japanese grocery stores in cans. The abalone in cans is so tender it need only be sliced and used.

1 *can abalone, drained and diced*
1 *small onion, chopped*
1 *clove garlic, minced*
1 *small green pepper, chopped*
tabasco sauce to taste
juice of 1 *lemon*
¼ *cup olive oil*
salt and pepper to taste
2 *tablespoons chopped cilantro* (*optional*)
2 *avocados*

Combine all ingredients except avocados. Chill. Before serving, peel avocados. Section each one into 3 pieces and remove pits. Place each avocado section on a bed of crisp greens. Spoon abalone mixture over avocados and serve.

Serves 6.

HAWAIIAN MARINATED RAW FISH

1½ *pounds very fresh swordfish, tuna or striped bass*
⅔ *cup Japanese soy sauce*
⅓ *cup lemon juice*
1 *teaspoon shredded fresh ginger, or pickled ginger*
½ *teaspoon wasabi paste* (*see page* 20)
1 *cup Japanese seaweed, cut up* (*see Shopping Sources*)

Cut fish into small pieces. Combine remaining ingredients. Pour over fish. Marinate several hours before serving on crisp shredded greens.

Serves 6.

CEVICHE

Ceviche is Mexican in origin. Nothing in it is cooked; yet the acid properties of the marinade give the seafood a cooked quality which makes this first course unusual and delicious. Of course the seafood should be very fresh!

1/3 pound scallops
2/3 pound shelled, cleaned shrimp
1/3 pound filet of sole, or other firm white fish, such as striped bass or halibut
1 cup lime juice
1 onion, minced
1 small green pepper, minced
1 small hot pepper, minced
2 cloves garlic, minced
2 canned pimentos, minced
2 teaspoons chopped fresh cilantro
2 sweet gherkins, minced
salt and pepper to taste
1 teaspoon sugar (approximately)
1/2 cup white vinegar
1 large avocado

Cut all seafood into tiny pieces. Combine in a bowl. Pour lime juice over. Cover bowl and place in refrigerator for at least 4 hours, or until seafood has changed color and looks somewhat cooked. (Filet of sole and scallops will be white; the shrimp will be pink, as if they had been cooked.)

Drain the lime juice from the seafood. Dry seafood with paper towels as thoroughly as possible.

Combine all the remaining ingredients—except avocado—in a separate bowl. Taste. The mixture should be quite well seasoned—slightly sweet and spicy. Pour over drained seafood and toss well. Place in refrigerator till serving time. Before serving, peel and dice avocado. Combine with fish mixture. Serve in red cabbage leaf cups.

Serves 6.

ZUCCHINI STUFFED WITH TUNA

4 medium zucchini
3 cloves garlic
⅔ cup olive oil
2 slices bread, soaked in water, then squeezed dry and crumbled
1 teaspoon pepper
1 cup chopped parsley
1 7-ounce can tuna fish, mashed up
½ pound small mushrooms
1 cup tomato purée or sauce
salt
½ cup stock

Cut zucchini into 2-inch pieces. Scoop out centers, using a small sharp knife or apple corer. Chop zucchini centers coarsely. Combine with garlic. Sauté in half of oil till soft. Mix with bread, pepper, half of parsley, and mashed tuna fish.

Sauté mushrooms in remaining oil till soft. Add tomato purée, a little salt and stock. Simmer 15 minutes.

Stuff zucchini shells with tuna fish combination. Place into tomato purée mixture. Bake in a 375 degree oven about 45 minutes, or until zucchini are very tender. Serve cold, sprinkled with remaining chopped parsley.

Serves 6.

STUFFED MUSSELS, MIDDLE EAST STYLE

5 pounds mussels
5 medium onions, chopped
5 stalks celery, chopped, including leaves
2 cloves garlic, minced
1¼ cups olive oil
¾ cup rice

½ cup pine nuts
½ cup currants
¼ teaspoon each: cinnamon, cloves and allspice
¼ cup water
salt
1 cup water (approximately)
lemon wedges

Scrub mussels very well with steel wool, a brush or a dull knife, removing all the hairy, crusty parts on shell. Open each mussel with a small, sharp knife, but do not separate shells.

Sauté onions, celery and garlic in 1 cup olive oil until soft. Add rice, pine nuts, currants and spices. Stir. Continue to sauté about 5 minutes. Add ¼ cup water and salt. When the water is absorbed, rice will be only half cooked.

With a knife, arrange mussels so that all of the fish is in one side of the shell. Fill other side of shell with half-cooked rice mixture. Close shells and place the stuffed mussels close together in a large, deep pot. Place a plate on top of mussels to keep them in place. Add water to approximately one third the depth of the mussels. Add ¼ cup olive oil. Cover pot and cook about 30 minutes. Cool in pot.

To serve, remove from liquid and serve with lemon wedges.

Serves 6.

SEAFOOD AND RAW MUSHROOM SALAD

1½ pounds fresh white mushrooms, sliced
⅔ cup Vinaigrette Sauce (page 57)
1½ cups cooked cleaned shrimp or lobster meat, cut up, or flaked crabmeat
½ cup chopped parsley

Place mushrooms in a bowl. Pour vinaigrette over them, and toss. Marinate for at least an hour. Just before serving, add seafood. Toss gently. Serve on a bed of crisp greens, and sprinkle with chopped parsley.

Serves 6 to 8.

STUFFED PEPPERS, ITALIAN STYLE

8 *small green peppers*
4 *cups soft white bread crumbs, prepared by cutting bread into tiny cubes slightly smaller than peas*
1¼ *cups olive oil*
4 *cloves garlic, chopped*
8 *chopped anchovies*
¼ *cup chopped parsley*
¾ *cup chopped ripe olives*
3 *tablespoons capers*
3 *tablespoons currants*
salt and pepper to taste

Remove stems and seeds from peppers so they may be stuffed. If they are large, cut them in halves.

If bread is very fresh or of the soft variety, place the little cubes on a flat baking sheet and allow them to dry out, slightly, in a 350 degree oven.

Combine crumbs with 1 cup olive oil and all remaining ingredients, tossing lightly.

Stuff peppers, being careful not to pack the stuffing down. Spoon a little more oil over each pepper. Bake in a 350 degree oven for 45 minutes. Serve at room temperature.

Serves 8.

TUSCANY BEEF

1 *large onion, finely chopped*
¼ *cup finely chopped celery, including leaves*
3 *cloves garlic, minced*
⅓ *cup olive oil*
1¼ *cups red wine*

¼ cup wine vinegar
1½ cups strong beef stock
2 cups chopped parsley
salt
freshly ground pepper
1 bay leaf, crumbled
2 pounds raw filet of beef, trimmed of fat and sliced very thin with slicing machine by butcher

Sauté chopped onion, celery and garlic in olive oil till soft and golden. Add wine, wine vinegar and beef stock. Cook over high heat till liquid is reduced by one third. Add ¼ cup chopped parsley. Season with salt, fresh pepper and crumbled bay leaf.

Spoon some of this spicy liquid into a deep dish. Add a layer of thinly sliced beef. Add more hot liquid. Repeat layers of beef and liquid until all is used up. Cover dish and refrigerate at least 24 hours, or up to 6 days.

Before serving, drain liquid from slices of meat. Arrange meat on a platter and sprinkle with plenty of freshly chopped parsley.

You may also roll each slice of meat up, jelly-roll style. Skewer with toothpicks, and dip each roll into plenty of freshly chopped parsley.

Serves 6.

SAUSAGE VINAIGRETTE

For this very simple dish, you need a good, cooked sausage such as Polish kolbasa or even knockwurst. Remove the casing from the sausage. Slice sausage very thin and arrange on a serving plate. Sprinkle with chopped scallions. Gently spoon enough Vinaigrette Sauce (page 57) over to moisten the sausage well. Let sausage marinate in vinaigrette at least an hour. Sprinkle with chopped parsley before serving.

PARSLIED CHICKEN LOAF

3 *cups double-strength chicken stock (Concentrate of Chicken, page 50)*
1 *cup Madeira*
5 *whole chicken breasts, boned, skinned and cut in half*
1/4 *pound smoked or pickled tongue, cut into tiny cubes*
1 *cup finely chopped parsley*
2 *teaspoons fresh tarragon (or 1/2 teaspoon dry)*
2 *envelopes gelatin*

Bring stock and 3/4 cup Madeira to a boil. Lower heat so that liquid is just simmering. Poach chicken breasts in simmering liquid for about 6 minutes, or till they are just cooked. Cool and cut into 3/4-inch dice. Mix with tongue cubes. Add chopped parsley and tarragon and toss gently. Pack chicken mixture into a 5 x 7 loaf pan.

Sprinkle gelatin into remaining Madeira in a small metal pan. Stir. Place over low heat until gelatin is completely dissolved. Stir gelatin into chicken stock. Pour stock over chicken in pan.

Chill till firm. Loosen loaf by sliding a knife around edges of pan and allowing air to enter. Unmold on a bed of crisp salad greens, and serve cold.

Serves 6 to 8.

Pates and Terrines

Pâtés make a perfect first course. They may be prepared days—even weeks—ahead of time. To keep them at their best, seal them well in the fat in which they were cooked. If pâtés are well sealed, you can count on most to keep 2 to 3 weeks, refrigerated. Home-canned Country Pâté will keep for a year or more. A recipe for Home-canned Pâté will be found on page 36.

The difference between a pâté and a terrine is principally in the serving. A pâté is unmolded, while a terrine refers to an earthenware mold from which the pâté is served.

Firm pâtés which are not canned should be weighted so they will slice well.

TO WEIGHT A PATE

After taking pâté from oven, do not remove mold in which pâté was cooked from underpan. There will be an overflow of fat after weights are placed on top.

Place a pan that is slightly smaller than the pâté mold right on top of the baked pâté. Fill pan with heavy objects, or place a heavy skillet on top. Do not remove weights until pâté is completely cool. Refrigerate until pâté is needed.

PATE DE CAMPAGNE

1½ *pounds fresh pork fat*
1 *pound boneless veal*
1 *pound boneless pork shoulder*
1 *pound ham*
½ *pound chicken or pork livers*
8 *cloves garlic*
¼ *cup heavy cream*
3 *eggs*
½ *cup cognac*
4 *teaspoons salt*
2 *teaspoons white pepper*
½ *teaspoon allspice*
½ *teaspoon cinnamon*
½ *cup flour*

Slice thinly ½ pound of the pork fat. Finely grind half of the remaining pork fat with all the veal and pork shoulder.

Line a 3-quart mold or two 1½-quart molds with the thin slices of pork fat, letting long ends hang over the edge of the pan.

Grind the ham and remaining pork fat, using the coarse blade of the meat grinder. If a coarse blade is not available, dice the meat finely with a sharp knife.

In an electric blender, purée the livers with the garlic, cream, eggs and cognac. Gradually add to the blender about a third of the finely ground veal-pork mixture.

In a mixing bowl combine all the ground and puréed meats and add the remaining seasonings and flour. Mix all the ingredients thoroughly.

Fill the prepared mold with the pâté mixture. Fold the overhanging strips of pork fat over the top. Cover tightly with a double thickness of aluminum foil. Place the mold in a pan of water and bake in a 400 degree oven 3 hours. Remove the aluminum foil and continue baking until the top of the pâté is brown, about 20 minutes longer. Weight the pâté according to directions given on page 81.

Yield: 3 quarts pâté.

Note: If desired, the veal and pork shoulder may be replaced by any available game, such as venison, hare or pheasant. Also, the amount of garlic may be regulated according to taste.

FINE LIVER PATE

This is one pâté that does not keep more than a few days. Because of the liver, it does not can well either. It is, however, delicate, rich and delicious, and makes an excellent first course for a party of 10 to 12.

1 *teaspoon rendered chicken fat, or rendered pork fat*
2 *pounds chicken livers*
3 *eggs*
⅓ *cup cognac*
1½ *cups heavy cream*
⅔ *cup diced fresh unrendered chicken fat or fresh pork fat*
1 *onion, coarsely chopped*
½ *cup flour*
5 *teaspoons salt*
1 *teaspoon ground ginger*
1 *teaspoon monosodium glutamate*
2 *teaspoons white pepper*
1 *teaspoon allspice*

Lightly grease a 3-quart mold with rendered fat.

In an electric blender, make a fine purée of the livers, eggs, cognac and cream. From time to time add a little diced fat, onion and flour. (It will not be possible to do the entire mixture at one time. Three or 4 separate blendings will be needed.)

Add all the seasonings to the purée, and mix well. Pour into the mold and cover the top with a double thickness of aluminum foil.

Place in a pan of water and bake in a 325 degree oven for 1 hour. Cool the pâté, then store it in the refrigerator. (This pâté should not be weighted.) If desired, the top may be decorated with slices of truffle and a clear aspic poured over, after the pâté has been chilled. Yield: 3 quarts pâté.

TRUFFLED PATE

1½ pounds fresh pork fat
1 pound lean boneless veal
1 pound pork shoulder
½ pound ham
½ pound tongue
4 chicken breast halves, boned, skinned and trimmed
1 pound chicken livers
4 eggs
⅓ cup cognac
½ cup chopped black truffles
½ cup pistachio nuts
4 teaspoons salt
1 teaspoon white pepper
2 teaspoons monosodium glutamate
1 teaspoon allspice
½ teaspoon cinnamon
¼ teaspoon ground cloves
⅓ cup flour

Slice ⅔ pound of pork fat thinly. Grind ⅛ pound each of the veal, pork shoulder, pork fat, ham and tongue. Grind each 3 times.

Wrap each chicken breast half in a thin strip of sliced pork fat.

Line two 1½-quart molds or one 3-quart mold with the remaining thin slices of pork fat, letting long ends hang over outside of the pan.

In an electric blender, purée half the chicken livers with the eggs and cognac. Gradually add all the ground meats to the blender. If necessary, use a little more cognac, an additional egg or a little cream to provide extra liquid so that the mixture is made as fine as possible.

With a sharp knife, cut the remaining pork fat and meats (except the chicken breast) into cubes less than ⅓ inch in size. Combine the finely ground meats with the diced meats. Add the truffles, nuts, seasonings and flour. Mix very well.

Fill the molds slightly less than halfway with the pâté mixture. Place wrapped chicken breasts on top of this mixture; cover with remaining pâté, filling pans to top.

Fold hanging strips of pork fat over the top of pâté. Cover each mold tightly with a double thickness of aluminum foil. Place in a pan of water and bake in a 400 degree oven 3 hours. Remove the aluminum foil and continue baking until the top of the pâté is brown, about 20 minutes longer. Weight the pâté according to directions on page 81. Yield: 3 quarts pâté.

PATE A LA PUGETOISE

1 *slice ham, cut ¼″ thick, then cut into long strips*
½ *pound fresh larding pork cut into 12 long strips*
⅔ *pound chicken livers*
1 *small pair sweetbreads, blanched for 10 minutes and trimmed, then cut into strips ½″ wide (see page 222)*
1 *teaspoon salt*
½ *teaspoon pepper*
1 *teaspoon monosodium glutamate*
¼ *teaspoon allspice*
¼ *teaspoon ginger*
4 *cloves garlic, crushed*
⅓ *cup cognac*

In a broad, shallow dish, arrange ham in one corner, then place the larding pork, chicken livers and sweetbreads in separate piles, side by side. Sprinkle with salt, pepper, monosodium glutamate, allspice, ginger, garlic and cognac. Place in refrigerator, and marinate for at least 2 hours. Drain marinade and place in a measuring cup before continuing with recipe.

1 *egg*
heavy cream
¼ *pound fresh larding pork, cut into small dice*
⅓ *pound chicken livers*
¼ *pound ground veal*
¼ *pound ground pork*

(continued on the next page)

1½ *teaspoons salt*
½ *teaspoon pepper*
½ *teaspoon monosodium glutamate*
¼ *teaspoon allspice*
¼ *teaspoon ginger*
¼ *cup flour*
2 *veal or pork cauls (see instructions below)*

To marinade in measuring cup, add egg, then enough heavy cream to make ⅔ cup liquid. Place this liquid in blender. Turn blender on, gradually adding diced pork fat and chicken livers till a fine purée forms. Gradually add as much ground veal and pork as the purée will absorb, keeping the blender working. Pour this puréed meat mixture into a bowl. Add to bowl any remaining ground pork and veal, and add all seasonings and flour. Mix very well, with your hands.

Now take 2 veal or pork cauls approximately 10 x 14 inches in diameter. (Cauls are a thin but strong membrane from the stomach of the animal. Order them from your butcher ahead of time to be sure he will have them. If you have difficulty obtaining them, use the skins of 2 large chickens or 1 large turkey.) Spread each caul (or skin) flat. If there are any holes, overlap to cover them.

Spread each caul with half of ground meat mixture, making the layers even.

Now, from the meat mixture which was marinated, take some larding pork and make a strip across the ground meat (cover the ground meat completely). Then make a strip of chicken livers; next a strip of sweetbreads, and one of ham. Repeat: using larding pork, chicken livers, sweetbreads and ham till the cauls are covered with alternating strips of meat. Turn in ends of cauls. Now roll cauls up, jelly-roll style, rolling as tightly as possible. Fit each roll into a 9 x 5 x 3 loaf pan. Cover tops tightly with aluminum foil. Place in pan of water, and bake in a 400 degree oven for 2½ hours. Remove foil covering, and bake ½ hour longer.

Remove from oven. Weight each pâté according to directions on page 81. When pâtés have cooled, remove them from pans. Wrap well in foil and chill before serving.

This is a particularly beautiful pâté which looks like a mosaic.
Yield: 2 to 3 loaves of pâté, serving 10 to 12 people.

COARSE LIVER PATE

1 *pound fresh larding pork, ½ sliced thinly, the rest ground*
2½ *pounds chicken livers*
⅔ *cup coarsely chopped pistachio nuts*
½ *pound ground veal*
½ *pound ground pork*
⅓ *cup Madeira*
2 *eggs*
1 *cup flour*
1 *tablespoon monosodium glutamate*
1 *tablespoon salt*
2 *teaspoons allspice*
1 *tablespoon coarsely ground pepper*
1 *teaspoon ginger*

Set oven at 375 degrees.

Line a 9 x 5 x 3 loaf pan with thin slices of larding pork, reserving some of the slices for the top of the pâté.

Grind ½ pound chicken livers; reserve remaining livers. With your hands mix ground livers, veal and pork with the rest of the ingredients. Cut reserved livers in half. When the ground mixture is thoroughly combined, add the halved livers and, still using your hands, mix well. Fill prepared pan. Bang pan against counter once or twice to settle ingredients. Arrange larding pork slices on top of pâté.

Place loaf in a pan of hot water, and cover top of pâté with aluminum foil. Bake in preheated oven for 3 hours. Remove pâté from oven and weight according to directions on page 81. This pâté will not keep for more than 10 days.

Serves 8 to 10.

RILLETTES

Rillette is a widely known item of charcuterie in France, often served as part of an hors d'oeuvre plate, taking the place of pâté. When properly prepared and stored, it will keep a long time—I have kept it in the refrigerator for as long as 6 weeks. It makes a wonderful spread for crusty bread or crackers.

½ *pound fresh pork fat*
1½ *pounds fresh boneless shoulder of pork*
1 *goose or 2 ducks, cut into quarters*
1 *bottle white wine (approximately)*
1 *tablespoon chopped black truffles (optional)*
1 *teaspoon allspice*
¼ *teaspoon cinnamon*
2 *teaspoons white pepper*
1 *teaspoon ginger*
salt to taste

Place pork fat, pork and goose or ducks (including fat) in a deep pot. Add enough wine to cover, and bring slowly to a boil. Cover pot and simmer till meats are tender.

Take pieces of goose out of pot; remove all bones. Return meat to pot and continue to simmer, uncovered, for 2 or 3 hours, or until all the liquid has evaporated and the meats are simmering in fat.

Remove meats from pot, and cool slightly (reserve fat). With 2 forks, pull meats apart till they are in small shreds. Then, with a wooden spoon, or with an electric mixer, beat, adding enough fat to bind meat together. Add truffles and other seasonings, and salt to taste.

Pack into small crocks, leaving ½ inch at the top. Heat remaining fat till it is boiling hot, and pour into crocks. Cover, and refrigerate.

Note: You may chill rillette mixture in refrigerator until it is very cold, and then form into sausage shapes 8 inches long, 2 inches in diameter. Place each one on a piece of aluminum foil, and spoon boiling hot fat over to form a shell around the sausage. Enclose in aluminum foil and store in refrigerator.

COUNTRY TERRINE, JIM BEARD

1 *8-pound turkey, boned (see page 268)*
¼ *teaspoon each: cloves, nutmeg and allspice*
2 *teaspoons monosodium glutamate*
½ *cup cognac*
1 *pound boneless veal*
1 *pound boneless pork*
1 *pound ham*
1 *pound unsmoked bacon (pork siding)*
½ *pound chicken livers*
4 *eggs*
5 *teaspoons salt*

Cut the meat of the boned turkey away from the skin, being careful not to tear the skin. Set skin aside.

Cut the breast into halves, and place the halves in a bowl. Sprinkle with spices and monosodium glutamate. Pour cognac over, and allow breast to marinate while you are continuing with recipe.

Cut two thirds of the veal, pork, ham and unsmoked bacon into large cubes, about 1 inch in diameter. Add to the turkey breast in the marinade.

Grind remaining turkey meat very fine with remaining veal, pork, ham and unsmoked bacon.

Purée chicken livers in blender, using eggs as liquid.

Combine puréed liver mixture with ground meats, mixing well. Add salt and marinade from cubed meats to ground meat mixture, and mix in well. Then mix cubed meats into ground meat mixture.

Line a 3-quart terrine with the reserved turkey skin, letting ends overlap sides of terrine. Add half of meat mixture to terrine, patting meat down firmly. Lay whole turkey breasts on top. Cover with remaining meat mixture. Fold skin over top.

Cover terrine, and place in a pan of water. Bake for 2 hours in a 425 degree oven. Remove cover. If the juices look clear, the terrine is sufficiently cooked.

Remove from the oven, and weight down till cooled (see directions on page 81).

Yield: 3 quarts.

JEWISH-STYLE CHOPPED CHICKEN LIVERS

My version of Jewish chopped livers has changed over the many years I have been making it. I originally learned from my mother, but then I went on experimenting until I arrived at my present version, which I do think is the ultimate.

1 *pound unrendered chicken fat*
4 *Spanish onions, finely chopped*
1 *pound chicken livers*
1 *teaspoon monosodium glutamate*
4 *hard-cooked eggs*
salt and pepper

Render chicken fat (see page 28) using half of 1 onion.

Drain grieben and reserve for later use.

Place remaining onions in a heavy skillet over medium heat. Do not add any fat or liquid. Cover skillet and allow onions to steam in their own juice until they are almost dry and sticking to the pan. Add approximately ⅔ cup rendered chicken fat, and sauté onions in fat until they are golden brown. When onions are golden, remove them from pan, leaving excess fat.

Add chicken livers to pan and sauté until no blood comes when livers are pricked with a fork. Sprinkle with a teaspoon of monosodium glutamate and some salt.

Grind onions, livers and grieben in a meat grinder, along with shelled hard-cooked eggs. Also add any pan drippings. After grinding, mix well with a spoon. Taste and correct seasoning. Add 4 or 5 tablespoons additional chicken fat. Pack into a 1-quart terrine. Cover top with a little chicken fat. This will keep for almost 2 weeks.
Yield: 1 quart chopped livers.

3. SOUPS

A GOOD WAY TO BEGIN to cook a soup is with soup stock. This gives extra rich flavor, even if canned stock is all that is available. If you keep a supply of homemade Chicken or Beef Concentrate, you always have the makings of delicious soup.

Most soups take well to home-canning after they are cooked. They may be canned in glass jars, following the directions given with the pressure-canner. Home-canned soups present an ever-ready supply of luncheon dishes, or even first courses. The jars need only be opened, and their contents brought to the boiling point and simmered for 10 minutes.

A Chinese and a Japanese soup are usually delicious, and they constitute entire meals in themselves. Their final preparation takes place at the table—and this is part of the pleasure of serving them.

Cold soups are in a category by themselves. They may take the place of the cold first course.

CHICKEN BROTH

This is no ordinary chicken broth. It is more than double rich in flavor.

1 *5- or 6-pound fowl, quartered*
4 *pounds chicken backs*
chicken stock, fresh-cooked, canned, or made from Concentrate (page 50). If canned stock is used, choose a good brand, such as College Inn. You will need enough of it to cover the chicken and chicken backs in a deep pot. If you must, use part water.
soup greens—4 or 5 large stalks celery, with leaves; a handful of parsley; 2 carrots; 1 large onion; a handful of fresh dill; 2 leeks, and a parsnip, if available
2 *teaspoons monosodium glutamate*
salt to taste

Combine quartered chicken and chicken backs in a deep soup pot. Add enough stock (or a combination of stock and water) to just cover the contents of pot. Bring to a boil, and skim foam from top of soup. Lower heat. Simmer slowly, uncovered, for about 2½ hours. Add all of the washed soup greens and the monosodium glutamate. Simmer until the vegetables are all very soft (about 45 minutes).

Remove from heat. Season to taste with salt. Remove chicken, chicken backs and soup greens from pot, being sure to press out all the liquid.

Cool soup; then chill so that fat will solidify at the top and can be removed.

Chicken broth can be used in many ways—as a light first course, with a garnish of finely chopped parsley or chives, with cooked noodles or rice, or with any garniture which suits your fancy. Vegetables are delicious when braised in broth.

The broth will keep in the refrigerator for 3 or 4 days. To keep it for a longer period, reboil, cool and chill it every fourth day.

BEEF BROTH

Follow the same procedure as for making chicken broth, substituting 5 pounds of cracked beef bones and a 3-pound piece of brisket or grainy chuck, and using beef stock, fresh, canned or made from Concentrate in place of the chicken stock. To give the soup a good color, brown the cracked bones well in a 400 degree oven before you add the bones to the soup pot. The seasoning is the same as for chicken broth.

CONSOMME

Sometimes it is desirable to have a completely clear consommé. To this you may add any number of garnitures: watercress, chicken breasts (diced, skinned and added raw if the consommé is very hot), parboiled vegetables of any kind, or croutons.

Clear consommé with an appropriate garniture makes a perfect first course for a heavy dinner. You may clarify your own homemade soup stock (which is preferable, of course), or you may use a good brand of canned stock. Be sure, always, that all the fat is skimmed from the top of the stock.

To Clarify Soup Stock

For each quart of stock, use 1 egg white. Beat the egg white to a froth which is not quite stiff. Stir into cold stock. Place over medium heat, continuing to stir. When stock begins to simmer at edges, stop stirring. Allow mixture to simmer about 10 minutes. By that time, the egg white will coagulate and gather with it all the little bits in the stock which have been making it cloudy. Turn off the heat and allow mixture to settle for about ½ hour. Remove as much of coagulated egg white in one piece as possible. Then strain remaining liquid through 3 thicknesses of cheesecloth.

LEEK SOUP

3 *tablespoons butter*
5 *large leeks, trimmed, cleaned and sliced thin*
4 *cups strong beef stock*
salt and pepper
½ *teaspoon monosodium glutamate*
croutons

Melt butter in a deep saucepan. Add sliced leeks. Sauté over low heat until leeks are soft. Add stock, salt, pepper and monosodium glutamate. Simmer until leeks are very tender. Serve hot with croutons.

Serves 6.

GARLIC SOUP

1 *cup peeled garlic*
1 *tablespoon chopped onion*
2 *tablespoons olive oil or lard*
⅔ *cup drained tomatoes*
1 *quart soup stock*
salt and pepper
1 *teaspoon monosodium glutamate*
1 *egg, slightly beaten*
2 *cups croutons*

Mince garlic. Combine with chopped onion. Heat oil or lard in a deep saucepan but do not allow to smoke. Add garlic and onion, and sauté slowly until they are soft but not brown. Add tomatoes, mixing in well. When tomatoes lose their shape in saucepan, add stock. Season with salt, pepper and monosodium glutamate, and simmer for 15 minutes. Reduce heat under soup. Stir in lightly beaten egg, adding it very slowly. Serve at once with croutons.

Serves 6.

BLACK BEAN SOUP

This recipe is adapted from one used by the very fine Coach House restaurant in New York City. This is a hearty soup—almost a meal in itself—and especially delicious.

2 *cups black beans*
2½ *quarts cold water*
1½ *stalks celery, chopped*
1½ *large onions, chopped*
¼ *cup butter or bacon fat*
1¼ *tablespoons flour*
¼ *cup chopped parsley*
rind and bone of a smoked ham
1½ *leeks, trimmed and sliced*
1 *bay leaf*
2 *teaspoons salt*
½ *teaspoon black pepper*
½ *cup Madeira*
1 *hard-cooked egg, peeled and chopped*
½ *lemon*

Wash beans. Soak overnight in water to cover. In the morning drain beans. In a deep pot, combine beans and 2½ quarts of water. Cook beans over low heat for 1½ hours.

In a soup pot, sauté chopped celery and onions in butter over low heat until they are tender. Remove from heat. Blend in flour and chopped parsley. Return to low heat for a few minutes, stirring constantly. Gradually stir in beans and their liquid. Add rind and bone of ham, thinly sliced leeks, bay leaf, salt and pepper. Simmer soup for 4 hours.

Discard ham bone, rind and bay leaf. Force beans through a sieve, or purée in blender. Combine the puréed beans, their broth and ½ cup Madeira. Reheat soup; remove from stove. Stir in 2 finely chopped hard-cooked eggs, and add a thin slice of lemon to each serving. Serves 10 to 12.

POTATO SOUP

4 slices bacon, diced
6 leeks, trimmed and sliced thin
3 large potatoes, peeled and sliced
1 quart chicken stock
salt and pepper
1 teaspoon monosodium glutamate
1 cup sour cream

Sauté bacon in a deep saucepan until most of fat is rendered, but bacon is barely crisp. Add leeks and sauté till soft. Add potatoes and stir. Add chicken stock. Simmer for about 45 minutes, or until potatoes are very tender. Season with salt, pepper and monosodium glutamate. Remove from heat. Put mixture, including bacon, through a food mill, or whirl in the blender till smooth. Return to saucepan. Stir in sour cream. Reheat if necessary, but do not boil. Serve hot.

Serves 6 to 8.

Each of the following eight soups is a meal in itself. They are especially appropriate on a cold winter day; they taste even better after being reheated.

DUTCH PEA SOUP

1½ *cups dried split peas, washed and soaked overnight in cold water*
1 *ham shank, preferably with a little meat on it*
3 *or* 4 *beef or veal bones*
2 *pigs' feet, if available*
2 *carrots, scraped*
4 *stalks celery, with leaves*
1 *large onion*
10 *cups water or, preferably, stock*
salt to taste
white pepper to taste
2½ *cups croutons (flavored with garlic)*

After split peas have been washed and soaked overnight, drain remaining water. Place split peas into a large, heavy pot. Add all remaining ingredients except croutons.

Cover pot. Cook over medium heat till almost boiling. Reduce heat so soup is just simmering. Remove ham bone after 1 hour. Cut off meat. Replace bone in soup, and dice ham for use later. Simmer soup for 2½ to 3 hours.

Taste for seasoning and correct if necessary. To serve, remove all bones and vegetables from soup. Cut meat off pigs' feet and add to diced ham. Dice carrots. Discard onion, celery and remaining bones. Add meat from ham and pigs' feet to soup. Add diced carrots. Serve piping hot with croutons.

Serves 10 to 12.

SPANISH SOUP

¼ pound dried chickpeas
¼ pound dried white marrow beans
¼ pound salt pork, diced
¼ pound smoked ham, diced
¼ pound chorizos (Spanish sausage; if this is not available use any garlic sausage)
8 cups water or stock
2 cloves garlic, finely minced
1 ham bone
2 tomatoes, chopped
1½ teaspoons ground cumin
4 small potatoes, peeled and diced
salt and pepper to taste
½ pound chopped dandelion greens (if these are not available, use spinach or other greens)
3 tablespoons butter
croutons

Wash chickpeas and marrow beans. Soak overnight in water to cover. Drain in the morning.

Sauté salt pork till lightly browned. Add ham and sausage. Sauté these meats until they are almost completely cooked. Remove them from pot. Discard fat. Cut sausage into thin slices, and reserve meats till later.

Add all remaining ingredients to pot except dandelion greens and butter. Simmer for 2½ to 3 hours, or until chickpeas and beans are completely tender.

Make sure dandelion greens are clean and well drained of water. Melt butter in a heavy skillet. Add greens. Toss over high heat until they are wilted and any liquid which comes out cooks away. Add to soup. If there is any meat on ham bone, cut it into dice; discard bone and add diced ham and other meats to soup. Correct seasoning. Serve with croutons. Serves 10 to 12.

MEXICAN BEEF SOUP

2 *pounds flanken, very grainy chuck, or brisket*
1 *large beef bone, sawed into* 3 *or* 4 *pieces*
8 *cups water or stock*
1 *tablespoon salt*
½ *teaspoon black pepper*
1 *teaspoon monosodium glutamate*
1 *cup chopped onion*
1 *cup chopped green pepper*
1 *cup sliced carrot*
1 *cup chopped celery*
1 *cup diced potato*
1 16-*ounce can tomatoes*
2 *tablespoons chili powder*
½ *teaspoon ground cumin*
1½ *cups sliced zucchini*
1 *cup uncooked elbow macaroni*

Place meat, bone, water, salt, pepper and monosodium glutamate in a soup pot. Cover and bring to a boil. Lower heat and simmer about 2 hours, or until meat is barely tender. Cool. Chill in refrigerator until fat on top of liquid has hardened and can be removed and discarded.

Add all remaining ingredients except zucchini and macaroni. Simmer for about 1 hour, or till meat is thoroughly tender. Remove from heat, discard bone and cut meat into small pieces. Add meat, zucchini and macaroni to soup. Bring to a boil. Lower heat and simmer until macaroni and zucchini are tender.

Serves 10 to 12.

CABBAGE SOUP

3 pounds brisket of beef
3 or 4 good marrow bones
3 cloves garlic, chopped
2 onions, chopped
2½ quarts stock or water
1 No. 2 can tomatoes
1 5-pound cabbage, shredded coarsely, core removed
½ pound sauerkraut, washed in cold water and squeezed dry
salt and pepper to taste
2 teaspoons monosodium glutamate
¼ to ½ cup lemon juice
¼ to ½ cup sugar to taste
2 tablespoons cornstarch
1 cup commercial sour cream

Put meat, bones, garlic, onions, liquid and undrained tomatoes into a deep soup pot. Bring to a boil and skim off foam from top. Add shredded cabbage, sauerkraut, some salt and pepper and the monosodium glutamate. Cover, lower heat and simmer for 2 hours. Add lemon juice and sugar to taste. Correct salt and pepper seasoning if necessary.

Stir ½ cup of liquid from soup pot into cornstarch. Then stir cornstarch mixture back into soup. Soup will thicken slightly. Do not cover soup again. By this time brisket will be tender. Remove it. Cut into bite-size pieces and replace meat in soup. Remove marrow from bones. Add marrow to soup and discard bones.

Serve soup very hot, in deep bowls, garnished in the center with a large spoonful of sour cream.

Serves 12 to 14.

BASIL VEGETABLE SOUP

1 *package frozen cut green beans, slightly thawed*
1 *can cooked white beans, with bean liquid*
3 *carrots, scraped and cut into thin rounds*
3 *zucchini, washed and cut into thin rounds*
2 *quarts good beef or chicken broth*
3 *cloves garlic, finely minced*
salt and pepper
2 *teaspoons monosodium glutamate*
1 *cup dry vermicelli*
½ *cup (tightly packed) fresh basil*
grated Parmesan cheese

Combine green beans, white beans with liquid, carrots, sliced zucchini, broth, and garlic in a deep soup pot. Bring to a boil. Lower heat and simmer, covered, until carrots are tender. Season with salt, pepper and monosodium glutamate. Add vermicelli. Simmer till vermicelli is tender.

While soup is cooking, chop basil very fine. When vermicelli is tender, add basil to soup. Simmer till basil is completely wilted. Taste for seasoning and correct if necessary.

Serve in deep bowls. Sprinkle each serving with a little grated Parmesan cheese. Serves 10 to 12.

HUNGARIAN LAMB SOUP

⅓ cup lard
2 large onions, chopped
2 pounds lamb shoulder, trimmed of fat and cut into 1" cubes
1 tablespoon sweet Hungarian paprika
8 cups stock, or half water and half stock
1 large bay leaf
salt and pepper
2 teaspoons monosodium glutamate
2 potatoes, peeled and cut into ½" cubes
⅔ cup green beans, sliced
1 tablespoon flour
1 cup sour cream

Heat lard in a soup pot. Add onions and sauté over low heat till onions are soft and golden.

Add lamb cubes to onion and continue to sauté until lamb loses its pink color. Add paprika and stir in quickly. Add liquid; bring to a boil. Lower heat, and simmer uncovered about 40 minutes or until lamb is almost tender. Add bay leaf.

Season to taste with salt, pepper and monosodium glutamate. Add cubed potatoes and sliced beans. Simmer till contents of pot are entirely tender. Taste for seasoning and correct if necessary.

Stir flour into sour cream, then stir this mixture into the simmering soup. Cook 5 minutes longer.

Serves 10 to 12.

SOUP OF LORRAINE

¼ pound salt pork
6 small carrots, cut in half lengthwise
8 small white onions, peeled
2 pounds fresh, lean pork, cut into cubes
1 large veal bone, cracked
1½ cups diced turnip
1½ cups diced, peeled potatoes
1 medium-size cabbage, core removed and shredded coarsely
1 bay leaf
2½ quarts stock or water
salt and pepper
2 teaspoons monosodium glutamate
soup greens: 4 or 5 stalks of celery, 1 parsnip, 2 leeks, parsley
1½ pounds garlic sausage

Pour boiling water over piece of salt pork to remove some of the salt. Drain and dry on paper towels, and cut into small dice.

Place salt pork into a deep soup pot, over low heat, until a good deal of the fat is rendered but the pieces remaining are not brown. Add carrots and small white onions to pot and toss in fat till lightly browned.

Add all remaining ingredients, except soup greens and sausage. Bring to a boil. Cover pot, lower heat, and simmer.

After 2 hours, add the soup greens and sausage. Continue to cook about 45 minutes. Taste and correct seasoning. Discard soup greens and veal bone; cut up sausage and add to soup. Serve very hot—and be sure that each person gets his share of each of the meats and vegetables. Serves 6 to 8.

IBERIAN CHICKPEA SOUP

1 *pound dried chickpeas*
3 *quarts stock*
a ham bone (preferably with a little meat on it)
pinch of dried saffron
2 *bay leaves*
4 *cloves garlic, finely minced*
2 *onions, chopped*
2 *cups diced, peeled, raw potato*
1 *or* 2 *cooked Spanish sausages (chorizo, or if this is not available, use peperoni)*
3 *cups finely chopped cabbage, core removed*
salt and pepper to taste
2 *teaspoons monosodium glutamate*

Pick over chickpeas. Soak overnight in water to cover. Drain in the morning. Add stock, ham bone, saffron, bay leaves, garlic and onions. Cover pot and simmer about 3 hours. Add diced raw potato, Spanish sausage, thinly sliced, and cabbage. Simmer over low heat for at least 1 more hour.

Season with salt, pepper and monosodium glutamate. Remove ham bone from soup. Cut off any bits of ham and return to soup. Discard bone. Serve hot.

If soup thickens upon standing—and this rule applies to any hot soup that thickens while standing—thin with additional stock.

Serves 8 to 10.

TAH PEEN LO

This is an especially wonderful Chinese soup which is served in the winter. It should be prepared for from 4 to 8 people. If you make it for less than 4, you necessarily have to limit the variety of ingredients. A party for more than 8 people usually proves awkward since each person should be able to choose and cook his own tidbits.

Pork stock is the base of this soup. It should be prepared well ahead of time so that any fat may be skimmed off and so that the stock itself will be strong. Make your pork stock with plenty of pork bones, salt, pepper and a little monosodium glutamate. Add a slice or 2 of fresh ginger if it is available. Place bones and seasonings in a deep soup pot and barely cover them with water. Bring to a boil. Turn down the heat and simmer the stock for 3 or 4 hours. Cool before straining off the broth. Discard bones. Skim fat off soup. Taste for seasoning and correct.

At the dinner table, use a deep chafing dish, Mongolian chafing dish, or any deep pot which is attractive and can be placed over an alcohol burner.

Have an assortment of any or all of the following *raw* foods arranged in small dishes around the cooking vessel:

> *strips of filet of yellow pike / squid which has been cleaned, cut into pieces and scored / oysters / bay scallops / flank steak or beef filet which has been thinly sliced diagonally / clams / shrimp / bean curd cut into cubes / chicken breasts which have been boned, skinned and cut into thin strips / a small pitcher of sesame oil / soy sauce / finely chopped fresh ginger / scallions*

Provide for each guest a small dish in which he may combine some soy sauce, scallions and ginger as a dip for his food.

When the pork stock begins to boil, add a tablespoon of sesame oil. Then ask your guests to choose from the variety of foods on the table. They should hold their tidbits with either chopsticks or fork and immerse them in the simmering stock until cooked. None of these foods needs to be cooked very long. A moment or 2 is all that is needed: most of these foods toughen when they are overcooked.

As the bits are taken out of the stock, each guest dips his into his own dish of seasoned soy sauce. Now and then you should add a bit more sesame oil to the stock to prevent it from boiling too rapidly, and to flavor the foods being cooked.

When the raw food is gone, or when all the guests have eaten their fill, the stock will be somewhat reduced and much stronger in flavor. At that point, bring to the table some cooked noodles and a bowl of fresh greens—spinach or watercress are best. Add the greens to the stock, along with some cubes of bean curd. As soon as the greens wilt and the stock again begins to simmer, give each guest a bowl of the rich soup, including some noodles, greens and bean curd.

MISU TAKI

This is not the original version of misu taki—but it is my own, and very good, I think.

- 1¼ *cups grated Japanese radish (daikon; see Shopping Sources)*
- 1 *cup soy sauce*
- ½ *cup grated ginger*
- ⅔ *cup lemon juice*
- 6 *cups well-seasoned chicken stock*
- 6 *whole chicken breasts, boned, skinned and cut into 1" cubes*
- 3 *cups cooked noodles*
- 3 *cups watercress*

It is preferable to cook this dish at the table as there is less chance of the chicken becoming overcooked.

Combine grated Japanese radish, soy sauce, ginger and lemon juice. Divide this mixture among 6 small bowls at the table.

Heat chicken stock in a chafing dish or in a heavy pot at the stove. As soon as it is simmering, taste it for seasoning and correct if necessary. When it is again simmering, add pieces of chicken all at once. Cook only a few minutes, until the chicken changes color. Be very careful not to overcook the chicken. Turn heat off. With a slotted spoon, remove pieces of chicken to 6 bowls. The pieces of chicken should be dipped into the prepared sauce and eaten. If not overcooked, they are delicious.

When all the chicken has been used, reheat the broth till it is again simmering. Place in each person's bowl some cooked noodles and watercress. Pour hot broth on top. Eat all together. Continue to add noodles, watercress and broth to the bowls as long as the supply lasts. Serves 6.

CREAM OF MUSHROOM SOUP

1 *pound fresh mushrooms, sliced*
3 *tablespoons butter*
3 *tablespoons flour*
1 *quart chicken stock*
½ *cup Madeira*
salt and pepper to taste
1 *teaspoon monosodium glutamate*
¼ *cup Preserved Cream (page 29)*

Trim mushrooms. Place in a heavy skillet, without any fat or liquid. Place over medium heat, covered, until the mushrooms are almost completely dry and begin to stick to the pan. Stir in butter. When it is melted, stir in flour and continue to cook, stirring, about 5 minutes in order to cook the flour. Beat in chicken stock with a wire whisk. Stir till stock is slightly thickened. Remove mushrooms from soup.

Place mushrooms into blender with Madeira and whirl until smooth. Add to soup. Cover pot and simmer gently for about 30 minutes. Season with salt, pepper and monosodium glutamate. Cool slightly. Stir in cream. Reheat and serve. Serves 6 to 8.

This may also be served cold, but more liquid—stock or cream—will be needed, as the soup will thicken upon standing.

CREAM OF SORREL SOUP

4 *tablespoons butter*
¾ *pound washed, finely chopped sorrel*
4 *potatoes, peeled and diced*
2½ *quarts chicken stock*
salt and pepper to taste
2 *teaspoons monosodium glutamate*
¼ *to* ½ *cup heavy cream*

Melt butter in a deep saucepan. Add chopped sorrel. Allow it to wilt and become soft. Stir in diced potatoes. Pour in stock, salt, pepper and monosodium glutamate. Cook about 45 minutes. Cool slightly, then purée the mixture in a blender, or put through a sieve. Cool. Stir in cream, using as much as needed to make a nice consistency.

This can be served hot or chilled. If it is served cold, the soup will probably need to be thinned with additional cream. Serves 10 to 12.

WATERCRESS CREAM SOUP

¼ *cup sweet butter*
6 *small white onions, sliced*
1 *large onion, sliced*
2 *celery stalks, cut into thin slices*
4 *potatoes, peeled and diced*
6 *cups chicken stock*
2 *cups watercress*
salt and pepper to taste
2 *cups light cream*

Melt butter in a deep saucepan. Add onions and celery. Cook over low heat till vegetables are soft. Add potatoes and chicken stock. Simmer till potatoes are completely soft. Add watercress and continue cooking only a minute or 2, or till watercress wilts. Cool slightly. Purée entire mixture in blender to make a smooth cream. Season with salt and pepper. Chill, if desired. Just before serving, stir in cream. This soup is a lovely light green color. Serves 8 to 10.

COLD CLAM SOUP

This is a quick recipe, but very good.

- 1 *can (10½ ounces) condensed cream of celery soup*
- 2 *cans minced clams with their juice*
- 1½ *to 2 cups heavy cream*
- *chopped chives, or very finely chopped scallions*

Combine cream of celery soup with minced clams in blender jar. Whirl until smooth. Stir in enough cream to make a desired consistency. Chill thoroughly. Stir again before serving. Serve cold, garnished with chopped chives.

Serves 6.

BLUEBERRY SOUP

This is not a sweet fruit soup, but more like a cold beet borsch.

- 2 *cups water*
- 1 *pint blueberries*
- ½ *cup sugar*
- 1 *lemon, thinly sliced*
- 1 *cinnamon stick*
- *sour cream*

Combine water, blueberries, sugar, lemon and cinnamon in a deep saucepan. Bring to a boil; lower heat, and simmer about 15 minutes. Then put through food mill, or purée in blender. Cool.

Beat in 1 cup of sour cream with a wire whisk. Chill thoroughly. Top with an additional spoonful of sour cream for each serving.

Serves 6.

GAZPACHO

1 *cucumber, unpeeled, seeded and diced*
1 *onion, chopped*
1 *green pepper, seeded and cut into pieces*
6 *fresh tomatoes, peeled and cut up*
2 *cloves garlic*
4 *tablespoons tarragon wine vinegar*
1½ *cups stock (canned, if necessary)*
½ *cup red wine*
¼ *cup olive oil*
salt and pepper to taste

Combine all ingredients in blender jar. Whirl till ingredients are smooth. It will probably be necessary to do this in 2 or 3 operations. Taste for seasoning and correct. Place in refrigerator and chill very well. Serve as cold as possible and pass small dishes of the following garnitures to be added to the soup by each individual:

peeled, seeded, diced cucumber
finely chopped onion
seeded, diced green pepper
Garlic-seasoned Croutons

Serves 6.

4. EGG DISHES

EGGS, A DELICIOUS, HIGH-PROTEIN FOOD, are too often misunderstood and abused. Slow, gentle cooking is the key to most egg cookery (except for omelets, which require a hot pan).

How often have you been served fried eggs which are hard and rubbery on the bottom and gooey on top? Yet there is no secret to preparing perfect fried eggs. Two methods may be employed: Simply melt a good-size lump of butter in a skillet. When the butter is completely melted, drop in the eggs. Now you have a choice. You may cover the skillet, continuing to cook over very low heat. The steam in the pan soon will cook the tops as well as the bottoms of the eggs. A very few minutes are needed. Remove the cover to check frequently.

The second method is to keep the pan uncovered and baste the top of the eggs with the hot melted butter in the pan. The heat of the melted butter should cook the top. This second method is not as foolproof as the first. If the top still seems uncooked when the bottom is almost cooked, gently scrape off that stubborn bit of egg white covering the yolk and add it to the remaining white surrounding the yolk. Thus it will get cooked. The advantage to the second method is that the butter flavors the eggs more thoroughly.

Several of the recipes given in this chapter call for poaching eggs in tangy sauce. This gives especially unusual results.

Needless to say, the best eggs for eating are the freshest ones you can find—no mean feat in the cities.

LOX AND EGGS

1 *large Spanish onion, chopped*
1 *green pepper, chopped*
½ *cup butter*
2 *cups sliced mushrooms*
½ *pound smoked salmon (lox) cut into small dice*
8 *eggs*
¼ *cup heavy cream*
1 *tablespoon chopped parsley*
¼ *teaspoon basil*
dash of tabasco sauce
1 *teaspoon monosodium glutamate*
½ *teaspoon pepper*

Place onion, green pepper and mushrooms in a heavy skillet. Cover skillet and allow vegetables to steam in their own juices, without butter, until they almost stick to the pan.

Add butter and stir. Add diced smoked salmon and continue to cook for a minute or 2, stirring until the salmon becomes light pink.

Beat eggs, adding cream, parsley, basil, tabasco and monosodium glutamate. Add eggs to skillet. Continue to cook over low heat, stirring constantly, until eggs begin to set but are still creamy. Stir in a little salt and pepper. Serve at once.

Serves 6.

HUEVOS RANCHEROS

3 *tablespoons olive oil*
1 *large onion, chopped*
1 *green pepper, seeded and sliced*
1 *small hot green pepper, seeded and minced*
2 *cloves garlic, minced*
3 *tablespoons chili powder*
½ *teaspoon cumin powder*
¼ *teaspoon oregano*
tabasco to taste
2 *cups drained tomatoes, chopped*
6 *eggs*
jack or mozzarella cheese

In a heavy skillet, heat olive oil till it is hot. Add chopped onion, green peppers and garlic. Sauté until vegetables are tender. Stir in chili powder, cumin, oregano and tabasco. Add well-drained tomatoes. Simmer over low heat until tomatoes melt into a purée. Break 6 eggs, one at a time, into sauce, making a depression for each egg so that eggs are partially covered with sauce. Dot top with bits of jack or mozzarella cheese. Cover pan and continue to simmer till eggs are set, or bake in a 350 degree oven until eggs are set. Serve at once.

Serves 6.

PIPERADE

¼ *cup olive oil*
6 *green peppers, seeded and sliced*
1 *large onion, chopped*
3 *cloves garlic, minced*
¼ *pound mushrooms, sliced*

3 *tomatoes*
½ *cup chopped, uncooked ham*
1 *teaspoon salt*
8 *eggs*

In a heavy skillet, heat olive oil until it is hot. Add peppers, onion, garlic and mushrooms. Sauté until soft but not brown.

Remove skin from tomatoes by plunging them into boiling water for a minute or 2, then peeling. Squeeze out and discard juice and seeds from tomatoes; then chop them coarsely. Add chopped ham to sautéed vegetables, then the tomatoes and salt. Simmer in skillet about ½ hour, stirring occasionally. Mixture should be very soft.

Break eggs into simmering mixture, one by one. Allow eggs to remain whole, or mix gently so that eggs are not too broken up. As soon as the eggs are set, serve.

Serves 6.

VIENNESE HAM AND EGG CAKE

1½ *cups milk*
2½ *cups soft bread crumbs*
6 *well-beaten eggs*
1 *cup chopped ham*
1 *tablespoon finely chopped onion*
salt and pepper to taste

Combine milk and bread crumbs. Beat in eggs and remaining ingredients. Pour into a greased baking dish. Bake in a 350 degree oven about 45 minutes, or until mixture is set and golden brown.

Serves 6.

ITALIAN GREEN BEANS AND EGGS

3 *packages frozen cut green beans, partially thawed*
3 *cloves garlic, minced*
1 *onion, chopped*
¼ *cup olive oil*
1 *teaspoon salt*
pinch of sugar
½ *teaspoon monosodium glutamate*
½ *teaspoon pepper*
pinch of thyme
½ *teaspoon basil*
¼ *cup tomato purée*
3 *egg yolks*
1½ *cups ricotta cheese*
¼ *cup grated Parmesan cheese*
¼ *cup chopped parsley*
6 *eggs*
½ *cup diced mozzarella cheese*

Place frozen green beans into a heavy saucepan. Add garlic, onion, olive oil, salt, sugar, monosodium glutamate, pepper, thyme and basil. Cover and begin to cook over medium heat. Raise heat to high, until beans are barely cooked, and all the water has evaporated, leaving beans in oil. Stir in tomato purée.

Stir the yolks of 3 eggs into ricotta cheese. Stir in Parmesan cheese and chopped parsley.

In a baking dish, starting with the green beans, make layers of beans and seasoned ricotta cheese. Top layer should be beans. Bake in 350 degree oven for 30 minutes. Remove casserole from oven. Break 6 eggs on top of beans. Dot with mozzarella cheese. Bake 25 more minutes, or until cheese is melted and eggs are set. Serve at once.

Serves 6.

CURRIED EGGS

3 *tablespoons clarified butter or vegetable oil*
2 *tablespoons mustard seeds*
2 *onions, chopped*
4 *cloves garlic, minced*
2 *tablespoons chopped fresh or pickled ginger (see Shopping Sources)*
½ *cup curry powder*
⅔ *teaspoon ground cardamom seeds*
1½ *teaspoons ground black pepper*
2 *cups stock*
2 *teaspoons tomato paste*
½ *teaspoon sugar*
salt
dash of tabasco
12 *eggs*
2 *tablespoons chopped fresh cilantro, if available*

Melt butter or oil in a broad saucepan. When it is very hot, add mustard seeds. Heat should be high. Seeds will pop, like popcorn. Cover pan and wait until popping sound of seeds has stopped. Immediately lower heat, uncover pan and add chopped onions, garlic and ginger. Sauté till tender. Stir in curry powder, cardamom and black pepper. Stir for 2 or 3 minutes. Add stock and tomato paste. Season with sugar, salt and tabasco. This part of recipe may be done ahead of time and allowed to stand till serving time.

Twenty minutes before serving, heat sauce to simmering point. Lower heat. Break eggs into sauce. Cover pan. Allow eggs to cook in sauce until they are set, about 5 to 10 minutes. Garnish with chopped cilantro. Serve with Fluffy, Steamed Rice and Onion Relish.

Serves 6 to 8.

EGG AND POTATO PIZZA

½ cup olive oil
3 cups very well seasoned mashed potatoes
1 large onion, peeled and sliced
2 cloves garlic, minced
2 cups mushrooms
1 green pepper, seeded and sliced
4 cooked Italian sweet or hot sausages
6 eggs
¼ cup grated Parmesan cheese
⅔ cup diced mozzarella cheese

Grease a large flat baking dish (such as a jelly-roll pan) generously with as much olive oil as necessary. Spread mashed potatoes evenly. With the back of a large spoon, make indentations in the mashed potatoes for the eggs which will be added later.

Bake potato-lined pan in a 400 degree oven for 30 to 40 minutes or until potato seems slightly crisp on bottom. Remove from oven.

While potato is baking, sauté onion, garlic, mushrooms and green pepper in remaining olive oil till soft. Slice cooked sausage ¼ inch thick.

After potato has been removed from oven, spread top of it with sautéed mixture and sliced sausage, leaving indentations clear. Break eggs into each of the indentations. Sprinkle with Parmesan cheese and dot with pieces of mozzarella cheese. Return to oven. Bake about 25 minutes, or until eggs are set and cheese bubbling. To serve, cut into wedges or squares. A green salad goes well with this.

Serves 6.

POTATO, EGG AND CHEESE CASSEROLE

4 medium potatoes, boiled, peeled and cut into slices about ⅓" thick

¾ *pound mozzarella cheese, sliced thin*
salt and pepper
½ *cup Parmesan cheese*
½ *cup chopped parsley*
½ *cup melted butter*
6 *eggs*

Into a broad buttered casserole place a layer of potatoes. Cover with slices of mozzarella. Sprinkle with salt, pepper, Parmesan cheese and chopped parsley. Add another layer of potatoes, and repeat seasoning. Repeat till all of these ingredients are used. There should be no more than about 4 layers. Brush top with half of the melted butter. Bake in a 350 degree oven about 40 minutes. Remove casserole from oven. Break eggs on top. Sprinkle eggs with remaining butter, some salt and pepper. Return casserole to oven and bake about 25 minutes longer, or until eggs are set.

Serves 6.

EGGS IN TARRAGON SAUCE

¼ *pound sweet butter*
½ *cup chopped shallots or scallions*
2 *teaspoons fresh tarragon, chopped*
½ *cup chopped parsley*
2 *cups white wine*
1 *tablespoon Concentrate of Chicken (page* 50*) (optional)*
salt and pepper
1 *teaspoon monosodium glutamate*
12 *eggs*

Melt sweet butter in a saucepan. Add chopped shallots. When they are soft, stir in tarragon and parsley. Add wine and Chicken Concentrate, if available. Raise heat, and reduce liquid to about a cup. Then lower heat so that the liquid is just simmering. Season with salt, pepper and monosodium glutamate.

(continued on the next page)

Break whole eggs into the simmering liquid. Cover pan. Poach eggs till just set, basting the tops of them occasionally with the pan liquid.

As soon as eggs are set, serve with Fluffy, Steamed Rice.

Serves 6 to 8.

SWISS EGG CASSEROLE

butter
6 *hard-cooked eggs, sliced*
salt and pepper
1 *cup soft bread crumbs*
4 *tomatoes, sliced*
4 *firm anchovies, minced*
1 *teaspoon basil*
½ *cup chopped scallions*
½ *cup chopped parsley*
6 *eggs*
2 *cups light cream*
¼ *teaspoon nutmeg*

Butter a casserole. Place a layer of hard-cooked egg slices on the bottom. Season with salt and pepper. Sprinkle with some soft bread crumbs. Cover with a layer of tomatoes. Sprinkle with minced anchovies, basil, a little salt and pepper, chopped scallions and parsley. Continue making layers with egg slices, seasonings, bread crumbs, tomatoes, etc.

Beat 6 eggs. Add salt, 2 cups cream and nutmeg. Pour over ingredients in casserole. Bake in a pan of water in a 350 degree oven about 40 minutes or until the custard is firm.

Serves 6.

EGG CUSTARD RING

butter
6 *eggs*
1½ *cups light cream, or part stock if desired*
1 *teaspoon salt*
pepper and dash of tabasco
¼ *teaspoon nutmeg*

Butter a 1½-quart ring mold. Set oven at 350 degrees.

Beat eggs, adding cream, salt, pepper, tabasco and nutmeg. Pour into mold. Set ring in a pan of hot water and bake about 40 minutes, or until custard is set. Remove from oven. Slide a thin knife around edges of custard in order to loosen. Invert a warm plate over the top and turn out custard.

Fill center with any hot, seasoned vegetables, such as Angèles Parisian Spinach or Cauliflower Polonaise.

Serves 6.

EGGS MALAGUENA

6 *Spanish sausages (chorizos)*
½ *cup olive oil*
3 *large onions, chopped*
2 *green peppers, seeded and chopped*
3 *cloves garlic, minced*
1 *cup drained canned tomatoes, chopped*
2 *tablespoons chili powder*
salt and pepper
18 *peeled, cleaned shrimp*
12 *eggs*

Place chorizos in a saucepan. Barely cover with water. Bring to a boil. Simmer for 15 minutes or until the sausages are cooked. Drain

(continued on the next page)

sausages, cool, and cut into 1-inch pieces. Set aside till later.

In a heavy skillet, heat most of the olive oil till hot. Add onions, green peppers and garlic. Sauté till soft. Add well-drained, chopped tomatoes and chili powder. Cook about 20 minutes, seasoning with salt and pepper.

Divide mixture among 6 individual shallow casseroles. Into each casserole, place 1 chopped chorizo and 3 raw shrimp and 2 eggs. Sprinkle with a little remaining olive oil.

Bake in a 300 degree oven about 25 minutes or until eggs are set.

Serves 6.

POTATOES, ONIONS AND EGGS

⅔ cup butter
4 potatoes, peeled and cut into dice
2 onions, sliced and separated into rings
1 teaspoon salt
pepper
½ teaspoon monosodium glutamate
¼ cup chopped parsley
12 eggs
¼ cup cream

In a heavy skillet, melt butter. Add potatoes. Sauté over low heat until potatoes are tender and golden but not very brown. Add onion rings and continue to sauté until onions are tender. Season with salt, pepper and monosodium glutamate. Stir in chopped parsley.

Beat eggs; add cream, and pour over potato mixture. Continue to cook over low heat, stirring constantly until the eggs begin to set. Remove them from heat and serve while they are still creamy.

Serves 6.

EGGS IN A CRUST

6 *hard-crusted round or oval rolls*
⅔ *cup butter*
12 *eggs*
salt and pepper
½ *teaspoon monosodium glutamate*
½ *cup cream*
paprika
chopped parsley

Remove tops from rolls. With a spoon or your fingers, scoop out the soft interior of the rolls. Brush insides generously with melted butter. Place rolls in a 350 degree oven until they are toasted and crisp.

Beat eggs with salt, pepper and monosodium glutamate. Add cream. Heat half of remaining butter in a heavy skillet. Pour in eggs. Cook over low heat, stirring constantly. As eggs begin to set, add remaining butter. Cook till eggs are just creamy.

Quickly stuff the toasted rolls with eggs. Sprinkle tops with a tiny bit of paprika and a bit of chopped parsley. Serve at once. Sliced mushrooms may be sautéed and added to eggs as they are being cooked. Serves 6.

EGGS WITH CHORIZOS

6 *Spanish sausages (chorizos)*
¼ *cup butter*
1 *onion, chopped*
12 *eggs*
½ *teaspoon monosodium glutamate*
¼ *cup cream*

Place sausages in a saucepan. Cover with water. Bring to a boil. Lower heat and simmer for 15 minutes, or until sausages are cooked.

(*continued on the next page*)

Remove sausages from water and cool. When they are cool enough to handle, remove casings and chop sausages fine.

In a heavy skillet, melt butter until it is hot. Add onion. Sauté till it is soft. Add chorizos and stir for 2 or 3 minutes.

Beat eggs, monosodium glutamate and cream together. Pour into skillet. Cook over low heat, stirring constantly, till eggs are just set. Serve at once.

Serves 6.

EGGS, JALISCO STYLE

2 *No. 2 cans pinto beans, packed in their own liquid*
1 *cup bacon fat or fresh lard*
3 *tablespoons additional lard*
1 *cup chopped onion*
4 *cloves garlic, minced*
2 *tablespoons chili powder*
salt
dash of tabasco
1 *cup drained tomatoes, chopped*
1½ *cups chopped ham*
6 *eggs*
6 *tortillas, fresh or canned, fried in lard until they are crisp but not brown*
1 *red onion, chopped*
⅓ *cup Parmesan cheese*
2 *tablespoons chopped fresh cilantro* (*optional*)

Remove beans from cans. Place in a colander or strainer, and rinse with water until they are completely free of their packing liquid. Drain well.

In a heavy skillet, heat ⅔ cup bacon fat or lard. Add drained beans. With a heavy fork, mash and turn them until they almost form a purée. Turn heat very low and continue to cook, stirring occasionally.

Melt 3 tablespoons additional lard in a saucepan. Add chopped onion and garlic. Sauté until soft. Stir in chili powder, salt and tabasco. Add tomatoes. Simmer over low heat till the sauce is almost smooth, about 25 minutes. Add ham.

In another heavy skillet, melt the remaining ⅓ cup bacon fat or lard. Fry eggs very slowly in this fat, basting tops of eggs with fat so that tops get cooked. Cook over low heat so that eggs do not toughen.

Heat fried tortillas in oven till they are hot. Spread each with some of the mashed bean mixture. Spoon a little of the tomato-chili-ham sauce over each tortilla. Then sprinkle with chopped red onion and Parmesan cheese. Place a fried egg on top. Spoon a little more sauce on egg. Then sprinkle with chopped cilantro if it is available. Serve at once so that tortilla does not get soggy. Serves 6.

CURRIED EGG CAKES

6 *tablespoons butter*
6 *tablespoons flour*
2 *tablespoons curry powder*
⅛ *teaspoon cayenne pepper*
2 *teaspoons salt*
1¼ *cups milk*
3 *eggs, beaten*
12 *hard-cooked eggs, diced*
⅔ *cup flour*
bread crumbs
clarified butter or salad oil ½″ deep in a skillet for frying

Melt butter in a saucepan. Remove from heat. Stir in flour, curry powder, salt and cayenne. Return to heat and cook, stirring, about 5 minutes. Remove from heat and stir in milk, using a whisk so sauce won't be lumpy. Place over low heat and stir. Sauce will be very thick.

Remove from heat. Add half of the beaten eggs. Beat in well. Fold in the diced hard-cooked eggs. Chill mixture.

With your hands, form the chilled mixture into flattened cakes.

(*continued on the next page*)

Roll cakes in flour, then in remaining beaten egg. Then roll in bread crumbs, coating all over.

Chill.

Heat fat until it is hot but not smoking. Place curried cakes into hot fat and fry on each side until all are golden and crisp. Drain on paper towels. Serve with tomato sauce, if you wish, or just as they are. Serves 6 to 8.

Crepes

These thin pancakes are useful in dozens of ways. They may be stuffed with any creamed mixture such as chicken or sweetbreads, or perhaps with deviled crabmeat. Chopped spinach in olive oil makes a delicious filling, especially if the crepes are then topped with a good homemade tomato sauce. Crepes freeze very well. And of course you can always prepare the traditional crepes Suzette using this recipe.

BASIC CREPES

4 *eggs*
1 *cup sifted flour*
salt
3 *tablespoons melted butter*
3 *tablespoons cognac*
1 1/4 *cups milk, approximately*
melted butter for greasing pan

Add eggs to flour and salt. Beat in well. (If you wish, this may be done in blender.) Add melted butter, cognac and then about half of the milk. Gradually add remaining milk. The consistency of crepe batter should be that of light cream. If you like, you can make this batter a day or 2 ahead of time. However, when you use it, you will find that the batter has thickened somewhat, and you will need to add more milk.

To bake the crepes, use a small, heavy skillet or an omelet pan 6 to 8″ in diameter. Heat pan till it is so hot that a drop of water shatters and bounces off it.

Brush pan with melted butter. Pour in a small ladleful of batter. Immediately pour any batter which does not cling to the bottom of the pan back into bowl of crepe batter. Keep heat under pan high.

After a minute or 2, the edges of the crepe will begin to curl away from the edges of the pan. If you can, use your fingers and quickly turn the crepe over to bake on the other side. A spatula may also be used. Bake for just a minute on the other side. Turn out crepe. Regrease pan and repeat till all crepe batter is used.

Yield: approximately 12 crepes. These will keep in the refrigerator for up to a week, or in the freezer, well wrapped and with wax paper between each crepe, for 2 to 3 months.

EGGS IN CREPES

⅔ *cup butter*
6 *slices of bread, crusts trimmed*
6 *soft poached eggs*
6 *crepes (see recipe above)*
salt and pepper
toothpicks
6 *slices cooked ham, ¼″ thick*
2 *cups Hollandaise Sauce (page 48)*

Melt butter in a heavy skillet. Add bread slices and sauté on both sides till crisp and golden brown. Set aside till needed (keep warm).

Place a poached egg in the center of each crepe. Season with salt and pepper. Gather edges of crepe together as if to make a bag. Secure with a toothpick. Place on a greased baking sheet. This may be done ahead of time. Place in 350 degree oven for about 5 minutes, or until the crepe packages are heated through.

In butter remaining in skillet from sautéing bread, sauté ham, just

(continued on the next page)

till edges frizzle and ham is hot. Place a slice of ham on each piece of sautéed bread. On the ham, place a hot crepe filled with a poached egg. Spoon Hollandaise Sauce on top and serve at once.

Serves 6.

Omelets

The only way to learn to make omelets is to make them. Arm yourself with a suitable skillet and several dozen eggs. Make the omelet mixture and cook it by the ladleful until you have achieved your goal. This sounds like gross waste, but it is necessary. In making omelets, as in a few other kinds of cookery (baking and sauce-making, for example), practice is essential.

BASIC OMELET

3 *eggs*
1 *teaspoon cold water*
dash of tabasco
½ *teaspoon salt*
2 *teaspoons butter*

Beat all ingredients except butter together till blended.

Preheat omelet pan (about 6 to 8 inches in diameter, preferably made of iron or cast aluminum) over medium heat for 5 minutes. The pan is ready when the lump of butter placed into it sizzles sharply but does not brown.

When butter is melted, pour eggs into pan. With your right hand, stir egg mixture and, with your left hand, shake the pan at the same time so that the omelet does not stick to the bottom. Just as eggs begin to set, stop stirring, but continue to shake pan. The whole procedure should take no more than 30 seconds. While the center of the omelet is still *very soft* remove pan from heat.

This is the time to add your filling in a strip down the center of the omelet—hot sautéed chicken livers or mushrooms, a spicy vegetable mixture, diced cheese, or whatever you have.

Now with a fork, starting from the edge nearest the handle, fold over one end of the omelet so that it covers a total of two thirds of the omelet. If necessary, loosen center of omelet with a spatula—this should not, however, really be necessary.

Have a warm plate ready and, with the help of your fork or spatula, turn out omelet, making the final fold on the plate, as the omelet comes out of the pan.

5. FISH

FISH GENERALLY is the most overcooked of foods. Even in Paris, a gastronomic capital, fish almost always is served overcooked and dry. This is particularly true of salmon. It is rare to come upon a moist and succulent dish of salmon.

When I order grilled fish of any kind, in France, or in the United States, I always tell the waiter that I don't want it too well done. In the United States I might as well not say anything. In France, that country where it is almost impossible to get a well-done piece of beef, the waiter looks at me with a most puzzled expression and protests, "But, madame, it is fish!"

In the United States, overcooked fish is even more of a problem. Swordfish, which can be juicy and succulent, almost invariably comes to the table shriveled and dried up, without a drop of melted butter or a sprinkling of chopped parsley.

Perhaps I am optimistic, but I hope this chapter will initiate a revolution in fish cookery.

Broiled Fish Steaks

Use steak-type fish, such as halibut, salmon or swordfish. Have steak cut thick, at least 1 to 1½ inches. Make sure your grill is very hot, whether you are using the broiling pan of your stove, or a charcoal grill.

Spread some flour mixed with a little monosodium glutamate on a sheet of wax paper. Dry fish well with paper towels, and coat it with flour mixture on both sides, brushing off any excess with your hands.

Melt plenty of butter in a small saucepan (about 1 cup of butter for 4 servings).

Stove broiling: Place fish on lightly greased broiling rack about 3 inches from flame. The thicker the fish, the farther it should be from the heat. Broil fish about 5 to 7 minutes. The flour will give it a crust and the fish will begin to brown. Brush fish with melted butter. Then turn it over. Broil till fish is crusty, brown and tender, but be careful not to dry it out. Serve with additional melted butter, and a good sprinkling of parsley, along with wedges of lemon.

Charcoal broiling: Place floured fish on ungreased grill about 3 inches above flame, or farther away for thicker fish. Broil about 5 to 7 minutes, or until crusty and brown. Brush with melted butter, and turn fish over. Broil other side about the same amount of time. Serve with additional melted butter, chopped parsley and lemon wedges.

With thick-sliced fish repeat same process 3 or 4 times, depending on the thickness. The fish is finished when it is fairly firm to the touch but not hard.

Remove from broiler or grill to a board. Cut fish into slices. Serve with hot melted butter, wedges of lemon and some chopped parsley.

Cold, broiled fish steak: If you have any fish steak left, slice it and pour a few spoons of Vinaigrette Sauce over it or just add olive oil, lemon juice, some parsley and perhaps a little mint. Serve cold as a first course, or for luncheon.

Broiled Individual Whole Fish

Use small fish, such as sea bass, red snapper or sole. Do not have fish fileted. The center bone helps keep the fish succulent. Except for shad and some of the more exotic fish, it is usually not difficult for the diner to remove the center bone and small side bones with a fork and knife.

Dry fish well with paper towels. Flour fish as for broiled fish steaks. Broil in the same manner, turning only once. Baste with melted butter.

Both sides of the fish should be brown and crusty; the inside should be very moist and succulent. Serve in the same manner as fish steaks, with plenty of hot butter, chopped parsley and lemon wedges.

Sauteed Fish

In France, this method of preparing fish is called *meunière.*

It is very simple—and very delicious. The fish should not be thick: sole, boned shad, sea squab, which is really a part of blowfish, frogs' legs and the like lend themselves particularly well to this method. If you like, you can have sea bass or some other small fish fileted, and then prepare it in this manner.

Dry the fish well on paper towels. Dip it on both sides into flour which has been seasoned with salt and monosodium glutamate. Heat clarified butter (or olive oil, if you prefer) in a heavy skillet, until it is hot. Place the fish in a pan and sauté until one side is golden. Turn and sauté the other side. Remove fish to a warm platter and keep warm.

Pour out the cooking fat from the skillet. Rinse pan. Add a large lump of fresh butter, or some fresh olive oil. When it sizzles, add a good handful of chopped parsley. Pour over the sautéed fish and serve at once with lemon wedges.

If you are preparing frogs' legs or sea squab, you might like to insert the flavor of garlic. In that case, before you add the parsley, add several cloves of finely minced garlic. Do not let the little pieces brown: they should only become soft. Then stir in the parsley and pour over the fish.

Always serve with wedges of lemon.

Note: There is a world of difference between the soles of any variety obtainable in the United States and the Dover sole which is served in Europe. The latter has a firmness of texture lacking in the sole available in this country.

SKEWERED SWORDFISH

2 *pounds swordfish steak*
3 *cloves garlic, finely minced*
¼ *cup olive oil*
3 *tablespoons lemon juice*
1 *tablespoon Japanese soy sauce*
1 *teaspoon monosodium glutamate*
salt and pepper

Dry fish well on paper towels. Cut into 1½-inch chunks.

Combine garlic, olive oil, lemon juice, soy sauce and monosodium glutamate. Place swordfish in a bowl and pour this mixture over the chunks. Marinate in refrigerator for at least 3 hours, turning occasionally.

Thread chunks on skewers. Broil, preferably over charcoal, turning occasionally, until the swordfish is lightly brown all over. This should not take very long. Season with salt and pepper.

Serve with the following sauce:

6 *tablespoons lemon juice*
6 *tablespoons olive oil*
½ *cup chopped parsley*

Mix ingredients and spoon over skewered swordfish. Serves 4 to 5.

SALMON AND CUCUMBER KEBABS

2½ *pounds center-cut salmon steaks, cut at least* 1¼″ *thick, bones removed.*
3 *cucumbers*
½ *cup dry white wine*
3 *tablespoons Japanese soy sauce*
1 *teaspoon sugar*
2 *tablespoons melted butter*

Cut salmon into 1½-inch chunks. Peel and cut cucumbers in half. Remove seeds with a teaspoon, and cut cucumbers into 1-inch chunks.

Combine wine, soy sauce, sugar and melted butter. Pour over salmon and cucumber chunks. Mix and allow to marinate in refrigerator for at least an hour.

Just before serving, thread alternate pieces of salmon and cucumber on skewers. Broil, preferably over charcoal, turning the skewers, until salmon is lightly browned all over. Brush occasionally with marinade while broiling. Serves 5 to 6.

FRESH CODFISH, PORTUGUESE STYLE

1 *eggplant, unpeeled, sliced* ¼″ *thick*
¾ *cup olive oil (approximately)*
3 *onions, chopped*
4 *cloves garlic*
1 *cup drained tomatoes*
3 *tablespoons capers*
2 *cups Fluffy, Steamed Rice (page* 301)
1 *teaspoon cumin*
2½ *pounds codfish steak, floured and briefly sautéed in olive oil until brown on both sides*
1 *teaspoon monosodium glutamate*
½ *cup white wine*
3 *tablespoons lemon juice*

½ *teaspoon paprika*
½ *cup chopped parsley*

Sauté eggplant slices in olive oil until they are tender and golden. Drain on paper towels, then arrange in a baking dish. Sauté onions and garlic in remaining olive oil until they are soft.

Combine tomatoes, capers, rice, cumin, and sautéed onions and garlic. Spread this mixture on eggplant in baking dish, and season with salt and pepper. Place codfish steak on top. Sprinkle with salt, pepper and monosodium glutamate; add white wine. Squeeze lemon juice over fish and brush with a little more olive oil. Sprinkle with paprika.

Bake in a 375 degree oven about 25 minutes, or until the fish is just cooked. Sprinkle with chopped parsley and serve with lemon wedges. Serves 5 to 6.

AN UNORTHODOX VERSION OF MATELOTE OF EEL

2 *large or 3 smaller eels*
¼ *cup olive oil*
½ *cup diced salt pork*
1 *onion, chopped*
6 *shallots, minced*
4 *cloves garlic, minced*
3 *tablespoons flour*
½ *cup armagnac or cognac*
2 *cups red wine (approximately)*
salt and pepper
1 *teaspoon monosodium glutamate*
½ *cup butter*
2 *cups small, peeled white onions*
½ *teaspoon sugar*
⅔ *cup chopped parsley*

Have eels skinned and fileted by your fish man. Cut into 2-inch pieces.

(continued on the next page)

Heat olive oil in a broad, heavy saucepan. Add pieces of eel and sauté lightly in oil. Remove eel pieces. Add diced salt pork. When some of fat has come out of pork, add minced onion, shallots and garlic. Lower heat. Sprinkle with flour and stir. Return eel to pan.

Warm armagnac or cognac slightly, pour over eel in saucepan and ignite. Shake pan until flames subside.

Add enough red wine to just cover eel. Keeping heat low, simmer 10 to 15 minutes. Season with salt, pepper and monosodium glutamate.

While eel is cooking, melt butter in a skillet, then add peeled white onions to melted butter. Sprinkle onions lightly with sugar. Cover pan and cook, stirring occasionally, until onions are golden and soft. Add to eel mixture. Also stir in ½ cup chopped parsley. Serve hot, garnished with remaining chopped parsley. Serves 6.

GEFULLTE FISH

2 *pounds whitefish*
2 *pounds yellow pike*
1 *pound carp*
a piece of roe from carp, as well as a piece of milch
6 *onions, sliced*
salt and white pepper
1 *tablespoon sugar*
2 *teaspoons monosodium glutamate*
⅔ *bottle white wine*
3 *eggs*
½ *cup water*
4 *carrots*

Ask fish man to filet and skin all the fish. It may be difficult to obtain both the roe and milch since the roe comes from the female carp and the milch from the male. However, the fish store may have both (especially during Jewish holiday seasons). Be sure to keep all fish bones and ask for any extra heads of freshwater fish which the fish store may have.

Place fish heads, bones and 4 sliced onions in a large, deep, heavy pot. Season with salt, plenty of white pepper, half of sugar, and 1 teaspoon monosodium glutamate. Pour three quarters of the white wine into pot. Place over medium heat to simmer while you are preparing fish.

Grind all fish together (excluding milch and roe), putting through the fine blade of the grinder. Grind remaining 2 onions with fish. Add eggs and remaining seasoning, being sure to add enough white pepper. The only way to be sure of the seasoning is to taste the raw fish mixture. This won't hurt you. This mixture, is, in fact, quite tasty. It should be spicy. Chop in a wooden bowl, or if you prefer, beat briefly with a wooden spoon. As you are beating or chopping, beat in water and remaining white wine. Beat or chop only until the mixture stands in peaks and holds its shape when the beater or chopper is withdrawn. If the fish is beaten too long, the resulting fish balls will be too hard and firm.

By this time the mixture in the pot should be simmering very well. Taste it for seasoning and correct, if necessary. Remove pot from stove.

Scrape carrots and cut into ½-inch slices. Sprinkle into pot. (Liquid in the pot should be just covering bones and onions.)

Dip your hands into cold water. Then scoop up a small handful of chopped fish. Pat into a smooth ball and lay on top of carrots. Rinse hands again in cold water and repeat procedure until all fish is used up. You can put fish balls quite close together—they won't stick.

Cover pot well and replace on stove. Simmer over medium heat for an hour. At this point, add any milch and roe you have. Continue to simmer for 30 to 40 minutes longer. Turn off heat and allow fish to cool in pot.

When pot is cool enough to handle, gently separate pieces of fish and place them in a serving dish. Arrange carrots, milch and roe around fish. Discard bones. Pour cooking liquid through a strainer over fish. This liquid will form a jelly when cold. It is delicious.

Cool fish at room temperature, covering it with wax paper. When cool, cover fish with aluminum foil and refrigerate till serving time. Serve with freshly grated horseradish, on a bed of crisp greens.

Keeps, refrigerated, for a week. Serves 10 to 12.

SHAD ROE POACHED IN BUTTER

Shad roe can be a true delicacy, tender and succulent; or it can be hard, grainy and almost inedible. The secret lies in not overcooking it—and in cooking it slowly.

¾ pound sweet butter
2 pounds fresh shad roe
monosodium glutamate
salt and pepper to taste
⅔ cup chopped parsley

Melt butter in a heavy skillet. Sprinkle shad roe with a little monosodium glutamate on both sides, and place in butter in skillet. Sauté slowly, only until roe is just barely firm, turning it once during cooking. As soon as the roe is just firm on both sides, remove from skillet to a heated platter. The roe should not be brown. If it browns, it will toughen. Season with salt and pepper.

Turn up heat in skillet. When butter is bubbling rapidly, stir in parsley. Pour over roe. Serve hot with wedges of lemon. Serves 4 to 5.

RED SNAPPER OR COD, VERACRUZANA

3 pounds fileted red snapper or a thick cod steak
olive oil (about ½ cup)
6 small green peppers, seeded and sliced
6 small onions, sliced
12 cloves garlic, minced
3 tablespoons chili powder
1 teaspoon basil
1 teaspoon oregano
1 large bay leaf, crumbled
1 teaspoon cumin (ground)

1 *cup canned tomatoes, drained*
½ *cup fish stock, or clam juice*
salt, pepper and a little sugar
cayenne pepper or tabasco, to taste
2 *teaspoons monosodium glutamate*
24 *black and green olives (mixed)*
1 *tablespoon cilantro (optional)*

Dry fish filets with paper towels. Sauté fish in a little olive oil very briefly, on both sides, until it is lightly browned. Arrange fish in a broad baking dish.

In the same pan, sauté the green peppers, onions and garlic in remaining olive oil. When vegetables are just soft, stir in chili powder, basil, oregano, bay leaf and cumin.

Place tomatoes in a small saucepan, and cook over low heat until they lose their shape and form a sauce. Add fish liquid to tomato sauce, then combine sauce with vegetable mixture. Season to taste with salt, pepper, sugar and cayenne pepper. Add monosodium glutamate. Spoon this mixture over and around fish. Place in a 400 degree oven for about 20 minutes.

Sprinkle olives and chopped cilantro over dish, and serve at once. This dish is also very good served at room temperature. Serves 6.

FRIED SQUID

3 *pounds small squid*
oil for deep-fat frying
2½ *cups sifted flour*
1 *teaspoon baking powder*
1 *teaspoon salt*
1 *cup white wine or beer*

Clean squid by washing under running water, rubbing off outer speckled skin and pulling out all entrails. The fish will then be shaped like tubes. Cut into ¼-inch slices.

In a deep pan, heat 2 or 3 inches of oil to 375 degrees.

(continued on the next page)

Sift flour, baking powder and salt together. Stir wine or beer briskly into sifted dry ingredients.

With a fork, dip slices of squid into batter and drop into hot fat. Fry only until golden brown. Serve at once. Serves 6.

STUFFED SQUID

6 medium-size squid
1 onion, chopped
6 cloves, garlic, minced
½ cup melted butter
½ cup chopped parsley
1 teaspoon tarragon
1½ cups finely chopped cooked shrimp
1½ cups finely chopped cooked crabmeat
salt and pepper
1 teaspoon monosodium glutamate
½ cup chopped scallions
1 cup tomato purée
1 cup beef gravy
½ cup red wine

Clean squid under running water, rubbing off outer dark-speckled skin and pulling out entrails to make each squid a hollow tube.

Sauté chopped onion and half of the minced garlic in half of melted butter. When vegetables are soft, add chopped parsley, tarragon, shrimp and crabmeat. Toss well together. Season well with salt, pepper and monosodium glutamate.

Stuff this filling firmly into the cleaned squid tubes.

Heat remaining butter in a saucepan. Add chopped scallions and remaining garlic. Sauté till tender. Add tomato purée, beef gravy and wine. Bring to a boil and simmer for 5 minutes. Lower heat. Add stuffed squid. Simmer until squid are tender, about 1½ hours. Serve garnished with additional chopped parsley. Serves 6.

SQUID IN ITS INK

2 *pounds squid*
3 *to* 4 *tablespoons olive oil*
1 *large onion, chopped*
5 *cloves garlic, minced*
1 *cup dry red wine*
1 *teaspoon monosodium glutamate*
salt and pepper
¼ *cup chopped parsley*
Fluffy, Steamed Rice for 6 *people* (*page* 301)

Clean squid, rubbing off the dark speckled outer skin and pulling out the intestines from the center. Reserve small black ink sack located near the tentacles. Cut cleaned squid ino bite-size pieces.

Heat olive oil in a heavy saucepan. Add squid and sauté over medium-high heat about 4 minutes. Lower heat, and add onion and garlic. Sauté until they are just soft. Add ink sacks, wine and monosodium glutamate.

Lower heat till liquid is just simmering. Cook about 1½ hours, or until squid is tender. Season with salt and pepper.

Serve sprinkled with chopped parsley and with Fluffy, Steamed Rice. Serves 6.

AIOLI DINNER

Aioli is, in reality, a sauce, but a sauce served in a very special way, to make a Provençal version of a boiled dinner (seafood and vegetables).

The Aioli Sauce is a garlicky mayonnaise. It may be made a day or 2 in advance and stored in the refrigerator, but it should be removed ahead of time, so that it can be served at room temperature.

Aioli Sauce

3 *egg yolks*
1 *tablespoon lemon juice*
½ *teaspoon powdered mustard*
salt and pepper to taste
12 *garlic cloves*
3 *to* 4 *cups olive oil, or use* ⅔ *olive oil and* ⅓ *salad oil*

Place egg yolks, lemon juice, mustard, salt and pepper and a few cloves of garlic in blender jar. Blend till smooth. Gradually add remaining garlic and blend smooth. Now, very gradually add oil in a thin stream. Stop blender occasionally and scrape down sides. Add as much oil as the mixture will absorb.

Transfer mixture, which should now be quite thick, to the small bowl of an electric mixer. Turn mixer to high speed. Continue to add oil, in a fine stream, until aioli is very thick and holds its shape. (If you do not have an electric mixer, use a wire whisk or a rotary beater.)

Note: If a blender is not available to start the aioli, pound the garlic in a mortar and pestle. Proceed to make the aioli in the electric mixer, or, very slowly, by hand with whisk or beater. It is finished when the sauce is very thick and yellow.

Serve with the following:

Aioli Vegetables

12 small potatoes, boiled in their skins
1 pound trimmed whole green beans
10 trimmed artichoke hearts
1 small cauliflower, separated into flowerettes
12 Brussels sprouts
12 carrots, trimmed to look like small carrots (or use canned small carrots)
2 turnips, cut into small shapes
12 trimmed leeks
broth or Court Bouillon (page 55)

All of the vegetables should be cooked, separately, in a well-seasoned broth or Court Bouillon until they are tender. They may be cooked ahead of time and left to stand in their broth until serving time; then quickly reheated, drained well and arranged around the fish (directions below) on a large platter.

Aioli Seafood

The fish can be any variety of seafood which is available and appetizing. For example:

12 shrimp, shelled, cleaned and poached in Court Bouillon (page 55) only till they turn pink
2 cooked lobsters, cut into chunks and well cracked so the pieces are easy to handle
12 mussels—very well scrubbed, then steamed in Court Bouillon only until the shells open. Be careful not to overcook them. Serve in their shells.
12 clams—well scrubbed and barely cooked in Court Bouillon until their shells open.
2 to 3 pounds cod or halibut. Tie this in a piece of cheesecloth and poach in Court Bouillon for 8 minutes per pound. Keep Court Bouillon just simmering until the fish is cooked.
2 large eels, skinned, preferably fileted, cut into 6 pieces,

(*continued on the next page*)

then poached for 10 minutes in a simmering Court Bouillon

The Court Bouillon may be used over again for each fish or for the vegetables. You will need about 2 quarts of Court Bouillon.

Also, prepare a dozen shelled hard-cooked eggs.

To serve, place the large piece of cooked cod or halibut in the center of a hot platter. Arrange the vegetables, eggs and additional seafood attractively around cod or halibut. Garnish with sprigs of parsley and lemon wedges. Serve with a bowl of aioli sauce.

Note: You can strain the Court Bouillon, after all the fish and seafood have been cooked, and serve it hot, as a fish broth before dinner, or chilled, as a fish cocktail. Serves 6.

LEON'S STRIPED BASS PLAKI

This is one of the best fish dishes I know. Adults love it, and so do children. It is also delicious cold since the sauce forms a wonderful aspic.

1 *3- to 4-pound striped bass*
2 *lemons*
salt and pepper
monosodium glutamate
1 *cup chopped parsley*
1 *cup chopped green onions*
2 *bay leaves, crushed*
½ *teaspoon oregano*
4 *cloves garlic, minced*
1 *teaspoon basil*
3 *tablespoons chopped celery leaves*
1 *large onion, sliced*
1 *large tomato, sliced*
¾ *cup olive oil*
½ *bottle white wine*

24 *scrubbed little-neck clams*
24 *well-scrubbed mussels*
24 *raw cleaned, shelled shrimp*
24 *bay scallops*

Have fish cleaned, but left whole. Make 3 or 4 diagonal gashes through top skin. Rub fish, inside and out, with ½ lemon. Season stomach cavity with salt, pepper and a little monosodium glutamate.

Combine parsley, green onions, crushed bay leaves, oregano, garlic, basil and chopped celery leaves. Put two thirds of this mixture into the stomach cavity of fish. Sprinkle remaining mixture over top of fish.

Place fish in a large, shallow baking dish. On top of gashes, arrange alternate slices of onion, lemon and tomato. Season top of fish with salt, pepper and monosodium glutamate.

Pour olive oil over fish.

Pour wine around fish. Place on a high rack in a 375 degree oven. Bake about 40 minutes, or until wine is simmering around fish. Scatter scrubbed clams and mussels around fish. Continue to bake in oven about 10 to 15 minutes, until clams and mussels are just beginning to open.

Add shrimp and scallops. Raise heat to 400, and bake 10 to 15 minutes longer. By this time, the shrimp will have turned pink and the scallops and the bass should be cooked. Remove from oven and serve with crusty bread to mop up the sauce. Serves 6.

BREADED ABALONE STEAKS

2 *cans abalone (see Shopping Sources)*
4 *tablespoons flour*
1 *egg beaten with* 2 *teaspoons water*
2 *cups dry bread crumbs*
salt and pepper
1 *teaspoon monosodium glutamate*
clarified butter, or butter and oil, for sautéing

Drain juice from abalone and use it for another purpose—a soup, or a chilled abalone juice cocktail.

Cut abalone into slices ¼ inch thick. Pat them dry. Flour lightly on both sides, then dip into egg and water mixture.

Season bread crumbs well with salt, pepper and monosodium glutamate. Dip abalone slices into seasoned bread crumbs. Place crumbed slices on a baking sheet which has been covered with a sheet of wax paper and sprinkled with remaining bread crumbs. Chill for at least 1 hour.

Just before serving, heat fat in a skillet. Sauté abalone slices until golden brown on both sides. This should not take very long, only a few minutes for each side.

Serve with lemon wedges, and, if you like, a little additional fresh melted butter and chopped parsley. Serves 6.

ABALONE, ENSENADA

4 *tablespoons sesame or other vegetable oil*
3 *stalks celery, finely sliced*
2 *green peppers, sliced*
2 *onions, chopped*
2 *cloves garlic, minced*
2 *cans abalone, drained and sliced, juice reserved*

3 tablespoons cornstarch
4 tablespoons sherry
4 tablespoons Japanese soy sauce
¼ cup tomato purée
2 small tomatoes, halved, cored and cut into small wedges
1 teaspoon monosodium glutamate
salt and pepper
½ teaspoon sugar

Heat oil in a heavy skillet until it is hot. Add celery, green peppers, onions, and garlic. Sauté over fairly high heat until vegetables are almost, but not quite, soft. Stir in sliced abalone. Lower heat.

Stir abalone juice into cornstarch, making a smooth mixture. Add sherry, soy sauce and tomato purée.

Add tomato wedges to abalone mixture. Sauté, for a minute or 2. Pour in cornstarch mixture, stirring constantly. Season with monosodium glutamate, salt, pepper and sugar. When sauce in skillet is slightly thickened, the dish is cooked. Serve with Fluffy, Steamed Rice. Serves 6.

MUSSELS EN BROCHETTE

6 pounds mussels
¼ cup soy sauce
2 tablespoons sherry
2 cloves garlic, finely chopped
1 teaspoon finely chopped fresh or pickled ginger
1 pound bacon

Wash mussels to remove surface dirt (it is not necessary to scrub them, since they won't be cooked in their shells). Open the mussels with a small, sharp knife. Rinse inside of shell under cold water. Remove mussels from shells, keeping them whole. Place the mussel meat in a bowl. Add soy sauce, sherry, garlic and ginger. Marinate for at least an hour.

Cut bacon slices into thirds.

(*continued on the next page*)

Wrap each piece of bacon around 2 or 3 mussels. Divide among 6 skewers.

Broil under medium heat, basting with the marinade once or twice and turning the skewers, until the bacon is golden brown on all sides. Serve at once. Serves 6.

MUSSELS IN SNAIL BUTTER

6 *pounds mussels*
2 *cups sweet butter*
12 *cloves garlic, finely minced*
1 *cup chopped parsley*
1 *cup finely ground pistachio nuts*
salt and pepper

Wash outside of mussels. It is not necessary to scrub them as you would if you were steaming them.

Open each mussel with a small, sharp knife. Rinse insides under cold water, then remove mussels from shells, keeping them whole.

Cream butter until it is soft. Beat in minced garlic, parsley, pistachio nuts, and salt and pepper to taste.

Using snail dishes or snail casserolettes, distribute the mussels in the hollows, allowing 2 or 3 mussels for each hollow.

Fill a pastry bag with the garlic-butter mixture. Press an even amount of the mixture on top of each mussel-filled hollow. Use all the butter.

Place in a 350 degree oven. Bake about 25 minutes, or until garlic butter is bubbling and mussels are just cooked.

Serve very hot, with plenty of crusty bread to mop up the sauce. Serves 6.

DEVILED CLAMS

2 *dozen cherrystone clams*
1 *cup dry white wine*
¼ *cup butter*
1 *green pepper, finely chopped*
1 *onion, finely chopped*
2 *cloves garlic, finely minced*
½ *cup chopped parsley*
½ *cup soft bread crumbs*
2 *teaspoons tomato paste*
salt and pepper
dash of cayenne pepper
3 *slices bacon, chopped*

Scrub clams to get sand off shells. Place them in a pot and add wine. Cook, covered, over low heat, just until the clam shells open.

Remove clams from pot, reserving liquid and half of each shell. Remove clams from shells. Grind clams, using fine blade of grinder.

Melt butter in a skillet. Sauté green pepper, onion and garlic till soft and golden. Add to clams, along with chopped parsley and soft bread crumbs. Stir in tomato paste. Season well with salt, pepper and cayenne pepper.

Fill reserved clam shells with this mixture. Sprinkle tops with chopped bacon, and place on broiling pan. Brown under medium heat of broiler till bacon is crisp.

Note: The broth remaining from steamed clams is very good and can be served either hot or icy cold. Serves 4.

SHRIMP WITH CUCUMBER, CHINESE STYLE

4 tablespoons sherry
2 tablespoons Japanese soy sauce
½ teaspoon sugar
2 tablespoons cornstarch
2 pounds shelled, cleaned raw shrimp
2 large cucumbers
2 tablespoons vegetable oil
Fluffy, Steamed Rice (page 301) (6 servings)
½ cup chopped scallions

Combine sherry, soy sauce, sugar and cornstarch. Marinate shrimp in this mixture.

Peel cucumbers and cut in half; scoop out seeds with a teaspoon. Cut into ¼-inch slices. Add to shrimp mixture.

Just before serving, drain shrimp and cucumbers from marinade but reserve marinade.

In a heavy skillet, heat vegetable oil until it is hot. Add shrimp and cucumbers. Sauté over high heat, stirring constantly, for 3 or 4 minutes, or until all shrimp are pink. Add marinade. As soon as sauce thickens, serve with Fluffy, Steamed Rice. Garnish with chopped scallions. Serves 5 to 6.

CURRIED SHRIMP

3 tablespoons clarified butter or vegetable oil
2 tablespoons mustard seeds
2 onions, chopped
4 cloves garlic, minced
2 tablespoons chopped fresh or pickled ginger
½ cup curry powder
⅔ teaspoon ground cardamom seeds
1½ teaspoons ground black pepper
salt

dash of cayenne pepper
½ *teaspoon sugar*
2 *cups stock*
2 *teaspoons tomato paste*
2 *pounds fresh, cleaned shrimp*
2 *tablespoons chopped, fresh cilantro* (*optional*)

Melt butter or oil in a saucepan. When it is very hot, add mustard seeds. Keep heat high. Seeds will turn black and make a popping sound. Keep pan covered while seeds are popping. As soon as popping sound has stopped, lower heat. Uncover pan and add chopped onions, garlic and ginger. Sauté till tender. Stir for 2 or 3 minutes. Then stir in curry powder, cardamom seeds and black pepper. Season with salt and cayenne to taste and a bit of sugar. Add stock and tomato paste. (You may prepare this part of the recipe well ahead of time.)

About 10 minutes before serving, heat sauce to the simmering point. Add raw shrimp. Simmer over low heat only until shrimp becomes pink and slightly firm. This will take no more than 4 or 5 minutes at the most. Serve at once with Fluffy, Steamed Rice. Garnish with chopped cilantro. Onion Relish goes well with this. Serves 6.

SAUTEED SHRIMP WITH MUSHROOMS

1 *pound small button mushrooms*
¼ *cup sweet butter*
5 *cloves garlic, minced*
2 *pounds raw, cleaned, shelled shrimp*
1 *teaspoon fresh tarragon, chopped*
½ *cup chopped parsley*

Trim mushrooms; place in a heavy skillet. Cover until mushrooms have steamed almost dry and are sticking to the pan. Add butter, and stir. Sauté for about 10 or 15 minutes. Add garlic, and sauté 2 or 3 minutes longer. Add raw, cleaned shrimp, raise heat, and continue to sauté over fairly high heat until shrimp turn pink. This will not take long—if you stir, only 3 or 4 minutes. Add tarragon and chopped parsley, and serve at once. Serves 6.

AN ELEGANT SHRIMP MOUSSE

2 *egg whites*
2 *cups heavy cream*
1½ *teaspoons salt*
½ *teaspoon white pepper*
¼ *teaspoon nutmeg*
1 *pound raw, cleaned, shelled shrimp*

Combine egg whites, cream and seasonings in a bowl or measuring cup. Pour a third of mixture into blender. Add a third of the shrimp. Blend to the consistency of a smooth paste. Use a rubber spatula when needed to remove shrimp from sides of blender. Empty blended mixture into a bowl. Repeat process until all ingredients are used. Mix together well in bowl.

Pour into a fancy 1-quart mold—perhaps a mold shaped like a fish, if you have one. Place mold in a pan of water, cover with aluminum foil, and bake at 350 degrees for about 40 minutes. Remove from oven, and let mousse stand in mold approximately 5 minutes. Then loosen edges, turn out on a warm platter and cover with Shrimp Mousse Sauce. (Incidentally, this mousse is very good cold, without the sauce. It is much like a pâté of fish.)

Shrimp Mousse Sauce

2 *tablespoons butter*
2 *tablespoons flour*
1 *cup heavy cream*
½ *cup dry white wine*
½ *cup clam juice*
½ *pound cooked, cleaned, shelled shrimp*
2 *teaspoons chopped parsley*
½ *teaspoon tarragon*

Melt butter in a heavy saucepan. Remove from heat; stir in flour. Return to heat and stir, over low heat, about 5 minutes. Again remove from heat.

With a wire whisk, stir in cream, wine and clam juice. Return to heat and cook, stirring constantly, until sauce thickens.

Cut shrimp into small pieces. Add shrimp, parsley and tarragon to sauce. Spoon over hot Shrimp Mousse. Serves 6.

SHRIMP STUFFED EGGPLANT

3 *medium eggplants*
¾ *cup olive oil*
1 *pound shrimp*
2 *medium onions, chopped*
2 *cloves garlic, chopped*
2 *stalks celery, chopped*
1 *green pepper, chopped*
¼ *cup chopped parsley*
¼ *cup chopped celery leaves*
¼ *cup tomato sauce*
½ *teaspoon aniseed*
bay leaf
salt and pepper
1 *teaspoon monosodium glutamate*

Set oven at 350 degrees.

Cut eggplants in half, and brush with some of the olive oil. Bake until eggplants are very tender. Scoop out center pulp, leaving shells about ¼ inch thick. Chop pulp coarsely.

While eggplants are baking, shell and clean shrimp and chop them coarsely.

Sauté onions, garlic, celery and green pepper in remaining olive oil.

When vegetables are tender, add chopped parsley, celery leaves, tomato sauce, aniseed and bay leaf. Cook till mixture is almost dry.

Add chopped raw shrimp. Continue to cook, stirring over high heat, only until the shrimp are barely pink. Be careful not to overcook.

Add chopped eggplant pulp. Season with salt, pepper and monosodium glutamate.

Fill eggplant shells with the shrimp mixture. Bake about 15 minutes, or until stuffed eggplants are thoroughly hot. Serves 6.

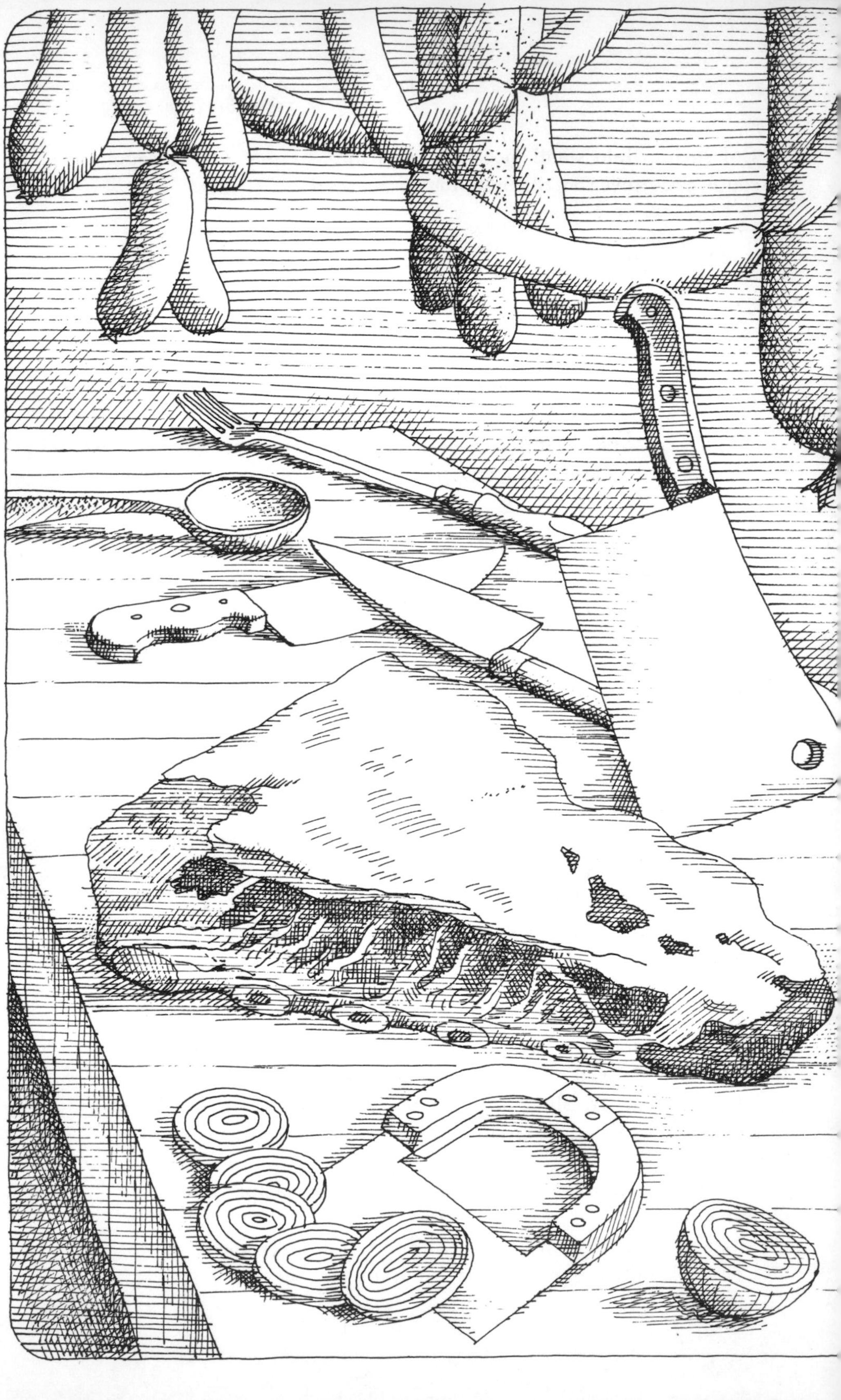

6. MEATS

EXCLUDING GAME, there are five types of meat which are generally used: beef, lamb, pork, veal and variety meats—liver, kidneys, sweetbreads and the like.

We are fortunate in the United States to have available very high quality beef: well marbled and often well aged. However, it is important to use the right cuts of meat for the particular dish involved. For example, filet of beef would be wasted in a stew. Leg of lamb would make a dry, stringy stew, whereas shoulder or neck of lamb makes succulent stew.

The best way to learn about cuts of meat is through experience and by asking questions.

A good butcher whom you know and trust can be an invaluable source of information. Not every butcher, however, will give foolproof advice regarding which cuts of meat to use for what dish. I have stood next to young housewives in butcher shops and heard butchers guarantee that a round roast of beef with absolutely no fat or marbling would make wonderful pot roast. Perhaps round of beef would make wonderful pot roast for someone who likes completely dry, stringy meat. But most people have something more juicy in mind when they think of pot roast.

Here are some tips I have learned over the years from the good butchers I have been lucky enough to deal with.

Beef: Grainy, well-marbled chuck, brisket or boned flanken are excellent in braised beef dishes. During the cooking, the graininess dissolves into a gelatinous matter and makes the cooked dish juicy and tender.

Lamb: Leg of lamb, if it is young, is naturally tender. It should be roasted to the pink or even to the rare stage and served with lamb juices created by simmering extra lamb bones in wine and/or stock as the leg is roasting. For further directions for making the juices for roasts, see page 52.

Pork: Pork can be succulent, or very dry and tasteless. For health reasons, pork must always be completely cooked so that there are no pink parts or juices. But it should never be overcooked so that it falls apart when sliced. A cut of pork excellent for roasting and for stew dishes alike is *un*smoked tenderloin. This cut is usually available only in foreign nationality butcher shops: German, Italian, Polish, etc. It is well worth seeking out because it is extraordinarily juicy. Boned pork shoulder, more easily obtained, is a fairly good substitute, if it is not too fatty.

Veal: Veal truly must be roasted only to the point where it is still just a little bit pink and yet not at all rare. Leg and rump of veal make beautiful roasts, as does the loin when it is boned and tied. For stews, the neck, breast or shoulder are best. Remember always that a little fat and graininess is a must for stew meat.

Generally we have very poor quality veal in the United States. It is usually not milk-fed, as it should be. Good veal is very light in color—light pink rather than red, and covered with a small amount of very white fat. Much of the veal sold in butcher shops tends to be far redder than it should be; it resembles a somewhat tasteless type of beef.

For sautéed dishes, loin or rib chops, or veal scallops (cut from the leg and pounded thin) are usually chosen. With a little imagination, many of the recommendations for cooking chicken breasts can be adapted to veal chops. For scallops of veal I often substitute chicken breasts which have been boned, skinned and pounded thin (see instructions on pages 238-39 and 248). These must be cooked and served very quickly or they will toughen. Properly prepared they are delicious, whereas the veal scallops are generally disappointing.

Mutton: Mutton, which is mature lamb, is not easily obtainable, although it is thoroughly delicious if properly aged and prepared. The leg or loin should be used for roasted or broiled mutton. Either of these cuts should be well aged by the butcher for several weeks. If the loin is used, the flank should be cut away and completely discarded. The loin may be cut into thick chops which may be broiled, or it may be boned, tied and roasted—but only to the point of rareness. Leg of mutton tastes even better when it has been marinated for at least 2 hours (or up to 3 or 4 days) in a very garlicky Vinaigrette Sauce. Really good mutton—either the leg or the loin—is comparable to the best beef you can imagine.

One final point: People are so often prejudiced against the variety meats because they are innards. Sweetbreads, veal hearts, calves' liver and the like are true delicacies and provide completely new taste and texture sensations.

Broiling

Broiling is an art rather than a science. Much depends on the thickness and type of meat, plus the heat of the broiler. Lamb and beef are best for broiling, although some cuts of pork—when there is marbling—lend themselves to this process.

Rubbing steaks or chops with a little Japanese soy sauce before broiling helps give them a nice color during cooking, even if the broiler is not as hot as it should be.

Steaks and chops may also be pan-broiled. The meat should be rubbed first with a little soy sauce and placed into a very hot iron skillet, without any fat at all.

It takes skill to know when meat is done to your taste. The finger test is the one I prefer. If the meat is still very soft when pressed with an index finger, it is very rare. The firmer the meat when pressed, the more well done it is. Pork should always be well done; lamb is best still pink, or at least medium rare.

I prefer beef rare. Two splendid, inexpensive cuts for broiling and serving rare are flank steak and skirt steak. These are best when marinated first for at least 20 minutes in a mixture of soy sauce, sherry, fresh ginger and monosodium glutamate. They should not be broiled till well done, or the meat will toughen. Either cut should be served thinly sliced, on the diagonal, across the grain. When not overcooked, they are tender and juicy.

There is a good trick for broiling extra-thick cuts of meat, such as triple lamb chops or 2½-inch steaks. The difficulty here, frequently, is that the outer parts of the meat brown beautifully, while the inside remains almost raw. It is important—particularly if your broiler is not a very hot one—to preheat your chops or steaks before placing them under the broiler. To do this, rub the meat with a little soy sauce, place on the broiling rack, and then into a low (300 degree) oven for 10 minutes or more, or just until you think the meat is warm throughout, though not completely cooked. At this point, transfer the broiler rack to a hot broiler, and proceed to brown the meat on both sides. Cook to the desired degree of doneness.

I also like to keep on hand rib or shell steaks cut ½ inch thick and pounded until they are just a bit more than ¼ inch thick, then individually wrapped and frozen. These are indispensable for last-minute meals since they thaw out in a hot skillet almost instantly. These also receive a preliminary rub with soy sauce before they are cooked.

BEEF

ROAST PRIME RIBS OF BEEF

Without doubt, well-aged prime ribs of beef make a superlative roast. To make carving simple, ask the butcher to make a standing rib roast by sawing off the short ribs at the narrow end, as well as the backbone. Do not discard these bones. Trim off as much fat as possible from the short ribs and use *all* the bones to make the sauce for the roast (see page 52).

There are several schools of thought regarding roasting temperatures for ribs of beef. There are those who believe in the searing process to begin with—to brown the roast—then lowering the temperature somewhat, to complete the cooking. This does brown the meat—as well as shrink it. There is an advantage in this method when the members of a household have varying degrees of taste regarding the doneness of meat. If you sear meat at the beginning, you will certainly have several rather well-done slices as you begin to carve. In my home this is not a popular procedure.

Then there are those who believe in a constant, rather moderate or low-moderate temperature of 325 degrees. This works fairly well, but not as well as the one I prefer, which creates a roast which is rare or medium from start to finish.

Start with a rib roast of at least three ribs. Make a mixture of minced garlic, monosodium glutamate, celery salt, commercial gravy coloring or a little soy sauce, thyme, crumbled bay leaf, chopped parsley and a little very strong stock, or slightly diluted Beef Concentrate of Beef. Rub the roast all over with this mixture.

Place the roast in a shallow pan. A rack is not necessary since the bones form a natural rack. Roast at the lowest possible temperature—less than 200 degrees, if possible. Insert a meat thermometer into the thickest part of the meat. For rare meat, remove the roast from the oven (or turn the heat off) when the thermometer registers about 130 degrees—about 10 degrees less than the thermometer says rare meat should be. The reason for this is that the meat continues to cook from its own heat and brings the temperature up a bit. Allow about 25 minutes per pound for rare meat. A meat thermometer is indispensable in this type of roasting. Always turn the oven heat off when the thermometer reads 10 degrees below the degree for which you are aiming. (150 degrees for medium beef. I am not going beyond this because I thoroughly disapprove of overcooked beef.)

Let the beef stand in a warm place (or in the oven with the heat turned off) for 15 to 25 minutes before carving it. This will allow the juices to settle and will make carving easier. Add any juices from the roast to the sauce you have already cooked. Have sauce warm, but not boiling hot, because boiling hot sauce, spooned on even very rare thin slices of roast beef, can cook them enough to make them well done. Serves 6 to 8.

BASIC BRAISED BEEF

In my experience, browning meat before braising only toughens the meat and creates smoke. Theoretically, browning is supposed to seal the juices in, but why, then, is it possible to have absolutely succulent boiled beef, which is not browned at all?

Here is my recipe for a basic braised beef which can also be turned into a curry, chili, paprikash, or any kind of stew you would like it to be. It can be kept in the refrigerator for as long as a week—even a bit longer if you take the trouble to reheat it to the boiling point every few days.

To make this properly, you need a heavy pot with a tight-fitting, heavy lid. With such equipment, you can practically dispense with any cooking liquid, unless you care to add some for flavor (such as a little wine or stock).

- 3 *pounds boned thick flanken* (*trimmed*), *or very grainy chuck cut into* 1″ *cubes*
- 2 *large onions, chopped*
- 4 *cloves garlic, finely minced* (*optional*)
- 2 *teaspoons monosodium glutamate*
- *salt and pepper to taste*
- ¾ *cup liquid* (*wine, beer, stock, tomato purée, or anything you choose*) (*optional*)
- 1 *cup beef gravy* (*see page* 53)

Place meat in a heavy pot. Add onions, garlic, monosodium glutamate and some salt and pepper. Cover tightly. Place in 325 degree oven. When meat and other ingredients begin to simmer, add any desired liquid. Liquid is *not* absolutely necessary, but helps make a more abundant sauce (almost too abundant!).

Continue to braise meat in covered pot about 1½ hours, or until the meat is barely tender. Skim off fat from top, and stir in beef gravy.

Serve with chopped parsley, or use this Basic Braised Beef to make any of the following four variations. All of these dishes taste better when they are cooked and then reheated on a second or third day.

Serves 6.

AMERICAN BEEF STEW

- *Basic Braised Beef* (*above*)
- 10 *tiny new potatoes, peeled*
- 2 *pounds green beans* (*ends trimmed*), *cut into* 1″ *pieces*
- *any other vegetable of your choice, peeled and trimmed*
- 2 *small cans tiny whole carrots, well drained*
- *chopped parsley*

Add all the raw vegetables to Basic Braised Beef before beef is completely tender. Bake, covered, in a 325 degree oven until the vege-

(*continued on the next page*)

tables and meat are thoroughly tender, 30 to 50 minutes. Add more salt, monosodium glutamate and pepper if necessary, as well as a pinch of sugar. Add well-drained canned carrots. If desired, stir in a few spoonfuls of tomato purée or even Madeira. Sprinkle with chopped parsley, and serve hot. Serves 6.

INDIAN BEEF CURRY

⅓ *cup oil, or fat skimmed from Basic Braised Beef* (*page* 166)
2 *tablespoons mustard seeds*
5 *tablespoons curry powder*
½ *teaspoon cinnamon*
1 *teaspoon black pepper*
2 *large potatoes, peeled and cut into dice, or* 3 *cups shredded cabbage*
salt
monosodium glutamate
½ *cup stock* (*optional*)
Basic Braised Beef
cayenne pepper
2 *tablespoons chopped fresh cilantro* (*optional*)

Heat oil or fat in a heavy pan, and add mustard seeds. Raise heat, cover pan, and let seeds turn dark in pan. Turn heat low. Add remaining spices: curry powder, cinnamon and black pepper. Stir for 2 or 3 minutes, then stir in diced potatoes or cabbage. Season with salt and a little monosodium glutamate.

Stir in Basic Braised Beef. Add stock if you like a liquid curry. Simmer over low heat until meat and vegetables are completely tender. Stir in cayenne pepper to taste.

Serve with Fluffy, Steamed Rice, and garnish with chopped fresh cilantro if it is available. Serves 6.

BEEF CHILI

½ cup oil, or fat skimmed from Basic Braised Beef (*page* 166)
5 *tablespoons chili powder*
2 *tablespoons sesame seeds, toasted in a dry frying pan till just golden, then pounded into a powder in a mortar or a blender*
½ cup well-drained and chopped canned tomatoes
1 *tablespoon tomato paste*
¼ ounce unsweetened chocolate
salt and pepper
2 *teaspoons monosodium glutamate*
Basic Braised Beef
2 *cans kidney or pinto beans, drained and rinsed in hot water*
cayenne pepper to taste (*optional*)
Fluffy, Steamed Rice
1 *cup chopped raw onion*
½ cup chopped cilantro (*optional*)

Heat oil or fat in a heavy pan. Stir in chili powder and ground sesame seeds. Add chopped tomatoes, tomato paste and unsweetened chocolate. Season to taste with salt, pepper and monosodium glutamate. Simmer until chocolate is melted.

Stir the above mixture into Basic Braised Beef. Let simmer until the beef is completely tender. Stir in well-drained beans. If you like your chili hot, add a little cayenne pepper.

Serve with Fluffy, Steamed Rice. Sprinkle chili with plenty of raw onion and chopped cilantro, if it is available. Serves. 6.

Note: If you like, eliminate the beans from the recipe and serve with Refried Beans and fried tortillas.

BEEF PAPRIKASH

½ *cup oil, or fat skimmed from Basic Braised Beef* (*page* 166)
5 *tablespoons sweet Hungarian paprika*
2 *teaspoons tomato paste*
Basic Braised Beef
½ *cup stock or wine*
1½ *cups sour cream*
¾ *cup chopped fresh dill, or* 1 *tablespoon dried dill*

Heat oil or fat in a heavy pot. Lower heat, and stir in paprika and tomato paste. Add Basic Braised Beef and mix well. Add stock or wine; simmer, covered, until the meat is tender. Stir in sour cream and half of dill. Serve hot, sprinkled with remaining chopped dill. Serve with buttered noodles. Serves 6.

OLD-FASHIONED POT ROAST

5 *pounds first-cut brisket of beef* (2 *or* 3 *thick slices of well-marbled flanken may be substituted*)
5 *onions, chopped*
4 *cloves garlic, finely minced*
salt and pepper to taste
2 *teaspoons monosodium glutamate*
½ *cup beef stock or red wine* (*optional*)

Combine all ingredients except liquid in a heavy pot. Cover tightly and place in a 325 degree oven. When mixture begins to simmer, add liquid, if desired. Continue to cook in oven until meat is completely tender, 2 to 3 hours. Serve hot, with pan juices, or serve at room temperature, sliced thin. Serves 6 to 8.

Note: If you use a heavy pot, the liquid is not really necessary, but, as with Basic Braised Beef, the liquid makes a more abundant gravy.

GREEK BEEF STEW

3 *pounds grainy chuck, or boned, trimmed flanken, cut into 1" cubes*
1 *tablespoon tomato paste*
½ *cup beef stock*
⅓ *cup chopped parsley*
1 *teaspoon oregano*
4 *cloves garlic, minced*
1 *bay leaf, crumbled*
4 *teaspoons salt*
2 *teaspoons pepper*
1 *tablespoon monosodium glutamate*
1 *teaspoon sugar*
1 *teaspoon cinnamon*
24 *small white onions*

Combine all ingredients. Mix well, using your hands, so that seasonings are evenly distributed.

Place mixture in a heavy pot, and cover tightly. Place in a 325 degree oven. Bake about 2½ hours, or until meat cubes and onions are completely tender. Serve hot, garnished with a little additional chopped parsley. Serves 6.

FRENCH BOILED BEEF

Prepared and served properly, this is one of the most attractive and delicious dishes in the world, and an excellent party dish. Fresh horseradish as an accompaniment adds greatly to the flavor, and it is unfortunate that this is not easily obtainable. However, there is a way to zip the taste of commercial horseradish. Japanese food supply stores sell a horseradish powder called wasabi. A spoonful or 2 mixed into a paste with water, then stirred into commercial horseradish, adds bite and flavor.

4 or 5 pieces of beef bone
4 stalks of celery (with the leaves left on)
1 small bunch parsley
1 large onion
salt
monosodium glutamate
6 beef consommé cubes or 6 tablespoons Concentrate of Beef
3 pounds brisket of beef, or thick flanken
1 medium-size cabbage, cut into small, even wedges
6 to 9 small potatoes (Scrub them; then cut away a strip of skin from around the center of each potato)
1 large turnip, cut into ¼″ slices, then cut into fancy shapes with a cooky cutter
6 celery hearts, washed, trimmed of leaves, but left whole
6 small zucchini, cut into 1″ slices
6 leeks, well trimmed and cleaned of sand
1 can tiny carrots, drained
horseradish, or hot Horseradish Sauce (page 50)
coarse salt

Place beef bones into a deep, heavy pot. Cover with cold water. Add celery stalks, parsley, onion, salt, monosodium glutamate and the consommé cubes or concentrate. Cook, uncovered, over high heat until liquid has reduced slightly. Taste and add more seasoning, if necessary. Add meat to the boiling liquid. When the liquid in the pot begins to boil again, cover the pot and lower heat so that liquid is barely simmering. Simmer slowly about 2½ to 3 hours, or until the meat is just tender when pierced with a fork. Turn off the heat and allow the meat to stand in broth until serving time.

Place each group of cleaned, trimmed vegetables into separate small pots. Add a little salt and monosodium glutamate to each vegetable, then ladle about a cup of beef broth over each. Cook over medium heat until the vegetables are tender. (Of course the carrots are already cooked, but reheating them in broth for a few minutes gives them extra flavor.) Turn off heat under vegetables as they are ready, and allow them to stand in the broth until serving time.

To serve (and this is *most* important): Slice meat neatly and arrange in the center of a large, hot platter. Arrange the hot vegetables around the meat, making separate bouquets of each vegetable.

Serve with horseradish (or Horseradish Sauce) and coarse salt. The broth may be used as a first course, or it may be served in bowls along with the meat and vegetables. Serves 6.

ROULADES PIQUANTES

The "beef birds" generally served in this country are rather dry and tasteless. Here is a French version that is delicious. The cut of beef used is all-important. If, for example, slices of round were substituted for brisket or chuck, the braised rolls would be dry and have an undesirable texture. This is because round of beef is not sufficiently marbled with fat and does not lend itself to the braising process.

¾ *pound pork, ground once*
¼ *pound ham, ground once*
1 *teaspoon salt*
1 *teaspoon pepper*
½ *teaspoon monosodium glutamate*
¼ *cup chopped parsley*
½ *cup chopped shallots or scallions*

Combine all ingredients. Mix well with your hands, then set aside while you prepare the meat slices (see instructions below).

2 *pounds brisket or grainy chuck, sliced ¼" thick (by the butcher)*
3 *tablespoons olive oil*
2 *large onions, chopped*
4 *cloves garlic, minced*
2 *cups dry red wine*
½ *cup beef gravy*
2 *teaspoons tomato paste*

(*continued on the next page*)

1 *teaspoon monosodium glutamate*
½ *teaspoon freshly ground pepper*
¼ *teaspoon allspice*
salt to taste
½ *cup chopped parsley*

Place slices of meat between 2 sheets of wax paper. Pound with a mallet or a bottle so that slices expand and become thinner.

Spread each slice with some of the ground meat mixture, making a layer slightly less than ¼ inch thick. Roll up each slice, jelly-roll style, and secure with toothpicks.

Heat olive oil in a heavy pot. Add chopped onions and garlic, and sauté over low heat until they are soft but not brown. Add red wine. Raise heat and boil rapidly to reduce liquid by ⅓. Stir in beef gravy, tomato paste, monosodium glutamate, pepper, allspice and salt.

Let this sauce simmer until it is syrupy, then place the beef rolls side by side in the sauce. Beef rolls should simmer in the sauce until they are tender—about 1½ hours. Sprinkle with chopped parsley, and serve. Serves 6.

BEEF, SAUSAGE AND CABBAGE, PEASANT STYLE

This dish has much the flavor of a traditional French chartreuse except that beef is used instead of the traditional game birds. Also, the dish is far less complicated to present.

6 *pounds cabbage*
½ *pound salt pork, cut into small dice*
2 *onions, peeled and chopped*
3 *carrots, scraped and chopped*
salt and pepper
1 *teaspoon monosodium glutamate*
3 *pounds brisket of beef, or flanken*
10 *juniper berries*
½ *cup chopped parsley*
1 *large bay leaf*

½ teaspoon thyme
1½ cups red wine
1 large garlic sausage (kolbasa, cooked salami, or whatever you can get)

With a sharp knife, remove core from cabbage. Cover the cabbage with water, and bring to a boil. Lower heat and simmer for 3 minutes, then drain cabbage and chop it fine.

Place diced salt pork in a heavy pot, and cook over low heat until it is almost crisp. Add cabbage, onions and carrots; season well with salt, pepper and monosodium glutamate. Place meat on top of the vegetables, then sprinkle with juniper berries, parsley, bay leaf and thyme. Add wine. Cover tightly and cook over low heat about 2½ hours, or till meat is barely tender when pierced with a fork.

Remove casing from sausage, and add sausage to pot. Continue cooking about 30 minutes longer, or till meat is completely tender and sausage is hot.

To serve, mound vegetables in the center of a platter and surround by alternating slices of beef and sausage. Serve hot. Serves 6 to 8.

FILET OF BEEF

For people who like tender, rare beef, filet is the natural choice. It can be cooked whole, as a roast, or cut into steaks (called tournedos in France) and sautéed. Filet of beef may also be cut into cubes or strips and combined with any number of distinctive sauces. It is considered an expensive cut of meat, but isn't really, when you consider how far it goes and how little waste there is.

French tournedos are generally cut about 1 inch thick, and the outer edges are wrapped in bacon. The tournedos are then sautéed in a mixture of sweet butter and a little oil until cooked to your taste. They may be served very simply, with a lump of creamed butter and parsley on top, or with a Bearnaise Sauce, with a reduced wine sauce made in the pan after the tournedos have been removed to a hot plate, or with any number of other French sauces and garnitures.

Presented here are four ideas for using filet of beef.

BEEF FILET IN MADEIRA SAUCE

6 *slices French bread, ½" thick, sautéed in butter on both sides till golden brown*
1 *cup beef marrow (see note below), poached in broth for 10 minutes, drained, then forced through a sieve*
1 *tablespoon olive oil*
3 *tablespoons sweet butter*
2 *pounds filet of beef, cut into ¾" cubes*
⅓ *cup finely chopped shallots or scallions*
2 *cups sliced mushrooms*
1¼ *cups Madeira wine*
⅔ *cup beef gravy (see page 53)*
salt and pepper to taste
2 *teaspoons monosodium glutamate*
½ *cup chopped parsley*

Spread sautéed bread with cooked marrow and place on a baking sheet to keep warm while the dish is being prepared.

In a heavy skillet, heat olive oil and butter. When fat is hot but not smoking, add beef cubes. Turn heat very high, and toss cubes in pan until they are *lightly* browned on all sides. They cook very fast, so be careful not to overcook them. Remove to a plate and keep warm.

Lower heat, then add to pan the finely chopped shallots and mushrooms. When they are soft—in just a minute or 2—add 1 cup of Madeira. Turn heat up very high and reduce until only about half of the liquid remains in pan. Stir in beef gravy. Season with salt, pepper and monosodium glutamate. When sauce bubbles, stir in remaining Madeira. Mix in beef cubes thoroughly so that beef and sauce blend well together.

Place bread slices spread with marrow on a hot serving plate, or on individual plates. Spoon beef in Madeira sauce on top. Sprinkle with chopped parsley. Serves 5 to 6.

Note on beef marrow: To obtain beef marrow, have your butcher crack marrow bones lengthwise so that the marrow can be removed easily with the point of a small knife. (Usually butchers will give you marrow bones for nothing.) Poach marrow in a little stock for about 10 minutes. Drain and force through a sieve while still hot.

BEEF LUCULLUS

½ cup sweet butter (approximately)
6 chicken livers, cut into quarters
1 small pair sweetbreads, blanched and trimmed (see page 222), then cut into ¾″ cubes
1½ pounds filet of beef, cut into ¾″ cubes
¼ cup minced shallots or scallions
1 cup sliced mushrooms
1½ cups dry red wine
½ cup beef gravy (see page 53)
1 cup chopped parsley
1 bay leaf
¼ teaspoon thyme
2 teaspoons monosodium glutamate
1 tablespoon salt
2 teaspoons pepper

Melt about half of the butter in a heavy skillet. Add quartered chicken livers and sweetbread cubes, and cook over high heat, turning constantly, until the livers and sweetbreads are golden. Remove to a platter and keep warm.

Add more butter to pan if necessary, and sauté beef cubes on all sides until lightly browned. Be careful not to overcook the beef, as it should be served rare. As soon as the beef has acquired a good color, transfer it to the platter with the sweetbreads and livers.

Add any remaining butter to skillet, then add chopped shallots and mushrooms. Cook over very high heat for a minute or 2. Then add the wine. Keeping heat high, cook wine down until there is about half left in the pan. Stir in beef gravy, half of chopped parsley and all remaining ingredients. The sauce should look syrupy—that is, slightly thickened. Pour it over meats. Toss all together gently, and serve sprinkled with remaining chopped parsley. Serves 6.

BEEF FILET NICOISE

½ cup olive oil
2 large onions, chopped
6 cloves garlic, minced
2 fresh tomatoes, skinned and cut into eighths
⅔ cup pitted black olives
2 tablespoons capers
½ cup tomato purée
¼ cup beef gravy (see page 53)
1 teaspoon basil
¼ teaspoon oregano
½ teaspoon sugar
2 teaspoons monosodium glutamate
salt and pepper to taste
1 cup chopped parsley
2 pounds filet of beef cut into ¾" cubes

Heat ¼ cup olive oil in a skillet. When it is hot but not smoking, add onions and garlic, and sauté over low heat till tender. Add fresh tomatoes, olives and capers. Raise heat slightly and, as mixture begins to bubble, stir in tomato purée, beef gravy, basil, oregano, sugar, monosodium glutamate, salt, pepper and half of chopped parsley. Cook this sauce down a bit, until it is slightly thickened. Set aside until needed.

Heat remaining olive oil in a separate skillet. When it is hot, add beef cubes. Sauté, stirring over high heat, only a minute or 2, coloring the meat on all sides. Be careful not to overcook the beef cubes. They should be rare when served.

Combine beef cubes and sauce. Mix lightly together. Taste for seasoning and correct if necessary. Sprinkle with remaining chopped parsley and serve. Serves 4 to 5.

CURRIED BEEF KEBABS

⅓ cup vegetable oil
2 tablespoons mustard seeds
1 onion, chopped
3 cloves garlic, finely minced
4 tablespoons curry powder
2 teaspoons tomato paste
1 teaspoon cardamom seeds
½ teaspoon cinnamon
1 teaspoon monosodium glutamate
1 teaspoon freshly ground black pepper
1 teaspoon very finely chopped fresh or pickled ginger
1 cup stock
2½ pounds filet of beef, cut into 1½″ cubes
2 tablespoons chopped cilantro (optional)

Heat oil in a deep pot. Add mustard seeds, and cover pot. Seeds will pop (like popcorn) and turn dark. Heat under pot should be medium high until this point. Now lower heat and add chopped onion and garlic. Sauté until soft.

Stir in curry powder, tomato paste and all remaining spices and seasonings. Stir all together for a minute or 2, then add stock. Cook, uncovered, over medium high heat until sauce is fairly thick. Cool thoroughly. This part of recipe may be done well ahead of time—as long as 2 or 3 days.

At least 2 hours before cooking, pour sauce over cubed beef in a deep bowl, and mix well.

Just before cooking, thread meat on 6 skewers. Preheat broiler so that it is very hot. Broil kebabs close to the flame, turning skewers so that meat browns all over. The meat is best served while it is still rare. Sprinkle with cilantro. Serve with Fluffy, Steamed Rice. Serves 6.

BARBECUED BEEF

2½ pounds boneless sirloin steak, or tender chuck steak, trimmed of all fat
½ cup Salsa Fria (page 60)
1 tablespoon chili powder
¼ cup tomato purée
2 tablespoons soy sauce
½ teaspoon hot sauce, or ¼ teaspoon cayenne pepper
½ teaspoon sugar
1 tablespoon salt
2 teaspoons monosodium glutamate
2 teaspoons pepper
¼ cup beef gravy
½ cup finely chopped raw onion

If sirloin steak is used, slice it thinly. If chuck is used, tenderize it by hitting it in all directions and on both sides of the meat with a sharp knife, until it can be pulled apart into strips.

Combine meat with all remaining ingredients except raw onion. Mix well with your hands so that seasonings are evenly distributed. Allow to stand at least ½ hour.

Preheat broiler. Arrange meat in a metal broiling pan, keeping the pieces so close together that they touch each other. Broil as close as possible to high heat. Do not turn the meat: the hot metal will cook the bottom of the meat. The meat can be broiled until well done, but it tastes much better rare or medium rare.

A good deal of juice will form in the broiling pan which should be served with the meat. Sprinkle with raw onion. Serve with Refried Beans and fried tortillas. Serves 6.

KOREAN MEAT

2½ *pounds sirloin steak, or tender chuck steak*
2 *tablespoons sesame seeds*
4 *cloves garlic, finely minced*
3 *tablespoons sherry*
6 *tablespoons Japanese soy sauce*
2 *onions, thinly sliced and separated into rings*
1 *teaspoon finely minced fresh or pickled ginger*
2 *tablespoons sesame oil*
2 *teaspoons sugar*
2 *teaspoons monosodium glutamate*

If sirloin steak is used, slice it thin. If chuck is used, tenderize it by hitting it in all directions and on both sides of the meat with a sharp knife until it can be pulled apart into strips.

Place sesame seeds in a small skillet over low heat, until they are golden and fragrant. Shake skillet frequently to prevent burning. Let the seeds cool, then grind them in a mortar and pestle, or pulverize in the blender.

Combine meat, ground sesame seeds and remaining ingredients, and mix thoroughly with your hands. Allow to stand at least 20 minutes.

Preheat broiler. Arrange pieces of meat in broiling pan very close together, so the pieces touch each other. Broil as close as possible to heat. It is not necessary to turn the meat unless you want it to be well done. (It tastes better rare or medium rare.) A good deal of juice will form in the pan; juice should be served with the meat. Serve with Fluffy, Steamed Rice. Serves 6.

LAMB

ROAST LEG OF LAMB

Roast leg of lamb makes a very satisfying main course—if it hasn't been overcooked and dried out. In France, lamb is eaten when it is still pink; occasionally it is even served rare. Prepared this way, lamb is amazingly delicious. Overcooked lamb, like overcooked beef, is very apt to be tough since the fibers of the meat contract. Also, the meat takes on a gray color.

- 9 *cloves garlic, peeled*
- 1 *leg of lamb, shank end chopped off by the butcher*
- 1 *tablespoon tomato purée*
- 2 *teaspoons monosodium glutamate*
- 1 *tablespoon soy sauce*
- 1 *tablespoon crushed dried celery leaves*
- 1 *tablespoon salt*
- ½ *teaspoon sugar*
- 2 *teaspoons pepper*

Cut 3 or 4 cloves of garlic into small slivers. Then, using a small pointed knife, make small, deep incisions all over the leg of lamb. Poke slivers of garlic into all the incisions.

Trim off surplus fat from lamb, and reserve for preparing beans.

Crush or mince remaining garlic as fine as possible, then combine it with all remaining ingredients. Rub this mixture over the lamb.

Preheat oven to 450 degrees. Place lamb on a rack in a roasting pan. Roast for 15 minutes in preheated oven. Reduce heat to 350 and roast 15 minutes longer. Then lower heat to 300 and continue to roast meat for 30 to 40 minutes. Turn off oven heat and allow lamb to stand in oven for 15 minutes before carving.

While the roast is cooking, make an unthickened sauce for it, following the directions on page 52. Use the shank end of the leg in making the sauce, as well as any extra lamb bones your butcher will give you. A little rosemary in the sauce improves it, since rosemary seems to have a natural affinity for lamb. Serve roast lamb with garlic-flavored White Beans (see page 305).

BARBECUED LEG OF LAMB

This is an unusual way of preparing a leg of lamb. If you attempt it in the kitchen, you should have a good strong fan to draw the smoke out of the kitchen. Barbecued out of doors, the smoke is no problem.

Note: An aged leg of mutton also lends itself very well to this preparation.

1 *leg of lamb, boned by the butcher, then cut so it will lie flat and be approximately the same thickness all over —if necessary, pound the thick parts so they are not too much thicker than the remaining meat*
1½ *cups Vinaigrette Sauce (made with a little more vinegar than usual) (page 57)*
3 *tablespoons soy sauce*
6 *cloves garlic, finely minced*
1 *bay leaf, crushed*
½ *teaspoon oregano*
2 *teaspoons monosodium glutamate*

Place boned leg of lamb in a wide, shallow pan or bowl. Combine all remaining ingredients, and pour over lamb. Turn meat once or twice so that all parts are in contact with the marinade. Marinate in the refrigerator for at least 2 hours, or up to 3 days, turning the meat frequently.

Preheat broiler, then turn heat to low. Broil, as far from a low flame as possible, turning meat frequently and basting with marinade. It will take about 40 minutes for the meat to cook to the medium rare stage. (It may be cooked longer if desired.)

To serve, slice diagonally with a sharp knife, cutting thin slices.

Serves about 6.

RACK OF LAMB

1 *double rack (ribs, not cut into chops) of lamb* (2 *pieces*)
2 *cups soft, fine, white bread crumbs, made in blender*
6 *cloves garlic, minced*
½ *cup chopped parsley*
½ *cup olive oil*
salt and pepper
1 *teaspoon monosodium glutamate*

Ask the butcher to french the bones—that is, cut off meat and fat from lower part, and remove bits of meat between lower part, leaving 2½ inches of plain bone tips showing—remove the backbone and saw through the beginning of each rib. Trim off completely the outer fatty shell from the rack so that you have only the eye of the meat remaining on the bones.

Combine bread crumbs, garlic, parsley, olive oil, salt, pepper and monosodium glutamate. Using half of this mixture for each rack, make an even layer on top of the meat, pressing the crumb mixture down firmly.

Preheat oven to 550 degrees. Place racks in a pan, bone sides down, in the preheated oven. Roast for 10 minutes. Reduce heat to 400 degrees and roast 10 more minutes. Turn off heat and allow racks to stand in oven for 5 minutes before carving. This makes rather rare lamb. If more well done meat is preferred, allow the racks to roast for a longer time.

To make a sauce for rack of lamb, follow directions given for making on page 52. You will need some lamb bones. Begin to cook the sauce well in advance so that it has some flavor by the time you are ready to serve the racks.

Serves 4 generously.

BASIC BRAISED LAMB

Basic Braised Lamb is made exactly like Basic Braised Beef, and it is just as useful. It can be combined with herbs and spices, well-drained canned tomatoes, and individual vegetables, such as eggplant, zucchini, artichoke hearts, leeks or Brussels sprouts. Many of these dishes have the flavors of the Middle East.

Lamb shoulder, boned neck or shanks are the best cuts to use when making Basic Braised Lamb or any lamb stew. It is best to prepare Basic Braised Lamb a day ahead of time so that it can be refrigerated and the fat removed easily.

Do not forget, when preparing lamb with eggplant, that such spices as cinnamon and allspice add much. The herbs mint and oregano go well with braised lamb, as do plenty of chopped parsley and garlic.

BAKED LAMB SHANKS WITH WHITE BEANS

6 *lamb shanks*
2 *tablespoons tomato paste*
3/4 *teaspoon celery seeds*
3/4 *teaspoon sugar*
2 *tablespoons olive oil*
1 *onion, chopped*
6 *cloves garlic, minced*
3/4 *teaspoon oregano*
salt and pepper
2 *teaspoons monosodium glutamate*
3 *cans white beans, drained, then rinsed in hot water*
stock

Have butcher chop off meatless bone tips of the shanks.

Combine tomato paste, celery seeds, sugar, olive oil, chopped onion,

(*continued on the next page*)

minced garlic, oregano, salt, pepper and monosodium glutamate. Rub lamb shanks all over with this mixture.

Place rinsed beans in a broad casserole large enough to hold the shanks as well. Add enough stock to barely cover the beans. Lay shanks on top of beans and cover casserole (with aluminum foil, if necessary). Place in a 325 degree oven for about 1½ hours, basting shanks with liquid in the pan occasionally, and adding more stock to beans when they begin to look dry.

When the shanks are almost tender, uncover the casserole and continue baking until the shanks are brown and the liquid in the casserole is somewhat reduced. Serves 6.

LAMB WITH GARLIC AND OLIVES

3½ *pounds shoulder of lamb, boned, trimmed of fat and cut into 1″ cubes*
1½ *cups black olives, pitted*
2 *cups coarsely cut garlic (or whole cloves may be used)*
⅔ *cup tomato purée*
1 *large onion, chopped*
1 *teaspoon basil*
½ *cup chopped celery leaves, or 1 teaspoon dry celery leaves*
½ *teaspoon oregano*
½ *cup chopped dill*
2 *teaspoons monosodium glutamate*
2 *teaspoons salt*
½ *teaspoon sugar*
1 *cup chopped parsley*

Mix all ingredients together, reserving ½ cup parsley. Place in a heavy pot which can be tightly covered, and cook in a 350 degree oven for 1 hour. Reduce heat to 300 degrees. Continue cooking 30 to 40 minutes longer, or until meat is tender. Skim off fat before serving. Sprinkle with remaining chopped parsley. Serves 6 to 8.

BAKED LAMB AND POTATO MOUSSAKA

3½ pounds shoulder of lamb, boned, trimmed of fat and cut into ½" cubes
⅔ cup tomato purée
2 large onions, chopped
2 cloves garlic, minced
1 teaspoon basil
2 teaspoons salt
pepper to taste
½ cup chopped parsley
3 pounds potatoes, peeled, then cut into thin matchsticks
¼ cup olive oil

Combine all ingredients except potatoes and oil. Mix well with your hands, then place in a rather broad-surfaced casserole (preferably one broader at the top than at the bottom). Press mixture down firmly. Arrange potatoes evenly on top of meat, and sprinkle potatoes with oil. Place the casserole in a 400 degree oven for about 1½ hours. Baste potatoes occasionally with meat juices from casserole. Potatoes should be very crisp when casserole is ready to eat. If this needs to be held over before serving, set oven to very low and leave casserole in oven.

Serves 6 to 8.

PASTETSEO

The exact origin of the dish Pastetseo is elusive. The name seems to be Greek, and yet it is on occasion described as Syrian. It is a version of macaroni and cheese, with additional ingredients: ground lamb, vegetables, spices and a delicate Cheese Custard covering the top.

1 large onion, chopped
4 cloves garlic, minced
4 tablespoons butter

(continued on the next page)

1 pound ground lamb
1 No. 2 can solid-pack tomatoes, well drained and chopped
salt and pepper
1/4 teaspoon nutmeg
1/2 teaspoon cinnamon
1 teaspoon monosodium glutamate
2 eggs, beaten
1/2 cup grated Parmesan cheese
1/3 pound elbow macaroni, cooked and drained
1 eggplant, peeled, sliced 1/4" thick, and sautéed in olive oil till tender and brown

Sauté onion and garlic in 2 tablespoons butter until soft. Add the meat and cook until the redness disappears. Add tomatoes, and cook until mixture is almost dry. Season well with salt, pepper, nutmeg, cinnamon and monosodium glutamate. Add eggs and 1/3 cup grated cheese.

Combine meat mixture with the cooked, drained macaroni, and pour into a deep, well-greased baking dish. The dish should be about half full. Place slices of sautéed eggplant over the meat-macaroni mixture. Pour the Cheese Custard (below) over all. Melt remaining 2 tablespoons butter and pour over top, then sprinkle with remaining grated cheese. Bake in a 350 degree oven for about 45 minutes, or till custard is set and browned. Serves 4 to 6.

Cheese Custard

1 tablespoon butter
2 teaspoons cornstarch
1 1/2 cups milk, heated
3 beaten eggs
1 cup ricotta cheese
salt and pepper

Melt butter in saucepan. Add cornstarch, and cook over low heat, stirring constantly. Add hot milk. Cook until slightly thickened. Pour some of the thickened hot sauce into the beaten eggs, beating constantly. Then pour warm egg mixture into the rest of the hot sauce, beating while you pour. Remove from flame, and beat in ricotta cheese. Season lightly with salt and pepper.

HAIDAGAN KEBAB

Haidagan Kebab, or lamb baked in papers, is a really outstanding dish. It is a Middle East version of lamb stew. The lamb is baked in its own juices in sealed individual packages.

2½ *pounds boneless lamb shoulder, trimmed of fat and cut into 1" chunks*
6 *pieces cooking parchment* 12" *x* 18" *or* 6 *pieces heavy aluminum foil*
6 *small potatoes*
3 *small zucchini, cut up*
6 *small ripe tomatoes, quartered, or* 1 *No.* 2 *can solid-pack tomatoes, well drained and cut up*
3 *green peppers, halved*
6 *small white onions*
2 *small eggplants, cut into cubes*
6 *whole mushrooms*
6 *tablespoons chopped parsley*
6 *cloves garlic, minced*
2 *tablespoons salt*
pepper, oregano, mint, thyme
6 *small pieces bay leaf*
sugar
3 *teaspoons monosodium glutamate*

Place ⅙ of the meat in the center of each of the 6 pieces of parchment or aluminum foil. Cover and surround the meat with all the vegetables, parsley and garlic, dividing them evenly. Season each mound with 1 teaspoon salt, a good pinch of pepper, oregano, mint, thyme, bay leaf and sugar. Use ½ teaspoon monosodium glutamate for each package.

If you are using parchment, gather the edges of the paper into a bag, twist very well and tie with strong cord so that no steam can escape. If you use foil, fold the edges of the packages so that the juices must remain inside. Place packages on a large cooky sheet and bake in a 325 degree oven for 3 hours. Do not turn or cover packages.

To serve, slit each package at top and pull paper partially away to expose food. Serve 1 package to each person. Serves 6.

SAVORY TURKISH DELIGHT

- 2½ *pounds boned neck or shoulder of lamb, trimmed of fat and cut into ½″ cubes*
- 2 *onions, peeled and chopped*
- 3 *cloves garlic, minced*
- 1 *teaspoon monosodium glutamate*
- ½ *teaspoon sugar*
- 2 *teaspoons salt*
- 1 *teaspoon oregano*
- ½ *teaspoon cinnamon*
- ½ *teaspoon mint*
- ½ *cup tomato purée*
- ⅔ *cup chopped parsley*
- ¼ *cup red wine*
- 3 *to* 4 *large, oval-shaped eggplants*
- 2 *to* 3 *cups olive oil*
- ½ *cup pine nuts*

Combine lamb cubes, onions, garlic, monosodium glutamate, sugar, salt, oregano, cinnamon, mint, tomato purée, 2 tablespoons chopped parsley and wine. Mix well together, and place in a heavy saucepan with a tight cover. Bake in a 350 degree oven for 1 hour, then reduce heat to 300 and continue to bake 30 minutes longer, or until meat is tender.

While meat is cooking, peel eggplants. Cut lengthwise into slices ¼ inch thick. Discard outer slices because they will be too small.

Pour olive oil into a heavy skillet to a depth of ¼ inch, and heat. Sauté eggplant slices on both sides until golden brown and tender. Drain slices on paper towels. (Add more olive oil as necessary.) Set sautéed slices aside to cool.

When the meat is tender, drain in a strainer or colander, being sure to save all the juices in a bowl. Cool meat slightly.

Place a tablespoon of meat in the center of each eggplant slice. Turn each end of eggplant slice over filling, overlapping ends and enclosing meat in center. Gently place filled eggplant rolls in a large, flat baking dish which may be used later for serving. Skim fat from reserved meat juices, then spoon skimmed juice over eggplant rolls. Sprinkle with pine nuts and remaining chopped parsley. Bake in a 350 degree oven for 45 minutes, or until juices are bubbling and eggplant is golden brown. Serve hot. Serves 6.

LAMB IN EGG AND LEMON SAUCE

Whole endive, celery hearts or almost any vegetable may be substituted for, or added to, the lettuce in this recipe.

½ *cup sweet butter*
8 *scallions, finely sliced*
2 *heads of Boston lettuce, washed and shredded*
2½ *pounds boned lamb shoulder, trimmed of fat and cut into 1" cubes*
2 *lemons (grated rind of 1; juice of both)*
¼ *cup chopped parsley*
½ *cup chopped dill, or 1 tablespoon dried dill*
salt
2 *teaspoons monosodium glutamate*
1 *heaping tablespoon Concentrate of Chicken (optional) (page 50)*
5 *egg yolks*

Melt butter in a heavy saucepan with a tight cover. Add scallions, and sauté until they are tender. Add shredded lettuce (or any other vegetable). Toss with a wooden spoon over high heat until lettuce (or vegetable) is wilted.

Stir lamb pieces into mixture in pan, and add lemon juice. Cover pan. Reduce heat so that entire mixture is just simmering. The liquid from the lettuce will be sufficient to cook the lamb in the heavy, tightly lidded pan.

Simmer about 1½ hours, or until meat is just fork-tender. Add chopped parsley and dill, and continue to simmer until these are wilted. Add salt and monosodium glutamate. If you have any Concentrate of Chicken, add a heaping tablespoon.

(continued on the next page)

The above procedure may be done well ahead of time and allowed to cool. At serving time, heat to the simmering point.

Stir egg yolks with a fork or wire whisk in a small bowl. Ladle some of the simmering liquid into the egg yolks, stirring briskly. Then pour this egg-yolk mixture into the saucepan, stirring constantly, over very low heat. As soon as the sauce has thickened slightly, remove from heat and serve at once. Serves 6.

KIMA CURRY

⅓ cup vegetable oil or clarified butter
2 tablespoons mustard seeds
1 large onion, chopped
6 cloves garlic, finely minced
6 tablespoons curry powder
1 teaspoon cardamom powder
½ teaspoon ground cinnamon
1 tablespoon salt
2 teaspoons monosodium glutamate
2 teaspoons freshly ground pepper
cayenne pepper to taste
2 pounds ground lamb
stock
2 cups green peas
2 tablespoons chopped cilantro (optional)

Heat oil in a heavy saucepan. Add mustard seeds. Cover pan and let seeds pop, over a medium heat, and darken. Lower heat, remove lid, and add chopped onion and garlic. Sauté until tender. Stir in curry powder and all remaining seasonings and spices. Stir for 2 or 3 minutes.

Add ground lamb, mixing it well into the spiced mixture. Cook over low heat until meat loses its red color and becomes somewhat crumbly. Add just enough stock to cover meat. Cover pan tightly and cook over low heat for 1 hour. Taste and correct seasonings. Stir in peas, and cook till they are tender. Serve with Fluffy, Steamed Rice, sprinkled with cilantro. (This dish tastes better when it is made ahead of time and reheated.)

Serves 6.

INDONESIAN SKEWERED LAMB

2 *teaspoons ground coriander*
½ *teaspoon ground hot pepper*
1 *teaspoon ground cumin seeds*
½ *teaspoon saffron, crushed*
1 *teaspoon powdered ginger*
3 *cloves garlic, minced*
1 *tablespoon salt*
2 *teaspoons pepper*
2 *teaspoons monosodium glutamate*
3 *pounds boneless, trimmed leg of lamb, cut into 1″ cubes*
⅔ *cup vinegar*
⅓ *cup peanut oil*

Combine coriander, hot pepper, cumin seeds, saffron, ginger, garlic, salt, pepper and monosodium glutamate. Add to lamb cubes and mix well with your hands so that meat is coated all over with the spice mixture. Add vinegar. Mix in well. Marinate meat in this mixture for at least an hour. Drain vinegar from meat.

Thread meat on 6 skewers, and brush with peanut oil. Broil with a high flame, turning skewers frequently, until meat is brown all over but still pink in the center. Serve with Fluffy, Steamed Rice.

Serves 6.

PORK

BARBECUED SPARERIBS

Succulent barbecued spareribs are difficult to find. Either they are meaty but greasy, or else they are very dry and tough. The first secret of good spareribs is to get good meat; then to trim off as much surface fat as you can; finally, to steam the ribs before brushing them with barbecue sauce and browning them.

Buy a sheet of spareribs. The best size to get are neither the extra large or tiny, but the medium-size. Have your butcher cut through rib bones at the top so they may be separated easily after cooking. Trim off as much fat as possible.

Place the sheet of ribs on a large sheet of heavy aluminum foil, and sprinkle both sides with a teaspoon of monosodium glutamate. Fold foil around ribs to seal completely in the foil. Place on a baking sheet in a 325 degree oven for 1 hour. This part may be done ahead of time.

Remove package of ribs from oven and open it up. There will be quite a lot of juice in the foil. Transfer the ribs (underside up) to a rack which has been placed in a shallow pan.

Add some of the pork juice in the foil to whichever barbecue sauce you have made. Baste the ribs with the barbecue sauce and place in a 375 degree oven. Baste twice more, at about 10-minute intervals. Turn ribs over. Baste. Baste again, 2 more times at 10-minute intervals. Continue to cook 10 or 15 minutes after last basting. Cut into serving portions and serve hot.

Hawaiian Barbecue Sauce

3 *tablespoons tomato purée*
3 *tablespoons soy sauce*
1 *teaspoon sugar*
2 *cloves garlic, minced*
1 *teaspoon grated, fresh ginger root, or pickled ginger*

Combine all ingredients and use for basting spareribs or pork.

Chinese Barbecue Sauce

4 *tablespoons soy sauce*
4 *tablespoons orange marmalade*
3 *cloves garlic, minced*
1 *teaspoon grated fresh ginger, or pickled ginger*
½ *teaspoon coarse black pepper*

Combine all ingredients and use for basting spareribs or pork.

Mexican Barbecue Sauce

3 *tablespoons chili powder*
3 *cloves garlic, minced*
3 *tablespoons tomato purée*
1 *tablespoon lemon juice*
2 *tablespoons soy sauce*

Combine all ingredients and use for basting spareribs or pork.

DUTCH BAKED HAM AND ENDIVE

12 *endive*
¾ *cup butter*
12 *slices cooked ham, ⅛″ thick*
butter for greasing casserole
¼ *teaspoon nutmeg*
salt and pepper
6 *hard-cooked eggs, diced*
½ *cup chopped parsley*

In a skillet, sauté endive in half of butter until lightly browned and tender. Cool slightly. Wrap a slice of ham around each endive and arrange in a shallow, buttered casserole. Melt remaining butter and spoon over top. Sprinkle with nutmeg, salt and pepper. Combine diced eggs with chopped parsley; sprinkle evenly over top of casserole. Bake in a 400 degree oven about 10 minutes. Hollandaise Sauce may be served with this dish. Serves 6.

HAM SLICES IN MADEIRA SAUCE

2 *pounds uncooked ham, sliced ¼" thick*
6 *tablespoons butter*
½ *cup minced shallots*
1¼ *cups Madeira*
½ *cup chopped parsley*

If ham is very fatty, trim away some of the fat.

Heat butter in a skillet, and sauté ham until lightly browned on both sides. Remove slices to a heated platter and keep warm.

Pour off most of fat remaining in skillet. Add shallots, and sauté for a minute or 2. Add 1 cup Madeira to the skillet; turn heat to high. Use wooden spoon to blend the browned bits in the pan with Madeira. Allow Madeira to reduce to one third the original amount. Stir in ¼ cup chopped parsley and the remaining Madeira. Return ham slices to pan, and combine well with sauce. Transfer to heated serving platter and sprinkle with remaining chopped parsley. Serves 6.

HAM, PEASANT STYLE

1 *cup rendered chicken or goose fat (approximately)*
8 *tart, hard apples, peeled, cored and chopped coarsely*
1 *large onion, chopped*
6 *slices white bread, trimmed of crust*
6 *slices ham, ⅓ inch thick*

Melt half of the fat in a heavy skillet. Add chopped apples and onion. Sauté over medium heat until they are tender and golden. Keep warm.

In another skillet, melt all but 2 tablespoons of remaining fat. Sauté slices of bread on both sides until they are golden brown. Remove bread slices to a serving platter and keep warm.

If necessary, add remaining fat to skillet. Sauté ham slices on both sides until they are just golden. Arrange a slice of ham on each crouton. Spoon some sautéed apples and onions on top. Serve hot. Serves 6.

MOCK WILD BOAR

- 1 *whole fresh ham (10 to 14 pounds)*
- 2 *tablespoons fresh pepper*
- ½ *teaspoon thyme*
- 1 *tablespoon monosodium glutamate*
- 1 *teaspoon allspice*
- 1 *large bay leaf, crumbled*
- 1 *teaspoon caraway seeds, crushed*
- 3 *cloves garlic, mashed*
- 4 *tablespoons salt*
- ½ *teaspoon celery seed*
- ½ *teaspoon cinnamon*
- 1 *teaspoon grated orange rind*
- 2 *onions*
- 1 *carrot*
- 2 *stalks celery, including leaves*
- ½ *cup olive oil*
- 1½ *cups red wine*
- 1 *cup wine vinegar*
- ⅓ *cup cognac*

Ask butcher to remove rind from ham, leaving just a band of it around the shank. Stick ham all over with a small knife to make slits. Combine next 11 ingredients, blending well. Rub ham all over with this spice mixture, then place ham in a large, flat casserole.

Prepare the following marinade (it should be cooled and then poured over the ham):

Chop onions, carrot and celery. Sauté briefly in olive oil, and add wine and wine vinegar. Bring just to a boil. Cool, then add cognac.

Let ham sit in marinade, in the refrigerator, at least 8 days—or up to 2 weeks. Turn it twice a day.

To roast ham: Remove meat from marinade. Do not dry or attempt to remove bits of vegetable clinging to it. Place on a rack in a flat pan, fat side up, and roast in a 300 degree oven for 4½ to 5 hours, or until a meat thermometer registers 175. If the ham should brown too quickly while roasting, cover it with brown paper.

(continued on the next page)

Place on carving plate. Turn off oven heat and allow the meat to rest in the oven for 20 minutes before carving. Serves 10 to 12.

Prepare the following sauce while meat is resting:

Sauce for Mock Wild Boar

strained marinade from meat
2 *cups red wine*
2 *cups beef gravy*
1 *cup stock*
2 *to* 3 *teaspoons currant jelly*
salt to taste
1 *teaspoon freshly ground black pepper*
2 *tablespoons finely chopped scallions*
3 *tablespoons finely chopped parsley*

Combine strained marinade, wine and beef gravy in a saucepan. Bring to a boil and allow to boil over medium heat until sauce is reduced by about half and is thicker than you would want it to be. (If you like, this part of the sauce can be made fairly early in the day—as soon as the meat has been removed from the marinade.)

Heat stock to boiling, and pour it into the roasting pan after the meat and excess fat have been removed. With a wooden spoon, loosen all the browned bits sticking to pan. Add stock to sauce, then add currant jelly and salt to taste, and next, pepper, scallions and parsley. Simmer a few minutes, taste, and correct seasoning if necessary. While Mock Wild Boar is being carved, add these meat juices to sauce.

SZEKELY GOULASH

3 pounds sauerkraut
3 large onions, chopped
4 cloves garlic, minced
⅓ cup lard
4 tablespoons Hungarian paprika
2 tablespoons caraway seeds
2 cups solid-pack tomatoes, well drained and chopped
3 pounds boned pork (unsmoked tenderloin or shoulder), cut into 1″ cubes
salt and pepper
2 teaspoons monosodium glutamate
2 cups stock
3 tablespoons flour
1 cup sour cream
½ cup chopped dill

Rinse sauerkraut in cold water, then press out all of the water. In a deep pot, sauté onions and garlic in lard until they are soft. Stir in paprika and caraway seeds, then add chopped tomatoes, pork, salt, pepper and monosodium glutamate. Add sauerkraut and toss gently to combine. Pour in three quarters of stock, and simmer slowly about 1½ hours, or until pork is just tender.

Stir remaining stock into flour. Stir in sour cream. Stir gently into meat-sauerkraut mixture, until entire goulash is thickened. Serve hot, garnished with chopped dill. Serves 6.

PORK AND RICE WITH BLACK BEANS

2 *cups dried black beans*
⅓ *cup olive oil*
3 *cloves garlic, minced*
1 *very large onion, chopped*
2 *small green peppers, seeded and diced*
2 *teaspoons salt*
½ *teaspoon coarse black pepper*
1½ *pounds unsmoked pork tenderloin, or pork shoulder, cut into 1" cubes*
¾ *pound Mexican sausage (if available), or fresh pork sausage*
⅔ *cup orange juice*
½ *cup dry red wine*
1½ *cups peeled, fresh orange slices*

Wash, pick over beans, and soak overnight in water to cover.

Heat olive oil in a deep pot. Add garlic, onion and green pepper, and sauté until tender. Season with salt and pepper. Add beans and enough additional water to cover them. Cover pot, and simmer about 45 minutes or until the beans are tender, adding more water if necessary.

Drain liquid from pot and reserve. Remove 2 cups of cooked beans from the pot. Cover remaining beans and keep them warm. Purée the 2 cups of cooked beans with as much bean liquid as necessary in blender. Stir bean purée into cooked beans and keep warm.

Brown pork cubes and sausage in their own fat in a skillet. Pour off fat when meats are golden all over, and cut sausage into 1-inch pieces. Add both meats to beans; season with additional salt and pepper, if required.

Pour orange juice and wine into the skillet that meats were browned in, and cook over high heat until liquid is reduced to less than half, scraping any brown bits in the pan into the sauce. Pour into bean mixture and stir to combine all flavors. Place in a 350 degree oven for 30 minutes.

Serve over Fluffy, Steamed Rice, garnished with peeled orange slices. Serves 6.

SOUTH AFRICAN BROILED PORK

½ cup dried apricots
1½ cups water
3 onions, chopped
3 cloves garlic, minced
¼ cup peanut oil
3 tablespoons vinegar
¼ teaspoon cayenne pepper
bay leaf, crumbled
2 teaspoons salt
2 tablespoons brown sugar
3 tablespoons curry powder
½ cup beef gravy
2 teaspoons monosodium glutamate
1 teaspoon coarse black pepper
2 pounds lean, boneless pork cut into 1″ cubes

Soak apricots in water overnight. The next day, cook slowly in the same water until the apricots are very soft. Place apricots and their liquid into a blender and purée.

Sauté onions and garlic in peanut oil until soft and slightly brown. Add to apricot purée, together with all remaining ingredients except pork cubes. Taste for seasoning. Sauce should be quite tart and slightly hot in flavor. Heat sauce in a saucepan until it begins to bubble. Be careful not to let it burn.

Pour sauce over pork cubes in a bowl. Marinate pork in the refrigerator for at least 6 hours, then thread meat on 6 skewers, reserving marinade for basting.

Preheat broiler. Place skewers on broiling rack as far away from heat as possible. Broil slowly 20 to 30 minutes, basting and turning skewers frequently, until the meat is crisp and brown on all sides and completely cooked through.

Reheat any remaining marinade until it is boiling. Serve with broiled pork cubes, along with Fluffy, Steamed Rice. Serves 6.

MEXICAN PORK ROLL

2½ *pounds pork tenderloin or boneless pork shoulder*
½ *pound chorizos (Spanish sausages), or a good garlic sausage*
2 *teaspoons monosodium glutamate*
Refried Beans (page 306)
1 *large onion, chopped fine*
2 *tablespoons chopped cilantro (optional)*

It is necessary to make this pork into a large sheet of meat. This is done by slicing it, with the grain, almost in half but not cutting through all the way (the 2 halves should remain connected). Then, if possible, slice it through the other way, against the grain, again not cutting all the way through. You should have a rectangular sheet of meat about ¼ inch thick. (Your butcher may be able to do this job for you.) If some parts of the pork sheet are thicker than the rest, place meat between sheets of wax paper and pound with a mallet or bottle until thickness of meat is fairly even all over.

Place chorizos in a saucepan, and add enough water to cover. Simmer about 15 minutes. Remove from water and cool. When cool enough to handle, chop chorizos coarsely.

Sprinkle pork sheet with monosodium glutamate, and spread with Refried Beans to a thickness of about ¼ inch. Sprinkle chopped chorizos evenly over beans, then sprinkle with most of the raw chopped onion and cilantro, if it is available. Press down this filling. Now, starting from the narrowest end of the pork sheet, roll it up tightly, jelly-roll style. Tie the roll in 4 or 5 places with string.

Place on a rack in a pan in a 325 degree oven and roast for about 2½ hours, or until pork is a deep golden brown. Transfer to a carving board and keep warm in oven for at least 15 minutes before slicing. Pour off fat from pan.

Pour some of the hot sauce (directions below) into the roasting pan. Scrape any bits of crust free with a wooden spoon. Pour back into remaining sauce.

Cut the pork roll into ½-inch slices. Spoon sauce over slices and garnish with chopped cilantro and the rest of the raw chopped onion.

Serves 6.

Sauce for Mexican Pork Roll

3 *tablespoons lard*
1 *onion, chopped*
4 *cloves garlic, minced*
3 *tablespoons chili powder*
½ *cup tomato purée*
¼ *ounce bitter chocolate*
2 *to* 3 *cups stock*
salt and pepper
cayenne pepper

Melt lard in a saucepan. When it is hot, add chopped onion and garlic. Sauté until soft. Stir in chili powder; then add tomato purée, chocolate and about a cup of stock. Season with salt, pepper and cayenne. Cook, stirring, until chocolate has melted. Raise heat to high, and continue to cook, stirring constantly, until mixture in saucepan thickens. Add enough additional stock to make a good sauce consistency. Taste, and correct seasoning if necessary.

MEXICAN PORK CHILI

- ½ *pound Spanish sausages (chorizos), or if these aren't available, any good garlic sausage*
- 2½ *pounds pork shoulder or unsmoked tenderloin, cut into 1" cubes*
- 4 *cloves garlic, minced*
- 1 *large onion, chopped*
- 4 *tablespoons chili powder*
- 3 *large tomatoes, peeled and chopped*
- 1 *to* 1½ *cups stock*
- *salt*
- 2 *teaspoons monosodium glutamate*
- 3 *large green peppers*
- 2 *small avocados, peeled and sliced thin*
- 2 *onions, thinly sliced and separated into rings*

Sauté sausages in a dry skillet until they are completely cooked. Remove from the skillet. Cool slightly, then cut the sausages into slices about ⅓ inch thick, and set aside. If there is a great deal of fat remaining in the skillet, discard most of it.

In a heavy pot, brown pork cubes in a little of the sausage fat. Generally, it is not necessary to brown meats before braising but pork is an exception because of its high fat content. The browning helps to get rid of some of the fat.

Discard most of fat after meat has browned. Add garlic and chopped onion to the pot, and sauté over medium heat until they are soft. Stir in chili powder, chopped tomatoes, stock, some salt and monosodium glutamate. The liquid in the pot should not quite cover the meat. Cover pot and simmer over low heat (about 1 to 1½ hours) until the meat is tender. Add sliced sausage.

Sear the green peppers over an open gas flame until the skins are charred and can be rubbed off easily. Halve the peppers; remove seeds and veins. Place halved, skinned peppers back over gas flame to char them a little more and to soften slightly. Cut the peppers into strips.

Serve pork chili garnished with pepper strips, avocado slices and raw onion rings. Refried Beans go well with this dish. Serves 6 to 8.

PORK VINDALOO

This is an Indian pork stew, rich-tasting and spicy. Tamarind, a dried fruit from the tropics, may be ordered by mail (see Shopping Sources). It is full of seeds and seems quite stringy. To obtain ½ cup of tamarind pulp, use about 1 cup of the whole fruit. Place it in a bowl, and add enough warm water to barely cover the fruit. Allow to stand for at least ½ hour. Then, with your hand in the water, work the pulp free of the seeds. You will finally have just a handful of seeds and strings, and several spoonfuls of thick tamarind pulp in the bowl. The seeds and strings should be discarded. (Or they may be rinsed off under running water and used for scouring dirty pots, as is done in some parts of India.)

½ *cup tamarind pulp*
2 *onions, chopped*
6 *cloves garlic, minced*
4 *tablespoons ground coriander*
2 *teaspoons turmeric*
1 *tablespoon coarsely ground black pepper*
1 *tablespoon cumin*
2 *teaspoons fresh, chopped, hot green chili* (*or substitute a little cayenne pepper or hot canned chilies which have been finely chopped*)
1 *tablespoon fresh or pickled ginger, grated*
1 *cup vinegar*
2 *pounds boneless pork tenderloin or shoulder, cut into* 1″ *cubes*
¼ *cup clarified butter*
1 *tablespoon mustard seeds*
salt
2 *tablespoons chopped cilantro* (*optional*)

Combine tamarind, onions, garlic, coriander, turmeric, pepper, cumin, chili, ginger and vinegar in a ceramic bowl. Add pork, and marinate in the refrigerator for 24 hours.

Heat clarified butter in a heavy saucepan until it is very hot. Add

(*continued on the next page*)

mustard seeds. Cover pan and allow mustard seeds to pop and become dark in color.

Lower heat. Remove lid from pot and add pork mixture. Cover pan tightly and simmer pork about 1½ hours, or until it is very tender. Season with salt. Sprinkle with chopped cilantro, and serve with plenty of Fluffy, Steamed Rice. Serves 6.

BRAISED SAUSAGE IN RED WINE

1 *garlic sausage, about* 1½ *to* 2 *pounds (Polish kolbasa is excellent for this—so is any other coarse, garlicky sausage)*
4 *tablespoons butter*
⅔ *cup chopped shallots or scallions*
1½ *cups dry red wine*
1 *teaspoon monosodium glutamate*
⅔ *cup chopped parsley*

Melt butter in a heavy pot. Add shallots and sauté until soft. Add sausage to pot and brown lightly on all sides, then add red wine and monosodium glutamate. Bring to a boil. Lower heat so that liquid just simmers, and cook sausage, turning occasionally, for about an hour. Remove sausage to a heated platter and keep warm.

Turn heat under pot to high and reduce liquid in pot to less than half. Pour over sausage. Sprinkle with chopped parsley. Serve with a Hot Potato Salad. Serves 5 to 6.

SAUSAGE-STUFFED TOMATOES

6 *medium-size tomatoes*
½ *teaspoon sugar*
½ *teaspoon dried basil*
2 *tablespoons salt*
½ *teaspoon freshly ground pepper*
3 *pounds pork* (¾ *lean,* ¼ *fat*), *or* 3 *pounds bulk sausage*
1 *teaspoon monosodium glutamate*
½ *cup chopped parsley*
2 *onions, chopped fine*
3 *cloves garlic, minced fine*
6 *slices bacon*

With a sharp knife, remove stem end of each tomato. Scoop out remaining tomato pulp, leaving hollow shells. Turn shells upside down on paper towels to drain well.

Sprinkle inside of each tomato with a little sugar, dried basil, and a little salt and pepper. Set tomatoes aside until needed.

Grind fat and lean pork once. Add remaining salt and pepper, the monosodium glutamate, parsley, onions and garlic. Mix well with your hands. (If you can buy good bulk sausage, you can eliminate the procedure of grinding the meat yourself and instead start with 3 pounds of sausage meat. If you buy ready-made sausage, do not salt it.)

Stuff each tomato firmly with the sausage mixture. Stretch the pieces of bacon so they can be completely wound around the tomatoes. Arrange bacon-wrapped tomatoes in a shallow baking pan. Bake in a 375 degree oven about 1½ hours, or until tomatoes are soft and bacon is crisp. Serve hot. Serves 6.

SAUSAGE AND LENTILS

1 *cup dried lentils*
salt
2 *tablespoons lard*
1 *onion, chopped*
3 *cloves garlic, minced*
1 *No. 2 can tomatoes, well drained and chopped*
1½ *pounds smoked sausage (Polish kolbasa, or even knockwurst)*
1 *bay leaf*
1 *teaspoon coarsely ground black pepper*
1 *teaspoon sugar*

Wash and pick over lentils. Place in a deep saucepan, and cover with water. Add a little salt. Bring to a boil, lower heat and simmer, covered, about 20 minutes, or until lentils are tender. Drain lentils, reserving the cooking liquid. Keep lentils warm.

Heat lard in a flameproof casserole. Add onion and garlic, and sauté until soft. Stir in tomatoes. Cook over medium heat till most of liquid has evaporated from tomatoes and mixture in pan is rather dry.

Remove casing from sausage and cut sausage into ½-inch slices. Gently stir sausage into casserole. Add all remaining ingredients, including the lentils and a little liquid. (More reserved liquid from lentils should be added if the casserole becomes dry during the cooking process.)

Place casserole in a 350 degree oven for 30 minutes. Serve hot. This is delicious when reheated. Serves 6.

LEEK AND SAUSAGE PIE

I can hardly claim this recipe as an original, since it appeared in the New York *Times* and is served at the Forum of the Twelve Caesars. Yet it is so good that I don't want to omit it. I have made only 1 or 2 minor changes.

1 *recipe Rich Tart Pastry, minus sugar and lemon* (*page* 348)
6 *leeks*
1 *cup stock*
12 *small pork sausages*
2 *tablespoons butter*
3 *tablespoons flour*
¾ *cup heavy cream*
2 *egg yolks*
1 *teaspoon salt*
freshly ground black pepper
3 *to* 4 *tablespoons horseradish, drained of all liquid*

Place a 9-inch, shallow flan ring on a baking sheet, then line it with unsweetened Rich Tart Pastry. Chill pastry-lined ring.

Trim the roots and green leaves from the leeks. Split the leeks lengthwise; then cut them crosswise into 2-inch lengths. Place in a saucepan, and add stock. Simmer leeks, covered, until almost tender. Drain leeks, but reserve ¾ cup of the liquid remaining in pot.

Sauté the sausage until it is browned and almost completely cooked. Drain on paper towels.

Melt the butter in a saucepan, then remove from heat. Stir in flour until blended. Meanwhile, bring reserved leek stock and cream to a boil. Add all at once to the butter-flour mixture, stirring with a whisk. When the sauce thickens, remove from heat and beat in the egg yolks. Return to heat and stir until the sauce is a little thicker. Season with salt, pepper and horseradish.

Arrange cooled leeks in flan ring. Pour sauce over and arrange sausages evenly on top. Bake in a 450 degree oven about 20 minutes, or until pastry edges are a nice golden brown. Serve hot, in wedges.

Serves 6.

COLD PORK PLATE

Pork is an excellent meat to serve, not icy cold, but at room temperature during the summer. Simply roast a piece of unsmoked pork tenderloin or boneless shoulder until it is well done—185 degrees on the meat thermometer. If you like, brush it with a little soy sauce or other seasoning ahead of time to give additional flavor. Allow the pork to cool at room temperature and, if possible, plan not to refrigerate it before serving, since refrigeration seems to rob meats of their juiciness. Slice the pork fairly thin and arrange overlapping slices on a platter. Place some deviled eggs around the pork, also some sliced tomatoes, and of course some greens. Serve with sweet-sour cucumber salad, or with any cold vegetable salad (such as green beans or broccoli). Strong mustard goes well with this, as does crusty bread and butter.

CARNITAS

These are crisp meat tidbits which are very popular in Mexico. They should be served with Salsa Fria (page 60), Guacamole (page 323), or both. Tostados also are a good accompaniment.

- 2½ *pounds unsmoked pork tenderloin or shoulder, cut into 1" cubes*
- 1 *pound Mexican sausage (chorizo), cut into 1" slices*
- 2 *teaspoons monosodium glutamate*

With your hands, mix meat cubes, sausage slices and monosodium glutamate. Arrange in a jelly-roll pan in 1 layer. The pieces can touch each other, however. Place in a 350 degree oven, and roast for 1 to 1¼ hours, or until meats are golden brown and crisp. Serve very hot. (Discard the fat left in the pan.) Serves 6 to 7.

VEAL

VEAL CHOPS, LANGUEDOC STYLE

6 *tablespoons butter*
1 *tablespoon olive oil*
6 *loin veal chops, cut 1" thick, tails removed*
2 *teaspoons monosodium glutamate*
1 *small onion, chopped*
⅔ *cup ham, peperoni or hard salami, cut into small dice*
6 *cloves garlic, minced*
⅔ *cup green olives, pitted and halved*
½ *cup chopped parsley*
salt and coarsely ground pepper

In a heavy skillet, heat butter and olive oil together until hot but not smoking. Sprinkle veal chops with monosodium glutamate on both sides. Sauté in hot fat, over medium heat, until the chops are golden brown on both sides, turning them frequently. Stir in chopped onion and ham, and continue to cook over low heat about 8 minutes more, turning chops occasionally so that they cook through evenly.

When the chops are still *slightly* underdone, remove to a platter and keep warm in the oven. Add to the skillet the minced garlic, olives and some of parsley. Season with salt and pepper, and spoon mixture in pan over chops. Sprinkle with remaining chopped parsley.

Serves 6.

TARRAGON VEAL CHOPS SAUTE

1 *teaspoon dried tarragon*
2 *teaspoons monosodium glutamate*
½ *teaspoon cinnamon*
¼ *teaspoon allspice*
⅛ *teaspoon cloves*
½ *teaspoon ground white pepper*
6 *loin veal chops cut 1″ thick, tails removed*
6 *tablespoons sweet butter*
1 *tablespoon olive oil*
salt
½ *cup chopped parsley*

Combine tarragon, monosodium glutamate, cinnamon, allspice, cloves and ground white pepper in a small bowl. Sprinkle veal chops on both sides with this mixture.

Melt butter and oil in a large heavy skillet. Add chops and sauté over medium heat, turning frequently, about 10 minutes or until chops are golden on both sides and just cooked through. Remove to a heated platter. Swirl an extra lump of butter in the pan. Pour drippings over the chops. Sprinkle with salt and chopped parsley and serve at once.

Note: If you wish, a more sophisticated sauce can be made after the chops are removed from the pan. For this, add a few chopped shallots to the fat remaining in the pan. When they are soft, add 1 cup white wine. Raise heat to high and reduce liquid to a third of the original amount. Season with additional salt and parsley, and spoon over the chops. Serves 6.

VEAL CHOPS IN MUSHROOM SAUCE

6 loin veal chops, 1" thick, tails removed
salt and coarsely ground pepper
2 teaspoons monosodium glutamate
½ teaspoon cinnamon
5 tablespoons butter
1 teaspoon olive oil
2 tablespoons Duxelles (page 21)
1 pound fresh mushroom caps, sliced
8 shallots, chopped, or ½ cup chopped scallions
1½ cups port wine
1 tablespoon Concentrate of Chicken or Beef (optional) (page 50)
3 egg yolks
¾ cup heavy cream (or 3 tablespoons Preserved Cream, page 29)
½ cup chopped parsley

Season chops on both sides with salt, pepper, monosodium glutamate and cinnamon. Heat butter and olive oil in a heavy skillet, and add chops. Sauté, turning frequently, until chops are golden brown on both sides and almost completely cooked. Remove chops to a heated platter.

Add Duxelles and fresh mushroom caps to pan. Sauté over high heat, then add shallots. When they are soft, add wine and Concentrate of Chicken or Beef. Cook over high heat until liquid is reduced to less than half.

Combine egg yolks with heavy cream, mixing well. Remove skillet from heat. Pour a little of skillet liquid into the cream mixture, stirring briskly. Then pour the cream mixture back into skillet, continuing to stir. Replace over very low heat and stir until sauce has thickened, or just coats a spoon. Spoon sauce over chops. Sprinkle with chopped parsley and serve. Serves 6.

VEAL CHOPS GRANDMERE

6 *loin veal chops, cut* 1½″ *thick, tails removed*
salt and pepper
2 *teaspoons monosodium glutamate*
6 *tablespoons butter*
1 *tablespoon olive oil*
2 *large onions, chopped*
4 *cloves garlic, minced*
3 *green peppers, seeded and diced*
6 *strips bacon, diced*
12 *mushrooms, sliced*
3 *large potatoes, cooked, chilled, peeled, then cut into dice*
1 *pair sweetbreads, blanched* (*see page* 00), *trimmed and cut into small dice*
1 *cup chopped parsley*

Season veal chops on both sides with salt, pepper and monosodium glutamate.

Heat butter and olive oil in a large skillet. Add onions, garlic and green pepper, and sauté until soft. Remove from pan, and place diced bacon in pan. When bacon is almost cooked but not crisp, drain and add to onion mixture.

Add mushrooms to pan, and cook until liquid evaporates from mushrooms. Add mushrooms to onion mixture.

Add diced potato and sweetbreads to pan. If necessary, add a little more fat. Sauté over high heat, stirring occasionally, until potatoes are lightly crisped on all sides. Add to onion mixture. Stir in half of parsley. Keep this warm.

Sauté chops in pan, adding more fat if necessary, turning frequently, until the chops are golden brown on both sides, about 5 to 8 minutes. Arrange the chops on a baking pan. Spoon the onion-sweetbreads mixture around and on top of the chops. Bake in a 350 degree oven 20 to 30 minutes, or until mixture around the chops is sizzling. Sprinkle with the remaining chopped parsley, and serve. Serves 6.

VEAL ROLLATINE

The meat is best served cold, cut into slices about ½ inch thick. This makes a very pretty summer meat course.

3 *slices leg of veal, cut about ½" thick*
¼ *pound prosciutto, thinly sliced*
¼ *pound Italian salami, thinly sliced*
1½ *cups soft, fine bread crumbs*
½ *cup chopped parsley*
¼ *cup grated Parmesan cheese*
1 *teaspoon coarsely ground pepper*
1 *teaspoon monosodium glutamate*
½ *cup olive oil*
6 *eggs*
½ *pound Italian sausage, cooked and cooled (sweet or hot may be used)*
6 *strips bacon*

Arrange leg of veal slices on wax paper so that the edges overlap, making a large, somewhat rectangular shape. Cover with additional wax paper. Pound with a mallet or bottle until veal is less than ⅓ inch thick and overlapping edges are stuck together. Remove top sheet of wax paper.

Arrange prosciutto slices on top of veal so that veal is completely covered. Make a layer of slices of salami on top of prosciutto.

Combine bread crumbs, parsley, cheese, pepper, monosodium glutamate and about half of olive oil. Pat a layer of this mixture firmly on top of salami, completely covering the area.

Heat remaining oil in a skillet. Beat eggs lightly—do not season them. Pour eggs into skillet, and cook, stirring constantly, until eggs are just set but still quite soft. Remove eggs from skillet and allow them to cool. When eggs have cooled, arrange them down one end (the shortest end) of the bread crumb mixture. The eggs should make a strip about 3 inches wide. Place cooked Italian sausage in center of eggs. If it extends beyond edges of meat, trim it off.

(continued on the next page)

Now, starting with the edge with the eggs, begin to roll up meat tightly, using the wax paper underneath the veal to help. Be careful not to allow pounded edges to separate during rolling. When meat has been completely rolled up, jelly-roll style, tie it with string in 3 or 4 places.

Entwine strips of bacon around various parts of the roll. Place on a rack in a shallow pan. Roast, in a 375 degree oven, about 1½ hours. The meat does not need to be basted because of the fat provided by the bacon, but if you like, baste it with a little white wine or Madeira. If served hot, top with a well-seasoned tomato sauce to which the pan juices have been added. The cold meat needs no sauce, but may be garnished with greens and cubed Aspic (page 56). Serves 6.

Braised Veal

There are many braised veal recipes, from the French blanquette to stews and pot roasts of other nationalities. For braised veal it is important to use an appropriate cut of meat—namely the neck, breast or shoulder. Veal shanks, used in the Italian dish osso buco, also make succulent fare. In braising veal, or meat of any kind, try to use either wine or stock as your liquid—never just water.

VEAL NICOISE

1 *tablespoon butter (approximately)*
1 *onion, chopped*
3 *cloves garlic, minced*
¼ *pound mushrooms, sliced*
2 *pounds boneless neck, breast or shoulder of veal cut into 1" cubes*
3 *tablespoons sherry*
2 *cups stock*
1 *tablespoon Concentrate of Chicken or Beef (page 50)*
1 *teaspoon tomato paste*
salt and pepper
1 *teaspoon monosodium glutamate*
1 *cup converted rice*
6 *small zucchini, cut into ½" slices*
1 *cup pitted black olives*
½ *cup chopped parsley*

Melt half of butter in a heavy pan. Add onions and garlic, and sauté until tender. Add mushrooms and continue to sauté for 2 or 3 minutes longer. Add pieces of veal; toss them around until they lose their color, but do not brown them. Add sherry and stock, Concentrate and tomato paste. Season with salt, pepper and monosodium glutamate. Cover pot and simmer over low heat for about 1¼ hours, or until the meat is barely tender. Add rice and continue to cook about 25 minutes longer.

Melt remaining butter in a separate pan. Add zucchini slices and sauté until barely tender. Add zucchini to veal and rice. Add olives. Cover pot and continue to cook a few minutes longer, or until rice and zucchini are completely cooked. Add chopped parsley, and toss gently. Serves 6.

VEAL POT ROAST, ITALIAN STYLE

½ *cup olive oil*
3 *onions, chopped*
5 *cloves garlic, minced*
3½ *pounds boned neck of veal, tied*
1 *No. 2 can solid-pack tomatoes, drained and chopped*
½ *cup Marsala wine*
2 *teaspoons monosodium glutamate*
2 *tablespoons Concentrate of Chicken or Beef (optional) (page 50)*
salt and pepper
1 *large bay leaf, crumbled*
1 *teaspoon basil*
½ *teaspoon oregano*
½ *teaspoon thyme*
⅔ *cup chopped parsley*

Heat olive oil in a large, heavy pot. Add chopped onions and garlic, and sauté until they are soft. Push them to the sides of the pot. Add veal. Sauté on both sides till color changes, but do not brown the veal. Add chopped tomatoes and wine. Sprinkle with monosodium glutamate and place in a 325 degree oven. Cover tightly. Allow to simmer 1½ to 2 hours, or until meat is tender. Remove meat to a carving board.

Place pot over high heat on top of stove. Add Concentrate of Chicken or Beef if you wish. Reduce liquid in pot to less than half. Season with salt and pepper. Turn off heat and add bay leaf, basil, oregano and thyme. Let sauce stand while you cut meat into slices about 1 inch thick. Replace slices of meat in sauce and spoon sauce over so that meat is covered with it.

To serve, reheat slices of meat in the sauce. Sprinkle meat with chopped parsley before serving. Serves 6 to 8.

ROAST STUFFED BREAST OF VEAL

2 *tablespoons olive oil*
3 *pieces of bacon, diced*
2 *onions, finely chopped*
2 *cloves garlic, minced*
2 *packages frozen, chopped spinach*
2 *teaspoons dried tarragon*
¼ *cup chopped parsley*
1 *cup soft bread crumbs*
salt to taste
1 *teaspoon coarsely ground pepper*
1 *egg*
½ *pound ham, ground*
½ *pound veal, ground*
1 *4-pound breast of veal, prepared for stuffing*
1 *teaspoon monosodium glutamate*

Heat 1 tablespoon olive oil in a skillet. Add bacon and sauté the pieces until they are almost crisp. Add onion and garlic and sauté until soft.

Thaw spinach slightly. Cook in a saucepan, over high heat, until soft; then drain very well, pressing out as much water as possible.

Place spinach in a bowl, and add sautéed mixture, 1 teaspoon tarragon, the parsley and bread crumbs. Season with salt and black pepper, and beat in 1 egg. Mix in ground meats, using your hands to mix with. Taste mixture and correct seasoning if necessary.

Pack stuffing into veal breast. Fasten opening with skewers or toothpicks and string, and place veal on a greased rack in a roasting pan, meat side up. Rub meat with remaining olive oil, and sprinkle with monosodium glutamate, salt and remaining tarragon. Cover meat (with aluminum foil if necessary), and roast for 2½ hours in a 350 degree oven. Remove foil and continue to roast until the meat browns—about another 15 minutes. Remove fastenings and cut into slices between the bones. If desired, make an unthickened sauce (page 52) with the pan drippings. Serves 8.

MIROTON OF VEAL

Several years ago, Poppy Cannon published a recipe for Miroton of Beef. I have adapted it somewhat, and I prefer it made with leftover roast veal.

- 2 *large Spanish onions, chopped*
- 1 *pound sliced fresh mushrooms*
- 3 *tablespoons butter*
- 3 *tablespoons flour*
- 2 *cups leftover veal gravy, or part stock, wine and a little beef gravy*
- 1 *teaspoon tarragon*
- ½ *cup chopped parsley*
- 1 *teaspoon monosodium glutamate*
- *salt and pepper to taste*
- 2½ *pounds leftover veal, thinly sliced*
- 2 *cups Croutons (see page* 30)

Place onions and mushrooms in a heavy skillet. Cover, and cook without any liquid or fat, over medium heat, until all the liquid cooks away and the vegetables are almost sticking to the pan.

Add butter to skillet, and stir. When butter has melted, stir in flour with a wooden spoon, and continue stirring over low heat for 4 or 5 minutes. Remove from heat. With a wire whisk, stir in the liquid. Continue to stir until contents of pan thicken to a medium cream-type sauce. Stir in tarragon and chopped parsley. Add monosodium glutamate and season with salt and pepper to taste.

Spoon several spoonfuls of this sauce into a casserole. Place slices of veal on top of sauce. Add more sauce, and continue adding layers of meat and sauce until all meat has been used. Pour any remaining sauce on top. This part of recipe may be prepared ahead of time and refrigerated.

Preheat oven to 350 degrees. Place casserole in oven, and bake about 25 minutes, or until sauce is bubbling. Sprinkle Croutons on top and bake 5 more minutes before serving. Serves 6 to 8.

Venison

VENISON CHOPS IN TRADITIONAL SAUCE

1½ cups red wine
1 onion, finely chopped
1 teaspoon pickling spices
¼ cup wine vinegar
⅔ cup chopped parsley
2 teaspoons coarsely ground pepper
12 venison loin chops, ¾" thick
½ cup clarified butter
⅔ cup beef gravy
1 tablespoon currant jelly
¾ cup heavy cream
salt to taste
1 teaspoon monosodium glutamate

Combine wine, onion, pickling spices, vinegar, ⅓ cup chopped parsley and 1 teaspoon black pepper in a dish large enough to hold all the chops. Trim tails from the chops and arrange the chops close together in the dish. Pour the wine mixture over them.

Marinate the chops from 2 to 4 days in the refrigerator, turning the chops once or twice a day.

Remove chops from marinade and pat them dry with paper towels. Melt clarified butter in a large, heavy skillet. Sauté chops on both sides, over high heat, until they are rare or medium rare.

While chops are cooking, prepare the sauce as follows:

Strain the marinade and discard the onion and spices. Place marinade in a saucepan and bring to a boil over high heat. Keeping the heat high, let the marinade reduce to half its original quantity. Stir in beef gravy and currant jelly. The sauce should now be slightly thicker than you would want it. If it isn't, continue to boil it down.

When the sauce is a little too thick, stir in the cream, the remaining pepper, the salt, monosodium glutamate and remaining parsley.

Arrange chops on a platter and pour sauce over the meat. Serves 6.

Variety Meats

BLANCHING SWEETBREADS

Veal sweetbreads are the type generally sold, although sometimes lamb sweetbreads also are available. While these have a definitively lamb flavor, they can be quite good.

To blanch sweetbreads, fill a rather deep pan with water. Season well with monosodium glutamate, salt, peppercorns, bay leaf, thyme, an onion and a carrot. Allow this mixture to cook down a little. While it is still boiling rapidly, add the sweetbreads. When the liquid boils again, lower the heat so that the liquid simmers rather than boils. Simmer sweetbreads in this liquid for 10 to 15 minutes, depending on the size of the sweetbreads. After they have cooked for the proper length of time, drain the sweetbreads and plunge them into a bowl of very cold water. If possible, keep cold water running into the bowl until the sweetbreads are at least lukewarm.

Make a bed of paper towels on a flat plate. Place sweetbreads on paper towels; cover with more paper towels, then another plate. Place a good, heavy weight on top of the plate to press the sweetbreads as they finish cooling.

After an hour or so, the sweetbreads should be completely cooled and pressed. With your fingers—and the help of a small sharp knife—peel off any membranes and veins you can see. After that, the sweetbreads are ready to be used in any number of dishes.

SWEETBREADS WITH PEAS AND MARROW

3 *pair sweetbreads, blanched (see above)*
1½ *cups beef marrow*
stock
Madeira
6 *slices bacon*
⅔ *cup chopped shallots or scallions*
salt and pepper
2 *teaspoons monosodium glutamate*
1½ *cups beef gravy*
4 *cups cooked tiny peas*
1½ *cups chopped parsley*

After sweetbreads have been blanched, weighted and trimmed, cut them crosswise into scallops ¼ inch thick.

Place marrow in a saucepan. Barely cover it with half stock and half Madeira, and bring to a boil. Lower heat and simmer for 20 minutes. Drain marrow, reserving liquid. Skim off as much fat as possible from liquid. Reduce remaining liquid by one half.

Cook bacon in a large skillet till almost crisp, then remove bacon from skillet. Add sweetbread scallops to hot fat and sauté on both sides until golden brown. Remove from pan and keep warm.

Place chopped shallots in skillet and sauté until soft, then add reduced liquid. Chop bacon, and return sweetbreads and bacon to pan, along with cooked marrow. Season with salt, pepper, and monosodium glutamate. Gently stir in beef gravy. Allow to cook, uncovered, for a few minutes over high heat to reduce sauce. Then stir in cooked peas, most of chopped parsley, and serve, sprinkled with remaining chopped parsley. Serves 6.

SWEETBREAD, CHICKEN LIVER AND SAUSAGE SAUTE

1 pound Italian hot sausages
1 large pair sweetbreads, blanched, trimmed and cut into cubes (see page 222)
¾ pound chicken livers, halved
1 onion, chopped
1 green pepper, diced
3 cloves garlic, minced
⅔ cup tomato purée
½ cup strong stock
1 teaspoon basil
½ teaspoon oregano
salt and pepper
2 teaspoons monosodium glutamate
½ teaspoon sugar
½ cup chopped parsley

Prick sausages with a fork. Place in a dry skillet over medium heat, and turn frequently until they are browned and cooked. Remove from skillet and keep warm.

If there is not much fat left in skillet, add a little olive oil, and sauté sweetbread cubes and chicken livers until golden brown on both sides. (Be careful not to overcook the livers.) Remove sweetbreads and livers from pan and keep warm.

Cut sausage into slices and mix with sweetbreads and livers. Set meat mixture aside.

Add onion, green pepper and garlic to skillet, and sauté until soft. Add tomato purée and stock. Season with basil, oregano, salt, pepper, monosodium glutamate and sugar. Return meats to sauce and stir in well. When mixture is bubbling, stir in chopped parsley and serve at once. Serves 6.

SWEETBREADS AND CHICKEN LIVERS, EN BROCHETTE

2 *pair sweetbreads, blanched, weighted and trimmed*
¼ *pound butter*
1 *pound chicken livers, halved*
6 *cloves garlic, very finely minced or crushed*
salt and pepper
½ *to* ¾ *pound good-quality sliced bacon*
1 *pound mushrooms, stems removed*

Remove as many membranes as possible from sweetbreads. Cut into 1-inch cubes.

Heat butter in a heavy skillet; add sweetbread cubes, and brown lightly on all sides. Remove from skillet. Then add chicken livers and brown lightly all over but do not cook through. Cool sweetbreads and livers. When cool enough to handle, spread each piece of sweetbread and liver with a little of the finely minced garlic. Sprinkle with salt and pepper.

Cut bacon slices in half, crosswise. Wrap each piece of sweetbread and liver in a piece of bacon. Divide among 6 skewers, occasionally interspersing the bacon-wrapped meats with whole mushrooms. (This procedure may be done ahead of time.)

Before serving, preheat broiler till it is very hot. Broil skewered meats on all sides until bacon is crisp. Serve at once. Serves 6.

SWEETBREADS IN CREAM SAUCE

- 3 *pair sweetbreads, blanched, weighted and trimmed* (*see page* 222)
- ⅔ *cup butter*
- ½ *cup chopped shallots or scallions*
- 1 *pound mushrooms*
- 1¼ *cups white wine*
- *salt and pepper*
- 1 *teaspoon monosodium glutamate*
- 1 *teaspoon tarragon*
- ⅔ *cup heavy cream, or* 4 *tablespoons Preserved Cream* (*page* 29)
- 4 *egg yolks*
- ½ *cup chopped parsley*

After sweetbreads have been blanched, weighted and trimmed, cut them crosswise into scallops.

Melt butter in a heavy skillet. Sauté sweetbreads on both sides until they are lightly browned. Remove to a heated platter and keep warm.

Add shallots and mushrooms to skillet. Sauté briefly. Add ¾ cup wine to pan, and add seasonings. Raise heat. Stir to loosen brown bits in the pan. Reduce liquid in pan to half.

Stir cream and egg yolks together. Stir a little of hot wine sauce into the egg mixture. Remove sauce from stove, and stir in egg mixture. If sauce does not thicken immediately, place over very low heat and stir till it thickens. Return sautéed sweetbreads and mushrooms to pan. Stir together. Sprinkle with chopped parsley before serving. Serves 6.

CALVES' LIVER IN SOUR CREAM

6 *strips bacon*
2 *onions, chopped*
½ *pound mushrooms, sliced*
3 *cloves garlic, minced*
1 *green pepper, diced*
½ *cup flour*
1 *teaspoon dry mustard*
salt and pepper
2 *teaspoons monosodium glutamate*
6 *slices calves' liver, ⅓″ thick, cut into strips of the same thickness*
¼ *cup white wine*
½ *cup sour cream*
½ *cup chopped parsley*

Cook bacon in a large skillet until it is crisp. Remove, drain and crumble, and keep warm.

Sauté onions, mushrooms, garlic and green pepper in fat remaining in skillet, adding a little butter if necessary. When vegetables are soft, remove them and keep warm.

Season flour with mustard, salt and pepper and monosodium glutamate. Toss calves' liver strips in flour mixture, coating the strips on all sides. Raise heat under skillet and add coated liver strips. Sauté them on all sides until lightly browned. Be careful, however, not to overcook liver. Remove strips from pan and add to sautéed vegetables.

Add white wine to pan. Keep heat very high and reduce wine till it is little more than a glaze in the pan. Stir in sour cream. Taste sauce for seasoning and correct if necessary. Return liver, vegetables and crumbled bacon to sauce. Toss and sprinkle with chopped parsley. Serve at once. Serves 6.

TRIPE, SPANISH STYLE

3 *pounds tripe, cut into pieces 1½" square*
3 *onions, 1 left whole, the other 2 chopped*
4 *cloves garlic, minced*
⅓ *cup olive oil*
1 *Spanish sausage (chorizo), cut into thin slices*
bay leaf
salt
1 *teaspoon coarsely ground pepper*
2 *teaspoons monosodium glutamate*
1 *teaspoon oregano*
1 *No. 2 can solid-pack tomatoes, drained and chopped*
4 *pimentos, diced*
⅓ *pound ham, diced*

Place tripe in a deep pot; cover with 1 quart of water. Add whole onion and a little of the garlic. Cover pot, and simmer over low heat about 3 hours, or until tripe is almost tender.

Drain tripe, reserving liquid for later use.

Heat olive oil in a flameproof casserole. Add chopped onions and remaining garlic, and sauté until tender. Add chorizo, then drained tripe. Add bay leaf, salt, pepper, monosodium glutamate, oregano, drained tomatoes and pimentos. Add enough of the reserved cooking liquid to barely cover tripe. Cover casserole tightly and cook over low heat or in a 325 degree oven for 3 to 5 hours—the longer the better. One hour before serving, stir in ham. (If necessary, add more liquid as tripe cooks.) Serve very hot. Serves 8.

VEAL KIDNEYS IN MADEIRA SAUCE

6 *veal kidneys*
6 *tablespoons butter*
3 *carrots, diced*
12 *small white onions, peeled*
1 *cup chopped parsley*
1½ *pounds mushrooms, sliced*
salt and pepper
½ *teaspoon thyme*
2 *teaspoons monosodium glutamate*
1 *large bay leaf*
1½ *cups Madeira*
1 *cup beef gravy (see page* 53)

Trim fat and core from kidneys. Slice ½ inch thick.

Melt butter in a heavy pot, then add kidneys and sauté in butter till they change color but do not brown. Stir in carrots, onions and a little parsley. Cover pot and continue to sauté in butter till vegetables are barely tender. Stir in mushrooms. Season with salt, pepper, thyme, monosodium glutamate and bay leaf. Add 1¼ cups Madeira. Cover pot tightly and simmer over low heat about 1½ hours, or until kidneys are completely tender.

Remove lid from pot, and skim off any fat. If liquid in pot more than covers kidneys, remove kidneys from pot, turn heat up high, and reduce liquid by about a third. Then return kidneys to pot.

Stir in beef gravy. When sauce begins to simmer again, add remaining Madeira. Sprinkle with remaining chopped parsley and serve hot. Serves 6.

BRAINS, FLORENTINE

3 *pair veal brains*
2 *packages frozen unchopped spinach*
⅔ *cup olive oil*
6 *cloves garlic*
salt and coarsely ground pepper
1 *teaspoon monosodium glutamate*

Separate brains. Drop into well-seasoned boiling water for 5 minutes to blanch. Drain well, and dry on paper towels.

Allow frozen spinach to thaw partially, then cook, in its own liquid, for just a few minutes. Drain very well and press all liquid out of spinach.

Heat olive oil in a skillet, and when it is hot but not smoking add minced garlic. Sauté garlic until soft but not brown. Add brains, and sauté on both sides till brains are lightly browned. Remove to a heated dish and keep warm. Sprinkle with salt and pepper.

Add well-drained spinach to olive oil remaining in skillet. Toss spinach in oil over high heat for just a few minutes, seasoning with salt, pepper and monosodium glutamate.

Arrange spinach on a heated platter. Place sautéed brains on top and serve at once. Serves 6.

POTTED LAMBS' TONGUES

(If desired, parboiled lung or heart of lamb may be included in this dish)

5 *pounds lambs' tongues*
4 *tablespoons chicken fat*
2 *large onions, chopped*
5 *cloves garlic, minced*
3 *tablespoons paprika*
⅔ *cup tomato purée*
salt and pepper
2 *teaspoons monosodium glutamate*
½ *teaspoon sugar*

Place lambs' tongues (and lung or heart, if desired) in a deep pot. Cover with water. Bring to a boil, lower heat and simmer until meat is barely tender. Drain water, reserving about 1 cup of it. Skin the while they are still warm.

Heat chicken fat in deep pot. Add onions and garlic, and sauté until very soft and beginning to brown. Stir in paprika. Add tongues (and any other meat) and mix well. Stir in tomato purée, a little tongue liquid, salt, pepper, monosodium glutamate, and sugar. Cover pot tightly and simmer over low heat about 1 hour, or until tongues are completely tender. If necessary, add more liquid as the dish cooks, but there should not be too much sauce. Serve hot. Serves 6.

TONGUE, VERACRUZANA

Follow recipe for Red Snapper, Veracruzana (see page 144), substituting slices of unsmoked, cooked, skinned beef or veal tongue for the fish filets. Make layers of tongue, then of sauce, etc., until you fill a casserole with tongue and veracruzana sauce. Bake this dish until it is good and hot. (It is even better when reheated a second time.)

BROILED VEAL HEARTS

One of my favorite dishes is broiled veal hearts. Correctly cooked, they are better and more tender than steak. To prepare them, split the hearts in two lengthwise—not cutting them all the way through. Allow 1 small heart per person. Wash out the inside of the hearts well and dry on paper towels. Be sure to remove all blood clots, and score the hearts, on the inside, in diagonal directions. Place in a shallow marinade of Vinaigrette Sauce (page 57) with a little soy added. Use plenty of coarsely ground pepper. Marinate at least 1 hour, or longer if desired, turning the meat frequently.

Before serving, preheat broiler until it is very hot. Place hearts on the broiling rack, scored side up, about 3 inches from heat. Broil 4 to 5 minutes on each side, basting with the marinade once or twice. The hearts should not be overcooked or they will toughen. Serve at once. They will be very tender and juicy.

SWEET-SOUR HEART AND LUNG PAPRIKASH

2 *veal hearts*
1 *veal lung*
4 *tablespoons rendered chicken fat*
1 *onion, chopped*
2 *cloves garlic, minced*
3 *tablespoons paprika*
2 *tablespoons flour*
1 *cup stock*
½ *cup tomato purée*
¼ *cup lemon juice*
salt and pepper
1 *teaspoon monosodium glutamate*
2 *tablespoons honey (approximately)*
¼ *cup chopped dill or parsley*

Trim hearts of fat and veins, and cut into cubes. Cut lung into cubes.

Heat fat in a heavy pot. Add onion and garlic, and sauté until tender. Add meats. Cook, stirring occasionally, till meats change color but do not brown. Combine paprika and flour. Stir into meats, over low heat.

Add stock, tomato purée, lemon juice, salt, pepper and monosodium glutamate. Cover pot and simmer over low heat about 2 hours, or until meats are tender. Add some of the honey. Taste for seasoning. The sauce should have a sweet-sour quality. If necessary, add a little more honey or lemon juice. Serve hot, sprinkled with chopped dill or parsley. Serves 6.

CHICKEN GIBLET CURRY

1/3 cup vegetable oil, or clarified butter
2 tablespoons mustard seeds
1 large onion, chopped
6 cloves garlic, chopped
4 tablespoons curry powder
1 teaspoon cardamom powder
1/2 teaspoon ground cinnamon
salt
2 teaspoons monosodium glutamate
1 teaspoon freshly ground black pepper
cayenne pepper to taste (optional)
2 pounds cleaned chicken gizzards, cut in two
1 pound chicken hearts
1 1/4 cups chicken stock (approximately)
1/2 pound chicken livers, quartered
2 tablespoons chopped cilantro (optional)

Heat oil in a heavy saucepan, and add mustard seeds. Cover pan and keep over medium heat until seeds pop and darken. Remove lid, lower heat and add chopped onion and garlic. Sauté until tender. Stir in curry powder and all remaining seasonings and spices. Stir for 2 or 3 minutes.

Add chicken gizzards and hearts. Stir all together. Add enough stock to barely cover giblets. Simmer over low heat about 2 hours, or until meats are very tender. Add chicken livers and continue to simmer about 15 minutes longer. Taste for seasoning. Correct if necessary. Serve with Fluffy, Steamed Rice, garnished with cilantro.

This tastes even better if it is made a day or 2 ahead of time and reheated. Serves 8.

CHICKEN GIBLET PAPRIKASH

½ cup rendered chicken fat
2 onions, chopped
3 cloves garlic, minced
3 pounds mixed chicken gizzards and hearts
1 tablespoon flour
5 tablespoons paprika
1 cup chicken stock (approximately)
½ cup tomato purée
salt and pepper
2 teaspoons monosodium glutamate
1 pound chicken livers, quartered
¾ cup sour cream
½ cup chopped dill

Heat chicken fat in a deep pot. Add onions and garlic, and sauté until soft. Stir in gizzards and hearts. Let them change color, but do not brown them. Mix flour with paprika and stir in. Then stir in chicken stock, and next tomato purée. Season with salt, pepper and monosodium glutamate. Cover pot and allow to simmer until meats are almost tender, about 1½ hours. Stir in quartered chicken livers and continue to cook till meats are completely tender.

Just before serving, stir in sour cream and sprinkle with chopped dill. Serves 8.

7. POULTRY

IT WOULD BE WASTEFUL to make a stew of filet mignon and utterly foolish to try to sauté a piece of chuck or brisket. All three cuts are from the same animal, but each has a completely different taste quality and requires a different culinary preparation.

This is also true of a chicken—the white and dark meats have different cooking times and characteristics. Until recent years it was necessary, for practical reasons, to buy an entire bird and to cook it all at once. Inevitably, the result was dry, overcooked white meat, even when the remainder of the bird was palatable.

Fortunately, fresh chicken in parts is now available almost everywhere. Now it is no more necessary to buy a whole chicken than it is to buy a whole steer.

Chicken breasts should be cooked for a very short time—from 5 to 12 minutes, depending on the recipe used. Cooked for a short time, they are tender and succulent, never dry, stringy or tough. For best results, chicken breasts should be skinned and boned. Boning chicken breasts is a simple process, best done with your fingers. Insert your fingers between the meat and bone and pry away the meat gently. Very little work with a knife is necessary. You may easily remove the skin, too, simply by pulling it off. The result of this minor effort is a lovely, white filet of chicken, the basis for many delicate recipes—provided you are careful not to overcook the chicken. Even when you are cooking chicken breasts in the conventional way, without skinning and boning them, it is equally important to guard against overcooking them.

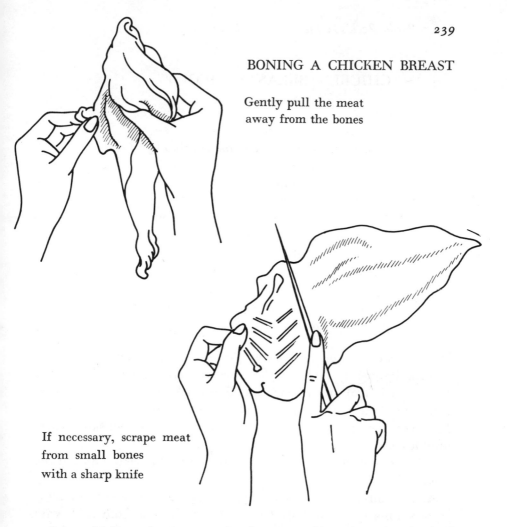

BONING A CHICKEN BREAST

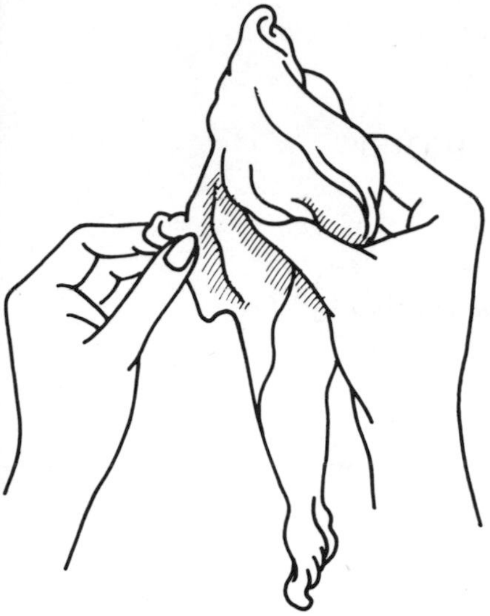

Gently pull the meat
away from the bones

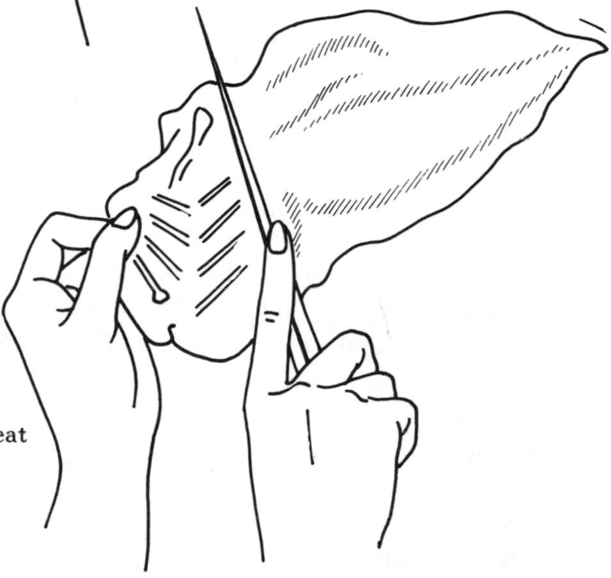

If necessary, scrape meat
from small bones
with a sharp knife

Legs, thighs and wings need a longer cooking time. For braised dishes, it is often better to remove the skin from the legs and thighs, as the skin tends to remain rubbery long after the meat has become tender. The exceptions to this rule are fried, broiled and sautéed chicken. (During these preparations, the skin of the chicken cooks comparatively quickly.) Even legs and thighs need far less cooking than conventional recipes call for, unless you happen to be cooking parts from a bird which you know is old. One small step that greatly enhances the appearance of braised chicken dishes (such as paprikash), is chopping off the small ends of the leg bones.

Note: Many of the recipes for chicken breasts may be used with chicken leg-thighs, if the cooking time is adjusted.

CHICKEN BREASTS NICOISE

¾ *cup olive oil (approximately)*
2 *large eggplants, peeled and cut into ½" dice*
1 *onion, minced*
4 *cloves garlic, minced*
1 *green pepper, minced*
½ *cup tomato purée*
1 *cup chopped parsley*
1 *teaspoon basil*
salt and pepper
½ *teaspoon sugar*
6 *chicken breasts, boned, skinned and cut in half*
1 *teaspoon monosodium glutamate*

Heat ½ cup olive oil in a heavy skillet. Add eggplant and brown, turning frequently. When it becomes soft and brown, add minced onion, garlic and green pepper, adding a bit more oil if necessary. Sauté until all of the vegetables are tender. Stir in tomato purée, ½ cup chopped parsley, basil, salt, pepper and sugar. Set skillet aside until needed.

Set oven temperature at 300 degrees, and heat a baking dish in the oven.

Add remaining olive oil to another skillet. Heat oil but do not allow it to become very hot. Sprinkle chicken breasts on both sides with monosodium glutamate, basil, salt and pepper; place in olive oil and sauté over low heat for only 1 minute. Turn chicken over. It will not be brown—just beginning to turn white. Sauté slowly for a minute on the second side.

Arrange chicken in the hot baking dish, and spoon eggplant mixture on top. Place in 300 degree oven for 8 minutes. Sprinkle with remaining chopped parsley and serve at once. Serves 6.

CHICKEN BREASTS AL VERMOUTH

¼ *cup butter*
2 *teaspoons salt*
2 *teaspoons monosodium glutamate*
½ *teaspoon allspice*
¼ *teaspoon cinnamon*
6 *chicken breasts, boned, skinned and cut in half*
3 *scallions, minced*
½ *cup dry vermouth*
⅔ *cup heavy cream, or 3 tablespoons Preserved Cream*
¾ *cup pitted green olives, cut in halves*
¼ *cup chopped parsley*

Set oven temperature at 300 degrees. Place baking dish in oven so it will be hot. Melt butter in a heavy saucepan. Combine salt, monosodium glutamate, allspice and cinnamon, and sprinkle this mixture on both sides of chicken breast.

Sauté chicken breasts in skillet over low heat. Turn them after 1 minute, and sauté on the second side for 1 minute longer. Transfer chicken breasts to hot baking dish and place in oven for 8 to 10 minutes.

While chicken is cooking, add minced scallions to remaining butter in skillet. Raise heat. When scallions are soft, stir in vermouth and cream. Cook over very high heat until liquid is reduced to less than half. Stir in olives. Season with additional salt to taste, and pour over chicken. Sprinkle with chopped parsley and serve at once. Serves 6.

SKEWERED CHICKEN BREASTS

Chicken breasts which have been boned, skinned and cut into large cubes are delicious when they have been marinated in a spicy sauce, threaded onto skewers and broiled very briefly either over charcoal or under a broiler flame. The combinations of spices and ingredients are almost endless. However, here are four suggestions for you to think about. Be sure not to overcook the skewered chicken. Turn the skewers every minute or 2. Remove from heat as soon as the chicken is golden, and serve at once.

ORIENTAL CHICKEN KEBABS

6 *whole chicken breasts, boned, skinned and cut into large cubes*
⅔ *cup Japanese soy sauce*
¼ *cup sherry*
¼ *cup sesame seeds, toasted in a dry frying pan till golden, then pulverized in blender or mortar and pestle*
1 *clove garlic, finely minced*
1 *tablespoon grated fresh or pickled ginger*
½ *teaspoon sugar*
1 *teaspoon monosodium glutamate*

Place cubed chicken breasts in a bowl. Add all remaining ingredients and mix well. Allow to marinate for at least an hour. Then thread on skewers and broil with high heat, very briefly, on all sides. Baste each side with the marinade as the skewers are being turned.

Serves 6.

INDIAN CHICKEN KEBABS

6 *whole chicken breasts, boned, skinned and cut into large cubes*
3 *tablespoons curry powder*
2 *teaspoons lemon juice*
½ *cup yogurt*
1 *small onion, chopped*
2 *cloves garlic, finely minced*
1 *teaspoon fresh or pickled ginger, minced*
1 *teaspoon ground cardamom*
1 *small hot green pepper, seeded and chopped fine*
salt
1 *teaspoon monosodium glutamate*

Place cubed chicken breasts in a bowl. Add all remaining ingredients and mix well. Marinate 3 to 4 hours before threading on skewers. Broil with high heat, briefly, on all sides, brushing with the marinade as the skewers are turned. Serves 6.

SPICY CHICKEN KEBABS

6 *whole chicken breasts, skinned, boned and cut into large cubes*
chicken liver halves, as many as you have chicken breast cubes
1½ *cups Vinaigrette Sauce* (*page* 57)
chopped parsley

Place cubed chicken breasts and chicken liver halves in a bowl. Add Vinaigrette Sauce. Marinate for 3 to 4 hours before threading the chicken breasts and livers, alternately, on skewers. Broil briefly on all sides, brushing with the marinade as the skewers are turned. Sprinkle with chopped parsley before serving. Serves 6.

CHICKEN BREAST KEBABS

6 *chicken breasts, boned, skinned and cut into 1" squares*
5 *cloves garlic, minced*
2 *tablespoons chopped parsley*
3/8 *cup olive oil*
1 1/2 *tablespoons wine vinegar*
1 *tablespoon soy sauce*
2 *teaspoons monosodium glutamate*
1/4 *cup sherry*
1 *teaspoon pepper*
1 *teaspoon salt*
8 *strips of bacon, cut into thirds, slightly cooked and cooled*
24 *cherry tomatoes*

Place squares of chicken in a bowl and add all remaining ingredients except bacon and tomatoes. Mix well, then place in the refrigerator to marinate for at least an hour.

Twenty minutes before serving time, preheat broiler. Remove chicken from refrigerator, and wrap each piece in a piece of bacon. Thread on 6 skewers, placing a cherry tomato between every 2 pieces of bacon-wrapped chicken. If there is any liquid left in bowl, brush over bacon.

Place skewers on broiling rack. Turn down heat slightly and broil 2 inches from heat for 3 minutes, or until bacon is brown. Turn skewers over, and broil 3 minutes longer. Serve at once. Serves 6.

CHICKEN BREASTS, MEXICAN STYLE

6 whole chicken breasts, boned, skinned and cut into 1" squares
4 cloves garlic, minced
1 onion, minced
2 cans peeled green chilies, minced
3 tablespoons chili powder
½ cup beef gravy
1 teaspoon soy sauce
salt and pepper to taste
2 teaspoons chopped cilantro (optional)

Place chicken pieces in a bowl. Combine all remaining ingredients and add to chicken. Mix well. Place in refrigerator and marinate chicken for at least an hour.

Preheat broiler for 20 minutes. Arrange chicken mixture in a metal pan large enough to hold it but small enough so that all the pieces touch each other. Place in broiler as close to heat as possible. Broil for 6 minutes, or until top is brown. Do not turn pieces. The combination of the high heat and metal pan will be enough to cook the chicken sufficiently. Serve at once with Refried Beans, and fried Tortillas. Serves 6.

CHICKEN BREASTS LORRAINE

2 *teaspoons salt*
1 *teaspoon pepper*
1 *teaspoon tarragon*
2 *teaspoons monosodium glutamate*
½ *teaspoon allspice*
¼ *teaspoon cinnamon*
6 *chicken breasts, boned, skinned and cut in half*
4 *slices bacon, diced*
1 *tablespoon butter*
3 *scallions, minced*
⅔ *cup chopped parsley*
⅔ *cup white wine*
⅔ *cup chicken stock*
2 *teaspoons lemon juice*
4 *egg yolks, slightly beaten*

Set oven at 300 degrees, and place a baking dish in it to warm.

Combine salt, pepper, tarragon, monosodium glutamate, allspice and cinnamon. Sprinkle chicken breasts on both sides with this mixture.

In a heavy skillet, sauté diced bacon in butter. When bacon begins to brown, lower heat and place chicken in skillet. Sauté for 1 minute. Turn chicken over and sauté on other side for another minute. Chicken will not brown at all—it will just begin to turn white. Transfer chicken and bacon pieces to hot baking dish and place in oven while sauce is being prepared.

Add minced scallions and half of parsley to fat remaining in skillet. Turn heat up high. When scallions are soft (in just a few seconds), add wine, chicken stock and lemon juice. Cook over very high heat until the liquid is reduced by about half. Remove from heat. Beat a little of this hot liquid into the egg yolks with a wire whisk. Then pour egg yolk mixture back into remaining hot liquid, stirring briskly.

Chicken should have been in the oven almost 10 minutes by now. Pour sauce over it. Sprinkle with remaining chopped parsley and serve at once. Serves 6.

TANGORE CHICKEN

This is a remarkable chicken dish, very highly spiced, and just as good served cold as hot. Served hot, it needs a bed of good, fluffy rice.

- ⅓ *cup lime juice*
- 1 *teaspoon paprika*
- 4 *teaspoons ground coriander*
- 4 *teaspoons ground cardamom*
- 1 *teaspoon salt*
- ⅔ *cup chicken stock*
- 1 *teaspoon tomato paste*
- 1 *teaspoon sugar*
- 6 *chicken breasts, boned, skinned and cut in half*
- 1 *tablespoon chopped cilantro* (*optional*)

Combine all ingredients except chicken breasts and cilantro.

Using a sharp knife, score chicken breasts on their smooth sides, about ⅛ inch deep. Place chicken breasts in a broad, heavy pot, and pour lime juice mixture over them. Marinate the breasts for at least an hour, turning once or twice.

Remove chicken from marinade, and place pot over low heat. Bring the liquid in the pot to a simmering point. Add chicken breasts. Simmer breasts for 7 to 10 minutes, or till they are just firm to the touch. Serve on Fluffy, Steamed Rice at once, sprinkled with cilantro, or chill and serve cold with a salad. Serves 6.

BREADED CHICKEN CUTLETS

Chicken cooked in this manner surpasses the finest veal available in this country. However, the chicken must go from the skillet to the table, because the interior of the chicken continues to cook even after it is removed from the heat. It can become overdone rapidly.

1 *small loaf firm-style white bread, crusts removed*
1 *teaspoon salt*
1 *teaspoon monosodium glutamate*
1 *teaspoon white pepper*
1 *egg*
2 *tablespoons milk*
3 *chicken breasts, boned, skinned and cut in half*
½ *cup sweet butter*
3 *tablespoons oil*
1 *lemon, cut into wedges*
chopped parsley

Place bread on a baking sheet in a slow oven for about 20 minutes, or until bread dries out slightly (but does not brown). Cut bread into dice and place in blender jar. Turn on blender and reduce the bread to crumbs. Turn out bread crumbs on a large sheet of wax paper. Add to it the salt, monosodium glutamate and pepper.

Beat egg lightly with the milk.

Pound each chicken breast half between 2 sheets of wax paper with a mallet or a bottle until the meat has flattened and is no more than ¼ inch thick.

Dip each chicken cutlet into the egg mixture, then into the seasoned bread crumbs, being sure that both sides are well coated. If possible, chill breaded chicken cutlets for at least an hour before cooking them.

Combine butter and oil in a large, heavy skillet. Place over medium heat. When fat is completely melted and hot, but not smoking or burning, add chicken cutlets. Sauté about 3 minutes (or less) on each side. Drain on paper towels and serve immediately, garnished with lemon wedges and chopped parsley. Serves 6.

POACHED CHICKEN BREASTS IN TARRAGON CREAM SAUCE

1 *cup dry white wine*
1½ *cups chicken stock*
1 *teaspoon monosodium glutamate*
6 *chicken breasts, boned, skinned and cut in half*
1 *package frozen tiny peas, completely defrosted and rinsed in hot water*
salt to taste
2 *teaspoons dried tarragon*
2 *egg yolks*
½ *cup Preserved Cream*
¼ *cup chopped parsley*

Combine wine, chicken stock and monosodium glutamate in a saucepan and bring to a boil. Lower heat so that liquid simmers. Add chicken breasts. When liquid begins to simmer again, poach chicken for 5 to 7 minutes, or until the breasts are just barely firm to the touch.

Remove chicken breasts from liquid with a slotted spoon. Place on a heatproof dish in a very low oven to keep warm while sauce is being made.

Raise heat under liquid in pan to very high and reduce liquid to about ½ of original quantity, or even a little less. Lower heat and add peas. Season with salt, and add tarragon.

Stir egg yolks into cream. Spoon a little of the hot reduced liquid into cream mixture and stir briskly. Then pour the warm cream mixture back into the saucepan, stirring quickly with a wire whisk. Cook over low heat until sauce is slightly thickened; then pour over chicken breast. Sprinkle with chopped parsley and serve hot. Serves 6.

CHICKEN SALTIMBOCCA

Bone and skin chicken breasts. With a mallet, pound each one thin between 2 sheets of wax paper. You now have chicken scaloppine—a wonderful substitute for veal. Why substitute? you may ask. The reason is that the veal generally available in the United States is of such poor quality. Chicken breasts, handled properly, have much of the wonderful delicacy of French or Italian veal.

6 *chicken breasts, boned, skinned and cut in half*
6 *thin slices of prosciutto, cut in half*
12 *pieces of mozzarella cheese, about ¾" square*
12 *pitted black olives, cut in half*
1 *teaspoon monosodium glutamate*
1 *teaspoon pepper*
½ *cup flour*
1 *egg*
3 *tablespoons milk*
2 *cups fine bread or cracker crumbs*
½ *cup butter*
2 *cloves garlic, finely minced*
½ *cup chopped parsley*
butter and olive oil, in equal parts, to cover the bottom of a skillet to a depth of ¼ inch

On one side of each thin chicken breast, place half a piece of prosciutto, a piece of mozzarella cheese and 2 olive halves. Sprinkle with monosodium glutamate and freshly ground pepper. Fold unfilled side over to cover filling, and press edges firmly together to enclose filling.

Flour each little package, so it is well dusted on all sides. Beat egg slightly, adding milk. Dip chicken packages into egg mixture, on both sides. Then dip into bread crumbs. Chill for at least ½ hour, or longer.

Melt ½ cup butter in a small saucepan. Add chopped garlic and parsley, and keep warm until the chicken is cooked.

Heat butter and olive oil in a skillet until the fats are hot but not smoking. Place breaded chicken in skillet, and turn heat to medium high. Sauté chicken quickly, only till golden, turning once to cook the other side.

Remove to heated serving dish; pour warm garlic-parsley butter sauce on top and serve at once. Serves 6.

CHICKEN SALAD

8 *chicken breast halves, not boned or skinned*
chicken stock
1 *cup diced boiled ham*
1 *cup sliced, blanched almonds, toasted in a* 350 *degree oven till golden*
1 *cup seedless grapes, halved*
½ *teaspoon tarragon*
2 *tablespoons chopped parsley*
1 *teaspoon monosodium glutamate*
salt and freshly ground pepper
1 *cup homemade Mayonnaise* (*page* 58)
3 *hard-cooked egg yolks, mashed*
watercress

Place chicken breasts in a low, wide saucepan. Add enough well-seasoned stock to just cover the chicken. Bring to a boil. Lower heat and simmer breasts for just 8 minutes. Remove chicken from stock (which will now be extra good since it is doubly rich). Reserve this stock for another purpose.

When chicken is cool enough to handle, pull off the skin and then pull the meat away from the bones. Cut the chicken into ¾-inch chunks. Place them in a bowl. Add ham, ¾ cup almonds, grapes, tarragon, parsley, monosodium glutamate, salt and pepper. Add mayonnaise to this mixture and toss lightly. Taste and correct seasoning if necessary.

Arrange the chicken salad on a platter. Sprinkle with mashed egg yolks and remaining almonds. Make a wreath of watercress around the chicken salad. Serves 8.

BEST-EVER FRIED CHICKEN

½ cup milk
½ cup heavy cream
6 leg-thigh pieces of chicken, cut in two
1½ cups flour
2 tablespoons salt
1 teaspoon celery salt
2 teaspoons pepper
2 teaspoons monosodium glutamate
1 teaspoon allspice
1 teaspoon cinnamon
clarified butter and peanut oil (half and half), or all lard, to cover bottom of skillet to a depth of ½″

Combine milk and cream in a bowl, then add chicken. Mix around so that all parts of the chicken get coated.

Combine flour, salt, celery salt, pepper, monosodium glutamate, allspice and cinnamon, mixing well. Place in a fairly large paper or plastic bag. Taking 2 or 3 pieces of chicken at a time from the liquid, place in flour mixture. Close top of bag tightly and shake until chicken is well coated with flour mixture. Remove chicken from bag and place on wax paper till needed.

Heat fat in skillet until it is hot but not smoking. Place floured chicken pieces into hot fat, skin side down. Have heat medium high. Allow the chicken to cook for 9 minutes. By this time it will be well browned. Turn pieces over and cook 7 minutes more. Turn them once more so the skin side is down, and cook 4 minutes longer. Drain on paper towels and serve either hot or at room temperature. Chicken will remain crisp. Serves 6.

CHICKEN SAUTE GRANDMERE

½ cup bacon fat
¼ cup butter
6 leg-thigh pieces of chicken, cut in two
monosodium glutamate
salt
3 medium-size cold boiled potatoes, skinned and diced
1¼ cups diced ham (sausage such as Italian pepperoni may be substituted)
1 large onion, minced
6 cloves garlic, minced fine
2 green peppers, minced
½ cup chopped celery leaves
1 cup chopped parsley
pepper

Set oven at 325 degrees. Place baking pan in oven.

Heat fat and butter in a heavy skillet until hot but not smoking. Sprinkle chicken with monosodium glutamate and salt, and place pieces in hot fat. Have heat medium high. Sauté chicken, turning the pieces, until they brown on all sides. Transfer to baking dish and place in oven.

Add diced potatoes to remaining fat in pan. Add more fat if necessary. Turn the potatoes frequently until they are golden. Add diced ham, then onion, garlic, green peppers, chopped celery leaves and half of parsley. Sauté over high heat till vegetables are soft. Season mixture to taste with salt and pepper. Spoon over chicken. If chicken has been in oven a total of 20 minutes, serve at once. Otherwise return to oven for required cooking time. Sprinkle with remaining parsley before serving. Serves 6.

CHICKEN ST. GERMAIN

6 *slices bacon, diced*
½ *cup butter, melted*
6 *leg-thigh pieces of chicken, cut in two*
salt
2 *teaspoons monosodium glutamate*
½ *pound mushrooms, sliced*
1 *large onion, minced*
3 *scallions, minced*
2 *cloves garlic, minced*
2 *cups chopped lettuce*
2 *packages frozen tiny peas, partly defrosted*
½ *cup beef gravy*
1 *teaspoon tomato paste*
1 *teaspoon soy sauce*
½ *teaspoon sugar*
pepper
½ *teaspoon thyme*
bay leaf
½ *cup chopped parsley*

In a heavy skillet, sauté bacon in melted butter until the bacon is almost brown. Remove pieces of bacon from skillet.

Season chicken pieces on both sides with salt and some of the monosodium glutamate. Place chicken pieces in fat remaining in skillet, and sauté over medium high heat, turning pieces frequently until chicken is golden on all sides. Transfer chicken to an oven-proof dish and place in a 350 degree oven.

Add mushrooms to remaining fat in skillet (add more fat if necessary), along with the onion, scallions and garlic. Sauté until vegetables are soft. Add chopped lettuce. Raise heat to high so that water cooks out of lettuce. Add peas, beef gravy, tomato paste, soy sauce, sugar, remaining monosodium glutamate, salt and pepper. Continue to cook over high heat until the peas are just cooked. Stir in thyme and bay leaf. Taste for seasoning.

Spoon this mixture over chicken in oven. Continue to cook in a

350 degree oven till chicken has been in oven a total of 25 minutes. Sprinkle with chopped parsley and serve at once. Serves 6.

CHICKEN PAPRIKASH

6 *leg-thigh pieces of chicken, cut in two, skinned, small end of leg bone chopped off*
5 *scallions, minced*
2 *teaspoons monosodium glutamate*
1 *tablespoon salt*
5 *cloves garlic, minced*
4 *tablespoons chopped dill*
2 *cups chicken stock*
1 *cup white wine*
4 *tablespoons Hungarian paprika*
¼ *cup tomato sauce*
¾ *cup sour cream*

Place chicken in a low, wide saucepan which may be covered. Add scallions, monosodium glutamate, salt, garlic, 2 tablespoons dill, chicken stock and white wine. Bring to a boil over a high heat. Lower heat and simmer chicken for 20 minutes. Remove chicken pieces from the liquid and place them in a baking pan in a 300 degree oven while preparing the sauce.

Skim off fat from liquid in pot. Reduce the liquid over high heat by a half. Stir in paprika and tomato sauce. If sauce is very thin, continue to cook it down until it thickens slightly. Remove sauce from stove, and stir in sour cream. Pour over chicken. Sprinkle with remaining dill and serve. Serves 6.

CHICKEN AND GARLIC STEW

3 *tablespoons olive oil*
40 *to* 60 *plump cloves garlic, peeled*
6 *chicken leg-thigh pieces, cut in two*
½ *cup chopped parsley*
½ *cup chopped celery leaves*
1 *teaspoon dried tarragon*
1 *tablespoon salt*
1 *teaspoon monosodium glutamate*
1 *teaspoon ground white pepper*
½ *teaspoon ground allspice*
¼ *teaspoon cinnamon*
1½ *cups dry white wine*

Place olive oil in a heavy pot which can be tightly covered. Add ⅓ of garlic and ⅓ of all remaining ingredients, including chicken. Add a second third of garlic and of the other ingredients. Add remaining chicken and remaining ingredients, then cover pot tightly, and place in a 375 degree oven for about 1¼ hours. The chicken will not brown, but will be moist and succulent.

Serve with crusty bread to mop up the sauce. Spread the soft garlic on some of the crusty bread. The garlic will spread like butter or a pâté, and the flavor will not be overpowering. Serves 6.

CHICKEN IN MUSTARD CREAM

1/3 cup sweet butter
6 leg-thigh pieces of chicken, cut in two, skinned, small end of leg bone chopped off
2 onions, chopped
1 1/4 cups white wine
salt and pepper
1 teaspoon monosodium glutamate
1 tablespoon Dijon mustard
1 tablespoon potato flour
1/2 cup heavy cream
2 egg yolks
1/2 cup chopped parsley

Melt butter in a broad, heavy pan. Add chicken, and sauté, turning pieces frequently until chicken loses the pink color on the outside. Add chopped onions. Stir and continue to sauté until onions are soft. Add wine; bring to the boiling point. Lower heat and simmer covered for 20 minutes, or until the chicken is just tender and the juices run clear when chicken is pierced with a fork. Remove chicken pieces to a hot platter and keep warm.

Raise heat and reduce liquid in pan by one half. Add salt, pepper and monosodium glutamate.

Combine mustard and potato flour and stir into pan liquid, using low heat. Combine cream and egg yolks. Remove pan from heat and quickly stir cream mixture into sauce, using a wire whisk if possible. If sauce has consistency of heavy cream, pour over chicken pieces at once. If not, return to low heat and stir with wire whisk until it thickens slightly. Pour over chicken pieces, sprinkle with chopped parsley and serve at once. Serves 6.

ROYAL CHAMPAGNE CHICKEN

½ cup butter
6 leg-thigh pieces of chicken, cut in two, skinned, small bone of leg chopped off
½ cup chopped shallots or chopped scallions
3 tablespoons flour
1 teaspoon tarragon
salt and pepper
1 teaspoon monosodium glutamate
2 cups champagne (approximately)
½ pound mushrooms, sliced and sautéed in ¼ cup butter
1 cup heavy cream, or 4 tablespoons Preserved Cream
3 egg yolks
½ cup chopped parsley

Melt butter in a broad, heavy pan. Add chicken pieces and sauté slowly, turning frequently, until chicken loses its pink color on the outside. Add shallots or scallions and continue to sauté until they are soft. Remove chicken from the pan and keep warm.

Stir flour into pan. Cook for a few minutes over low heat, stirring constantly. Add tarragon, salt, pepper and monosodium glutamate. Remove from heat and, with a wire whisk, stir in champagne.

Return pieces of chicken to sauce. Cover pan and simmer about 20 minutes, or until chicken is just tender and the juices run clear when pierced with a fork. Remove chicken pieces to a platter and keep warm.

Add sautéed, sliced mushrooms to sauce. If the sauce seems very thin, raise heat to reduce it a little, while stirring, being careful not to scorch the sauce. Remove from heat.

Stir cream and egg yolks together, using a wire whisk. Stir this mixture into the sauce. Replace over low heat, stirring constantly, until sauce thickens a little more. Taste for seasoning, and correct if necessary. Pour over chicken, and sprinkle with chopped parsley. Serve at once with braised celery (see Braised Vegetables, page 279). Serves 6.

BASQUE CHICKEN SAUTE

⅔ *cup pork fat, cut into very small dice*
¼ *cup olive oil*
6 *chicken leg-thigh pieces, cut in two*
12 *small white onions, peeled*
½ *teaspoon sugar*
6 *cloves garlic, minced fine*
⅔ *cup ham, cut into small dice*
2 *green peppers, seeded and cut into strips*
salt and pepper
1 *teaspoon monosodium glutamate*
⅔ *cup white wine*
¼ *cup tomato purée*
1 *teaspoon basil*
½ *cup chopped parsley*

Place diced pork fat in a broad, heavy skillet, and render fat over low heat until pieces are crisp and there is fat in pan. Remove crisp bits and reserve them. Remove ½ of liquid pork fat and keep in case additional fat should be needed later. Add olive oil to fat in skillet.

Add chicken to hot fat, and brown lightly on all sides, turning frequently. Remove chicken from pan and keep warm in a low oven. Add small onions, and sprinkle them lightly with sugar. Raise heat and brown onions lightly. When they are golden on all sides, reduce heat.

Add browned chicken, pork bits, garlic, ham and green peppers to skillet. Sauté until everything is tender, turning the chicken pieces frequently. (This should take 20 to 25 minutes.) Season with salt, pepper and monosodium glutamate, and arrange chicken and vegetable mixture on a platter. Keep warm.

Pour wine into skillet. Raise heat to high and reduce by half. Add tomato purée and basil, and season the sauce to taste. Spoon over chicken and vegetables. Sprinkle with chopped parsley and serve at once. Serves 6.

CHICKEN IN EGG AND LEMON SAUCE

4 *tablespoons butter*
3 *onions, chopped*
6 *scallions, chopped*
2 *small heads Boston lettuce, core removed and chopped*
6 *chicken leg-thigh parts, cut in two, skinned, small bone of leg chopped off*
⅔ *cup white wine*
½ *cup chopped fresh dill*
2 *teaspoons cornstarch blended smooth with a little cold water*
3 *egg yolks*
juice of 2 lemons and grated rind of 1 lemon
salt and pepper to taste
1 *teaspoon monosodium glutamate*

Melt butter in a heavy saucepan. Add chopped onions and scallions, and sauté until tender. Add chopped lettuce. Stir till lettuce is wilted, then add chicken pieces. Turn them frequently until they lose their pink color. Add wine. Cover pan and simmer over low heat about 25 minutes, or until chicken is just tender and the juices are clear when the chicken is pierced with a fork. Remove chicken pieces to a platter and keep them warm in a low oven.

Stir chopped dill into saucepan, then stir in cornstarch mixture. The sauce will thicken slightly.

Mix egg yolks, lemon juice and rind together in a small bowl. Stirring briskly, add some of the hot sauce from the saucepan—about ¼ cup—to the egg yolk mixture. Now pour the egg yolk mixture back into the saucepan, stirring the entire mixture briskly. Stir over low heat until the sauce thickens a little more. Season to taste with salt, pepper and monosodium glutamate. Pour over chicken and serve at once. Serves 6.

NEAR EAST CHICKEN IN PAPER

6 *pieces of extra-heavy aluminum foil,* 40 *inches long*
6 *chicken leg-thigh parts, cut in two, skinned, small end of leg chopped off*
6 *small potatoes, peeled*
6 *small white onions, peeled*
6 *large fresh mushrooms, trimmed*
2 *green peppers, cut into strips*
6 *cloves garlic, minced fine*
1 *tablespoon tomato paste*
¾ *cup raw rice*
salt and pepper
2 *teaspoons monosodium glutamate*
1 *bay leaf cut into* 6 *pieces*
1 *teaspoon thyme*
chopped parsley

Fold aluminum foil in half to make each piece 20 inches long.

On each piece of aluminum foil (not quite in the center—about a third from one end) place 2 pieces of chicken. Surround with a peeled potato, a small onion, a mushroom, some green pepper strips and finely mined garlic, a little tomato paste, and a proportionate amount of rice. Season with salt, pepper, monosodium glutamate, bay leaf and thyme.

Fold aluminum foil, folding edges doubly or triply, to seal ingredients in. Be sure that there are no holes in the foil and that the edges are tight.

Place the six packages in a 450 degree oven and bake about 1 hour. To serve, place a package on each plate. Open by making a cross in the center and pulling top of paper away. Serve as is, in the paper. Sprinkle with some chopped parsley. Serves 6.

BROILED CHICKEN

Broiling, like roasting, is more of an art than a technique. A good deal of practice is necessary. When broiling chicken, it is important to know that some shrinkage occurs, but not so much that the chicken need be dried up. When served, the chicken should be crisp on the outside, moist and juicy within. The chicken should not be at all rare, but it should never be overcooked.

Chicken may be broiled without any basting whatsoever. However, basting the chicken with a tasty liquid gives noteworthy results. Even plain melted butter or olive oil is better than nothing.

Chicken breasts are not a good choice for broiling because they cook through too quickly. The best parts of the chicken for broiling are the leg and thigh, cut apart.

To broil chicken, preheat the broiler for about 15 minutes. Place the pieces, skin side down, on the broiling rack. Brush with basting liquid. (There are several basting suggestions below.) Place the broiling rack as far as possible (usually about 4 inches) from a medium low flame. Broil, brushing once or twice more, for about 10 minutes, or until the chicken is golden brown. Turn pieces over. Brush with basting liquid. Continue to broil until skin is crisp. If the chicken is of broiler size (under 2½ pounds) this should not take more than 10 additional minutes. If necessary, raise heat a little. Brush with basting liquid at least once during final period. When skin is crisp, the chicken should be done. If you wish, test it with a fork. When the fork is withdrawn, the running juices should be *almost* completely clear, but not pink or red.

BASTING LIQUIDS FOR BROILED CHICKEN

I

¼ pound butter, melted and heated
1 teaspoon soy sauce
1 teaspoon tarragon
1 clove garlic, minced fine
1 tablespoon chopped parsley
1 teaspoon monosodium glutamate

Mix all together. Use a brush for basting.

II

¼ pound butter, melted and heated
juice and grated rind of 2 lemons
1 clove garlic, minced fine
1 teaspoon monosodium glutamate
1 tablespoon chopped parsley
1 teaspoon chopped dill weed
salt and freshly ground pepper

Mix all together. Use a brush for basting.

III

Take 2 tablespoons chili powder, and add enough wine vinegar to make a loose paste. Add a few drops of soy sauce. Season with 1 clove of garlic (minced), a little cayenne pepper, a dash of sugar, ½ teaspoon monosodium glutamate, freshly ground pepper and salt. Add a teaspoon or 2 of tomato purée. Do not brush on the first side with this basting sauce until the chicken is almost ready to be turned; baste on the second side only during the final few minutes of cooking. (The sauce will char if the chicken is basted at the beginning.)

IV

Use well-seasoned Vinaigrette Sauce for basting.

V

- ½ *cup soy sauce*
- 2 *teaspoons finely chopped or grated fresh or pickled ginger*
- ½ *teaspoon sugar*
- 2 *cloves garlic, minced fine*
- 2 *tablespoons sherry*

Mix all together. Use a brush for basting.

BROILED SQUAB

Squab is a special breed of pigeon. It has only dark meat which is especially succulent if it isn't dried out by overcooking. It is best when served slightly rare.

- 6 *squabs*
- 1 *cup sweet butter*
- ¼ *cup chopped parsley*
- 1 *clove garlic, minced fine*
- 3 *tablespoons soy sauce*
- 1 *teaspoon monosodium glutamate*
- 2 *tablespoons cognac*
- 6 *slices French bread, cut 1" thick*

Remove the giblets of the squab (these are generally found in small paper bags inside each squab). Reserve the livers.

With a cleaver, or a heavy bottle, bash down the breasts of the squabs to flatten them. Turn squabs breast side down and bash again. (This enables them to cook more evenly.)

Melt ⅓ cup of the butter in a small saucepan. Add chopped parsley, minced garlic, soy sauce and monosodium glutamate. When mixture boils, remove from heat. This is the basting liquid.

Remove broiler tray from broiler and arrange squabs on it, breast side down, wing tips turned to the back. Preheat broiler for about 20 minutes. Brush squabs with basting liquid and place in preheated broiler as far from heat as possible. Turn heat low and place squabs into broiler, as far as possible from the flame. Broil about 20 minutes, brushing once more with basting liquid. Turn the squabs over so that breasts are now facing the heat. Increase heat slightly. Brush breasts with basting liquid. Continue to broil only until the squabs are a rich golden brown, about 5 more minutes.

While the squabs are broiling, sauté the livers in a tablespoon or 2 of butter, cooking them only till they lose their pink quality in the centers. Season livers with salt, pepper, a tiny bit of monosodium glutamate and the cognac. Remove from pan and mash livers with a fork till they are a paste.

In a skillet, melt all the remaining butter. Place slices of French bread into melted butter and sauté on both sides until golden brown. Remove from the skillet and keep warm.

Just before serving, spread the sautéed bread slices with the prepared liver paste. Place a squab on top of each piece of bread and serve. By all means, do not hesitate to use your fingers to help you extract every bit of delicious meat from the tiny bones.

This method of cooking squab may be used to cook squab chickens, which are about the same size. The cooking time should be increased by a few minutes, although not on the breast side, since, as you already know, chicken breasts dry very quickly.

ROYAL SQUAB CHICKENS

This is one of the few recipes in which I recommend using whole chickens instead of the parts. It is a little complicated to prepare, but well worth the effort.

6 *squab chickens, or squabs*
½ *cup Madeira*
2 *tablespoons Japanese soy sauce*
½ *teaspoon each: cinnamon, allspice and ginger*
salt and freshly ground pepper
1 *teaspoon monosodium glutamate*
3 *slices boiled ham, cut in halves*
6 *Crepes*
6 *tablespoons Duxelles*
3 *tablespoons chopped parsley*
6 *slices of bacon*

Bone squab chickens by making an incision down the center of the breasts. Using your fingers and a sharp knife, pull and scrape meat from bones. Do not attempt to bone wings or legs. Leave them intact. When you get to these parts, cut through joints, leaving them on the chicken. Perhaps your butcher will do this job for you, if you explain what is necessary. Bone the chickens (or have it done) the day before you will be cooking them.

Combine Madeira, soy sauce, spices, salt, pepper and monosodium glutamate in a large, flat dish. Add boned chickens to this marinade, spooning the marinade over all parts of the chickens. Place in refrigerator overnight.

In the morning, remove the chickens from the marinade, preserving the marinade for the sauce. Place chickens flat, skin side down, on wax paper. Place on each opened chicken a piece of boiled ham and a Crepe. Spread each Crepe with 1 tablespoon of Duxelles. Sprinkle with a little chopped parsley.

Tightly roll both sides of the breasts inward, toward the center, so that the breasts are inside and meet in the center. Take a piece of bacon for each chicken and wind it around, starting at one end and ending at the other, to hold chicken in shape.

Refrigerate until needed. Roast chickens on a rack in a 500 degree oven for 20 minutes, then transfer to a warm platter. Keep in a warm oven while the sauce is being prepared.

Sauce

1 cup beef gravy (see page 53)
1 1/2 cups chicken stock
2 teaspoons apricot jam
1 tablespoon Duxelles (page 21)
2/3 cup heavy cream
1/2 cup chopped parsley
pan drippings
marinade from chicken

Combine all ingredients in a saucepan. Boil over high heat until liquid is reduced and of sauce consistency. Spoon this over the chickens. Sprinkle with chopped parsley, and serve at once. Serves 6.

PAN-FRIED DUCKLING

There are many recipes which use duckling, but few as simple and satisfactory as this one.

salt and pepper
2 teaspoons monosodium glutamate
1 tablespoon soy sauce
1 tablespoon sherry
5- to 6-pound duckling, cut up for frying

In a small bowl, combine salt and pepper, monosodium glutamate, soy sauce and sherry. Rub this mixture into both sides of the pieces of duckling.

Place the duckling pieces in a large ungreased skillet, skin side

(continued on the next page)

down. Cover the skillet and place over a medium flame for 20 minutes.

Turn pieces of duckling over and cook, covered, 20 minutes more. Turn the pieces again so that the skin side is down. Cook *uncovered* for a final 20 minutes. Serve hot or cold. This method of preparation ensures a very crisp bird. Serves 4.

HOW TO BONE A TURKEY

Boning a turkey isn't difficult, but it can be a little frightening if you are doing it for the first time. You might want to experiment first with a chicken. In fact, the same method applies to boning all poultry.

The thing to remember when boning any poultry is not to panic. There is a point when it looks like a shapeless mass. It is important to continue right along, scraping the meat from the bones methodically, until the carcass (which is good for soup) is completely free of meat.

With a boning knife (see illustration—it must be very sharp, with a blade approximately 5 to 6 inches long), cut off the first 2 joints of each wing bone, leaving the third bone on each side attached to the turkey. Cut off the triangular "behind" of turkey.

Turn turkey so that the breast is down. With the knife, make an incision down the back of turkey, cutting through to the bone. On one side of incision, slip knife under skin and flesh and cut and scrape flesh away from the bones. When you get to the wing bone, cut meat free from end of bone which is attached to the carcass of the turkey, detach bone from carcass and scrape meat downward toward the outer end of bone. Then, cut around the other end of wing bone, scraping upward, until the meat is completely free. Then, from the inside end of bone, draw out the entire bone.

Keeping the knife as close to the bones as possible, cut and scrape one side of breast meat free, up to the top (sharp edge) of the breast bone.

You are now ready to remove the bones from the thigh and drumstick from one side. Working in the inside of the turkey, cut and scrape meat free from thigh bone, working downward toward drumstick.

Detach bone from carcass. Continue to push meat down on thigh bone until you reach the joint connecting the thigh bone and drumstick. Cut through joint and remove thigh bone. Beginning at upper end of drumstick bone, push and scrape meat down toward lower tip.

Then, cut around lower tip of drumstick, right through to the bone. This may be a little difficult because many turkeys have strong tendons in the drumsticks. When you have completely cut through flesh and tendons, and scraped drumstick upward until it is free of flesh, draw out the entire bone from the upper end. Remove tendons from boned drumstick by holding on to the protruding ends of them with paper towels and scraping the meat free, while pulling at the tendons at the same time.

Repeat the entire procedure on the other side of the turkey, starting at the back. You will have a turkey completely free of bones.

If desired, the entire wings and the drumsticks may be left on the turkey. The thigh should be boned, however. In this case the turkey may be sewed up the back and at one end, losely filled with a stuffing of your choice, sewed completely, and then trussed for roasting. The turkey is roasted as usual, although you should be more careful than ever not to overcook it. During the roasting, the turkey will swell and will look almost the same as an unboned turkey.

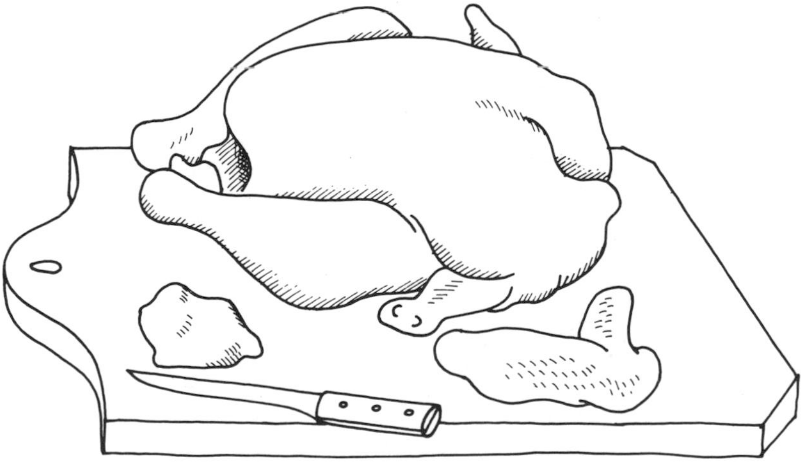

1. Turkey ready for boning, with first two joints of wing bone and triangular tail piece removed

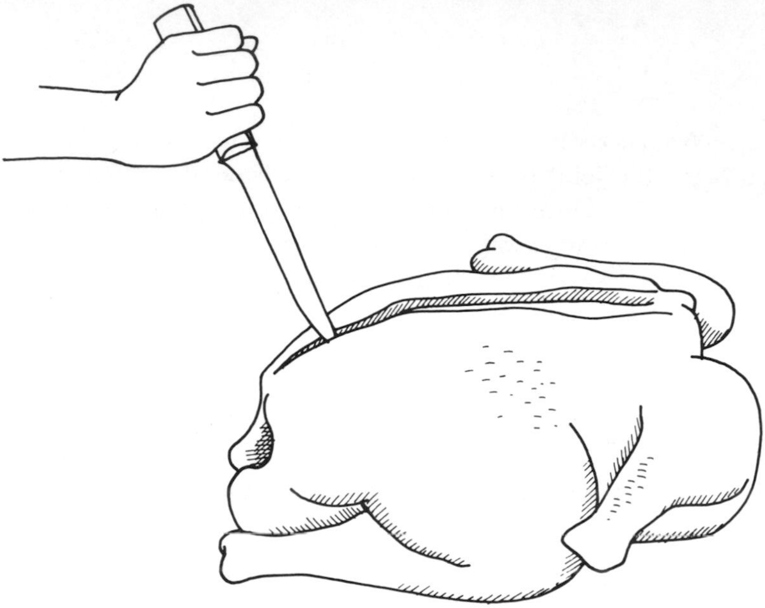

2. Making an incision down the back of the turkey with sharp boning knife

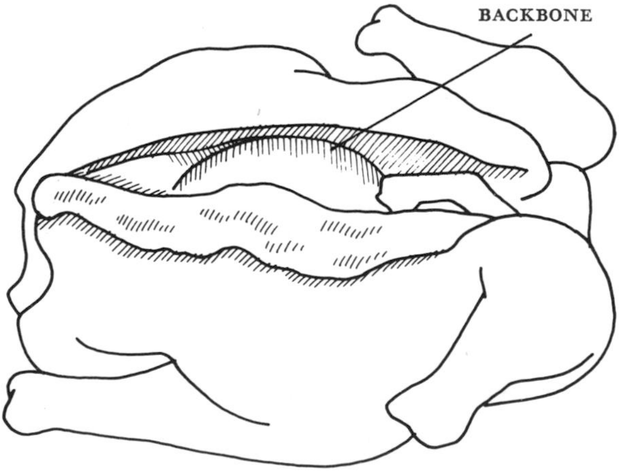

3. Meat partially scraped away from carcass, working down from backbone

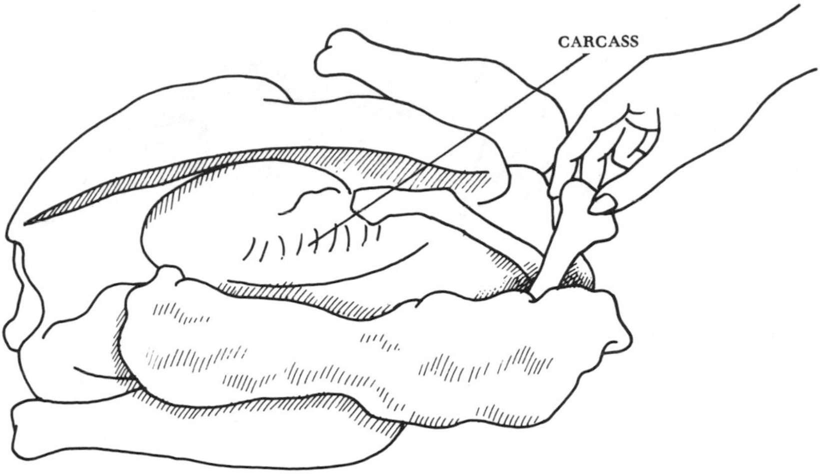

4. Wing bone, detached from carcass, is partially freed from surrounding flesh

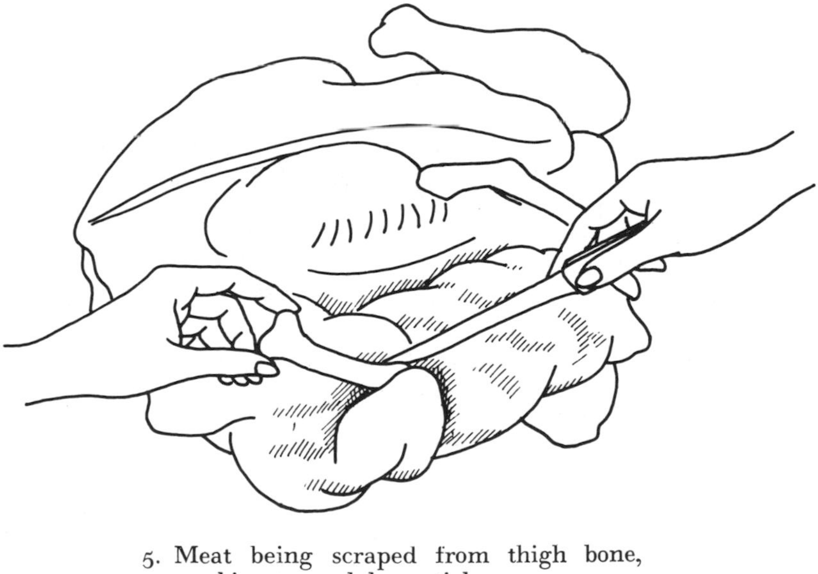

5. Meat being scraped from thigh bone, working toward drumstick

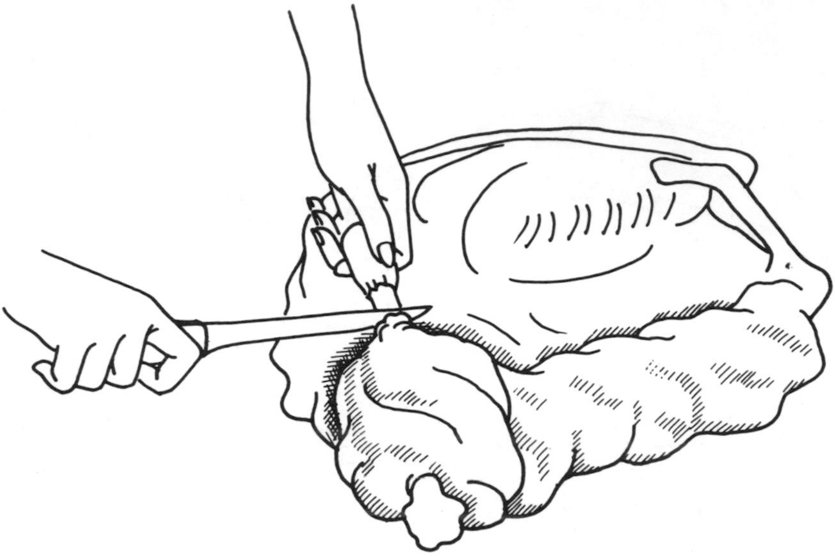

6. Second stage of boning drumstick: pushing flesh up from lower tip of drumstick

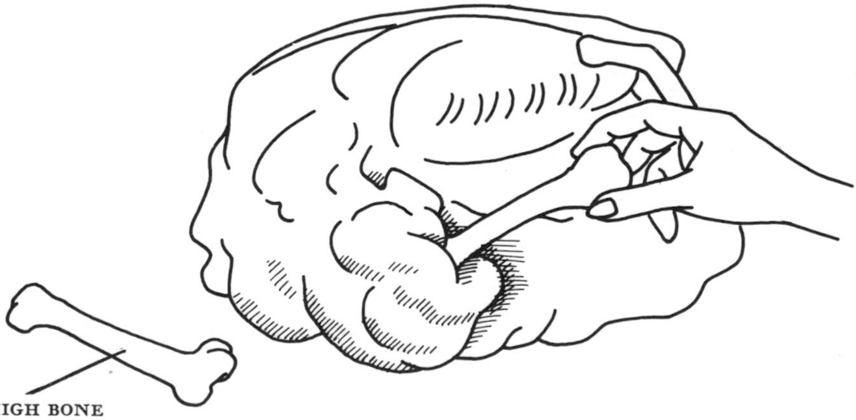

7. Removing drumstick, held at end that was attached to thigh bone

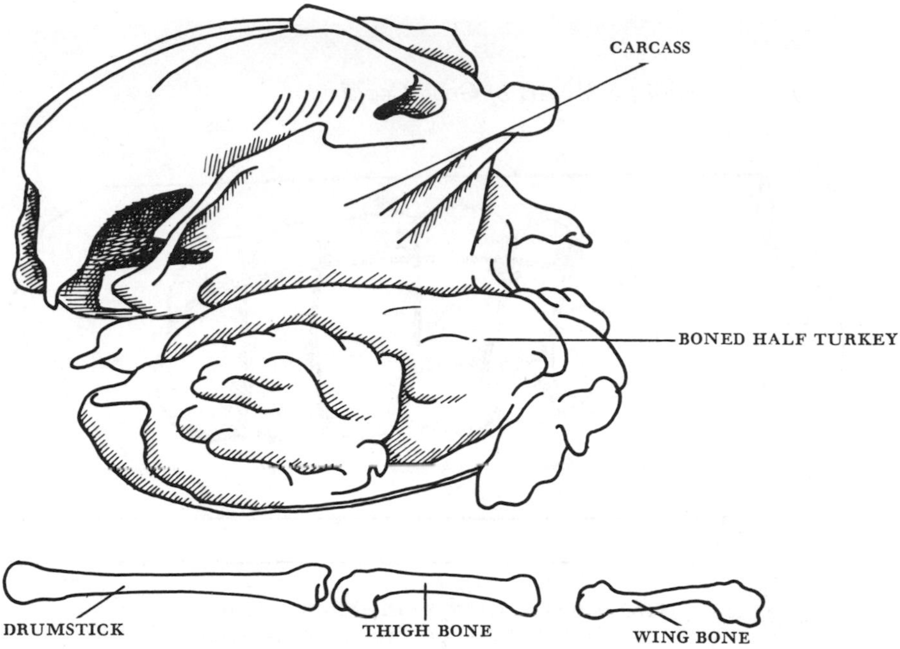

8. Turkey half boned, carcass exposed from backbone to breast bone

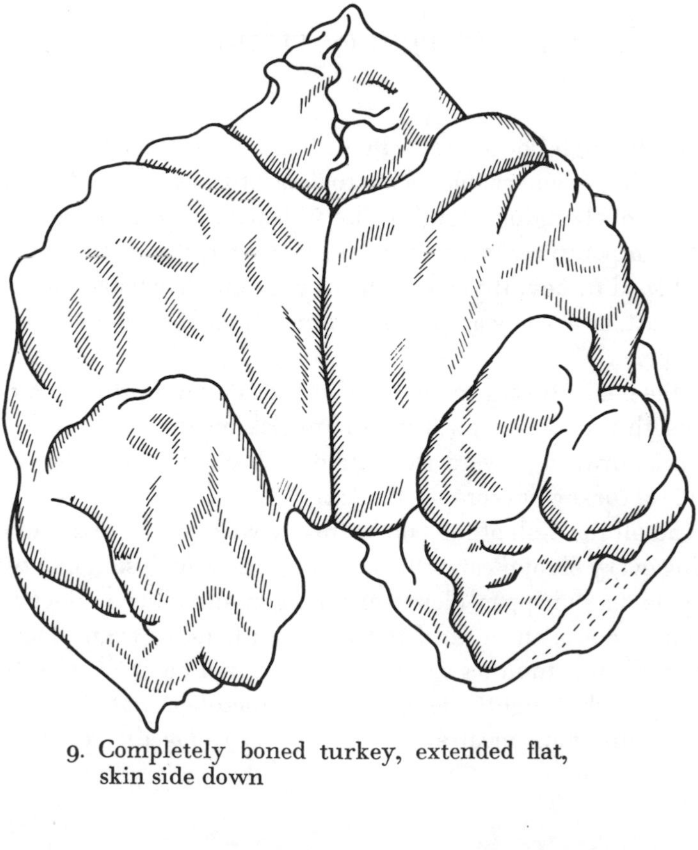

9. Completely boned turkey, extended flat, skin side down

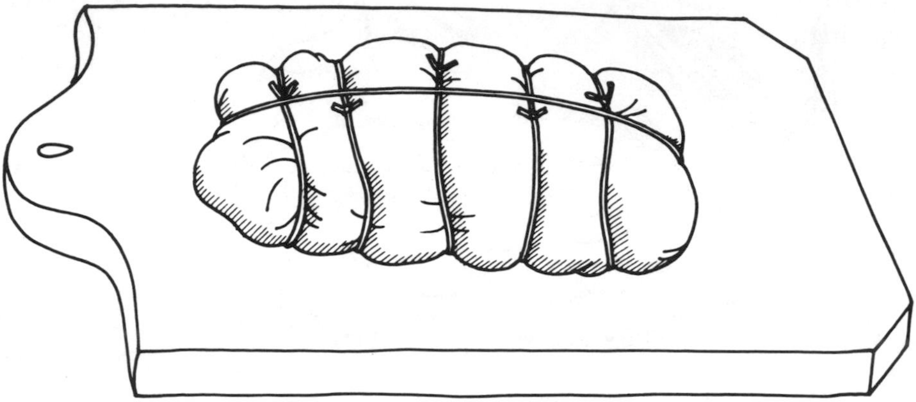

10. Boned turkey, rolled and tied (and stuffed, if desired), ready for roasting

BONED BUTTERED TURKEY

Turkey, although not my favorite of birds, is very popular at parties. Jim Beard has a remarkable recipe for roast turkey, which I have taken the liberty of changing slightly. The finished bird is good either hot or at room temperature. It is never dry. However, it is necessary to start with a boned turkey. If you can, have your butcher bone your turkey. If you must, or if you want to do it yourself, see instructions preceding this recipe.

Lay the boned turkey open flat, skin side down. Putting your hands underneath the turkey, push the drumstick meat as well as the wing-bone meat inward, toward the boned flesh of the turkey, so that the skin side of turkey lies completely flat.

Spread all the flesh of the boned turkey with plenty of sweet butter, covering every bit of meat with butter. Sprinkle with salt, monosodium glutamate, fresh pepper, plenty of tarragon and a little minced garlic. Chill on a cooky sheet until the butter is firm, or even place in the freezer for a few minutes so that the meat will be easier to roll up.

Roll up turkey tightly lengthwise (remember that the drumstick meat and the wing meat are on the inside). Tie the roll in several places so that it makes a nice compact roast. Weigh boned turkey before placing in oven. Allow about 15 to 20 minutes per pound. Roast in a 350 degree oven, basting with melted butter to begin with, then with pan drippings. The turkey should be golden brown when it is cooked.

ROAST TURKEY

To roast a regular turkey—perhaps for Thanksgiving—a good method is to rub it inside and outside with plenty of butter. Or make a good rich stuffing for the inside, and butter only the outside. Tie a piece of salt pork over the breast and be sure that the bird itself is well trussed: the legs tied together close to the breast, the wing tips turned over so that the wings themselves are firm against the carcass.

Place the turkey, breast *down*, on a roasting rack. Roast in a 325 degree oven until golden brown, basting frequently with the pan juices. The total roasting time for a 15-pound turkey should be no more than 2½ hours. Longer roasting will result in a dry, tasteless bird.

When the turkey is golden brown and almost done, turn it over so that the breast is up. This is most easily accomplished by picking up the turkey with two clean dish towels. Raise oven heat to 350. Continue to roast, basting often, until the breast is just golden. Turn off oven heat. Allow turkey to stand about 20 minutes before carving. If you are making Giblet Gravy (page 53), add pan drippings to it.

8. VEGETABLES

COOKING VEGETABLES PROPERLY calls for some technique. In France, green vegetables are first blanched in a great deal of boiling water for 3 or 4 minutes, then rinsed in very cold water. This preliminary preparation presumably sets the green color. Next, the vegetables are sautéed, creamed or flavored in a special manner, which makes them very good to eat.

My method with vegetables is easy and somewhat different. It doesn't guarantee that bright green color, unless you are very careful not to overcook the vegetables. However, the way I describe gives delicious results, without the loss of nutrients which inevitably takes place with all that blanching and rinsing.

First, you need a heavy pot with a tight cover. Enameled ironware is a good choice. The simplest, most basic preparation is to cook the vegetable in a butter (or olive oil) sauce. Cut the vegetable (unless it is peas, Brussels sprouts or fresh limas) into bite-size pieces, and place in a heavy pot. For 2½ cups of raw vegetable, add ⅓ to ½ cup of sweet butter or oil. Season with salt, a touch of sugar and ½ teaspoon monosodium glutamate. Pour about ½ cup stock (canned, if necessary) into the pot. A little diced onion or minced garlic may be added if you like (particularly if the fat is olive oil). Cover the pot tightly; bring to a boil over medium high heat. If the pieces of vegetable are fairly large, lower the heat until the vegetable has steamed tender. If the vegetable is peas, or something which has been cut into very small pieces, keep the heat fairly high so that the vegetable becomes tender and the stock cooks away at the same time. In either case, you should, at the end, have vegetables in butter or olive oil—the stock having evaporated. It may be necessary to practice a bit to perfect this technique for cooking vegetables. If you find that your vegetables are becoming soft and that a lot of liquid remains in the pot, turn the heat up very high and remove lid so the liquid can evaporate.

If you have any Concentrate of Chicken or Beef, a spoonful or 2 stirred in at the end adds good, rich flavor. Always sprinkle the cooked vegetables with plenty of chopped parsley before serving.

The best way to cook frozen vegetables is to thaw them a little, and place in a heavy pot with a good-size piece of butter, or some olive oil, and salt, sugar and monosodium glutamate. Proceed as for fresh vegetables. The heat under frozen vegetables should be kept high, however. Do not add any extra liquid. By the time the liquid has evaporated from the frozen vegetables, they should be cooked. If you don't overcook them, they will keep their color. Again, serve with chopped parsley.

BRAISED VEGETABLES

Braising is a topnotch method for cooking vegetables. Use it for almost any vegetable, but particularly for lettuce, celery hearts, leeks, endive, fennel, or Brussels sprouts.

The principle is simple: Place the trimmed, raw vegetable in a heavy saucepan with a little hot fat— butter, bacon fat or olive oil. Toss the vegetable in the fat (gently, so that it is not broken), until the outer parts are lightly browned. Then add enough stock to come about a quarter of the way up the vegetable. Place the pan over fairly high heat and cover tightly. Cook until the vegetable is tender. In the course of cooking, the stock should reduce and make a rich sauce for the vegetable. Sprinkle generously with chopped parsley, and serve.

CHICORY IN EGG AND LEMON SAUCE

½ cup butter
2 cloves garlic, minced
1 large bunch scallions, cut into 1" lengths
1½ pounds curly chicory, washed, dried and cut coarsely
⅔ cup chicken stock
juice of 2 lemons
grated rind of 1 lemon

½ teaspoon sugar
1 teaspoon monosodium glutamate
salt and pepper
½ teaspoon oregano
1 teaspoon cornstarch
2 whole eggs, lightly beaten
2 tablespoons chopped dill

Melt butter in a heavy saucepan, and add minced garlic and scallions. Sauté until soft, but not brown; then stir in coarsely chopped chicory. Stir until greens are coated with butter. Add chicken stock, lemon juice and rind, sugar, monosodium glutamate, salt and pepper. Cook over a brisk flame until liquid is reduced to less than half. Add oregano.

Remove from heat. Stir a little of pan liquid into cornstarch. Then stir cornstarch mixture back into pot. Cook over low heat, stirring constantly until mixture thickens slightly. Stir some of the slightly thickened liquid into the eggs, then stir egg mixture back into pot, being sure to stir constantly. Keep heat low. Mixture should just coat the vegetables; it should neither be too thick nor too thin. Sprinkle with chopped dill, and serve at once. Serves 6.

OTHER VEGETABLES IN EGG AND LEMON SAUCE

The inspiration for this preparation is the Middle East. Almost any vegetable is good prepared in this style. Green beans are especially flavorful, as are broccoli and the leafier vegetables such as lettuce and endive.

You begin by following the recipe for Braised Vegetables (page 279). The difference is that you cook over a low heat after stock is added so that the stock will not cook away. In addition to the stock, add the juice of 1 or 2 lemons, as well as the grated rind of 1 lemon.

When the vegetable is tender to your taste—and while there is still enough liquid to almost cover the vegetable—mix 1 tablespoon cornstarch with just a little of the liquid from the pot. Then stir the cornstarch mixture into the pot. Cook over very low heat until the cornstarch has just thickened the liquid.

Now, take 2 whole eggs which have been lightly beaten. Stir a little of the hot liquid into the eggs, then stir the egg mixture back into the pot. If the sauce around the vegetables doesn't thicken a little more almost at once, keep stirring the mixture over very low heat until the vegetables are surrounded by a very delicate, light yellow, slightly thickened sauce. Sprinkle with chopped dill or parsley before serving.

PUNJABI VEGETABLE CURRY

½ cup clarified butter
¼ cup mustard seeds
1 green pepper, chopped
2 onions, chopped
4 cloves garlic, minced
1 tablespoon grated fresh ginger
5 tablespoons curry powder
cayenne pepper to taste
salt and coarsely ground pepper
½ teaspoon sugar
1 small cauliflower, cut into flowerettes
2 potatoes, peeled and diced
⅓ cup stock
½ cup tomato purée
½ pound fresh cut green beans, or 1 package frozen cut green beans, partially thawed
1 package frozen tiny peas, partially thawed
juice of 1 lemon
¼ cup chopped cilantro (optional)
¼ cup grated coconut

Heat clarified butter in a deep pot, and add mustard seeds. Cover pot and allow seeds to pop and turn dark. Remove lid from pot; lower heat. Stir in green pepper, onions, garlic and ginger, and sauté until

(*continued on the next page*)

tender. Stir in curry powder, a little cayenne, salt and pepper and sugar. Add cauliflower and diced potatoes and toss in spicy mixture. Add stock and tomato purée.

Cover pot and simmer over low heat until cauliflower and potatoes are almost tender. Add green beans, then peas. Continue to cook until all vegetables are tender. If necessary, turn heat up high near the end of the cooking—there should not be too much sauce surrounding vegetables. Add lemon juice. Taste for seasoning and correct, if necessary.

Just before serving, sprinkle with chopped cilantro and grated coconut. Serve with Fluffy, Steamed Rice.

VEGETABLE FRITTO MISTO

This is a unique way of serving vegetables to vegetarians, or to cocktail party guests. You can turn this into a complete meal for non-vegetarians by adding blanched sweetbreads or brains to the mixture being fried. Chicken livers also are good, as are various seafoods. These need only be dipped in batter, fried and served.

Almost any vegetable may be used for Vegetable Fritto Misto. The usual ones are peeled, diced eggplant; cauliflower flowerettes; celery root slices; strips of pepper; artichoke hearts; onion slices; broccoli; spinach leaves, and green beans. Green beans should be left whole.

The harder vegetables, such as cauliflower, celery root, broccoli and artichoke hearts should be parboiled for a few minutes so that they lose their initial toughness.

First make the following batter:

2½ *cups sifted flour*
1 *teaspoon baking powder*
1 *teaspoon salt*
1 *cup white wine or beer (approximately)*

Sift flour, baking powder and salt together, then stir in wine or beer. This should make a batter thick enough to coat anything dipped into it.

Use a deep pot. Heat 2 or 3 inches of oil to 375 degrees. With a fork, dip each piece of vegetable into the batter until the vegetable is completely coated. Place batter-coated vegetable into hot fat, and fry, turning once, until the pieces of vegetable are golden brown all over. Drain on paper towels and serve at once.

SAUTEED APPLES WITH RED CABBAGE

4 *pounds hard, tart cooking apples (preferably greenings)*
1 *cup butter*
1 *tablespoon sugar*
grated rind of 1 *lemon*
4 *pounds red cabbage, coarsely shredded*
1/4 *cup dry red wine*
salt to taste

Peel and core apples, and chop coarsely. Melt half of butter in a large skillet. Add apples, and sprinkle with sugar and lemon rind. Sauté apples over medium heat, turning with a spatula occasionally so that they become lightly golden and soft but not mushy.

While apples are cooking, melt remaining butter in a large heavy saucepan. Add shredded cabbage and stir to distribute butter through cabbage. Add wine, cover pot tightly, and cook over high heat till cabbage is tender and liquid has evaporated, about 10 minutes. If liquid has not evaporated, turn heat up very high and cook uncovered a few more minutes.

Season cabbage to taste with salt.

Combine sautéed apples with cabbage by tossing together lightly.

All of this may be prepared ahead of time, placed in a casserole, and reheated in the oven at serving time. Serves 8 to 10.

CABBAGE CUSTARD

1 *cup butter*
6 *cups shredded cabbage*
5 *eggs*
2 *cups heavy cream*
1 *teaspoon nutmeg*
salt and pepper
1 *teaspoon monosodium glutamate*

Melt butter in a heavy skillet, then add cabbage. Cook over medium heat, tossing cabbage frequently, until the cabbage is tender and golden.

Beat eggs until they are frothy; stir in cream. Season with nutmeg, salt, pepper and monosodium glutamate.

Arrange sautéed cabbage in an even layer in unbaked, unsweetened tart shell. Pour egg mixture into shell. Bake for approximately 45 minutes in a 350 degree oven—or until custard is set and lightly browned. When the pastry is golden and the custard set, serve at once as a vegetable, or as a first course.

Instead of a tart shell, a shallow baking dish may be used. Place the dish containing the sautéed cabbage and the egg mixture in a pan of hot water in a 350 degree oven. Bake about 45 minutes.

Serves 6.

POLISH SWEET-SOUR CABBAGE

6 *cups cabbage, finely shredded*
½ *cup stock*
2 *green apples, peeled, cored and chopped*
salt, sugar and pepper to taste
1 *teaspoon monosodium glutamate*
4 *strips bacon, or (preferably) unsalted pork fat*
1 *tablespoon flour*

Place cabbage into pot with stock. Add chopped apples, and cook, covered, over fairly low heat, until half cooked. Stir in salt, sugar, pepper and monosodium glutamate.

Render bacon or pork fat. Chop crisp bacon or cracklings fine. Stir flour into remaining fat and cook over low heat for a few minutes, stirring constantly. Add this mixture to cabbage. Continue to cook cabbage until its liquid has thickened. Stir in crisp bacon or cracklings. Serve hot. Serves 6.

CABBAGE IN WHITE WINE

½ *cup butter*
6 *cups cabbage, finely shredded*
salt and pepper
1 *teaspoon monosodium glutamate*
½ *teaspoon sugar*
1 *to* 2 *cups white wine*

Heat butter in a skillet and add cabbage. Toss over fairly high heat. Add salt, pepper, monosodium glutamate and sugar. Add enough wine to come a third of the way up the cabbage. Raise heat and cook rapidly until wine has completely evaporated. Taste for seasoning and correct if necessary. This cabbage is especially good with pork.

Serves 6.

SAUTEED CABBAGE AND NOODLES

⅔ *cup bacon or chicken fat*
6 *cups cabbage, finely shredded*
1 *teaspoon monosodium glutamate*
salt, pepper and nutmeg to taste
½ *pound noodles, cooked*

Heat fat in a large skillet, and add cabbage. Sauté, over fairly low heat, stirring frequently, until cabbage is soft and lightly browned. Season with monosodium glutamate, salt, pepper and nutmeg.

Combine cabbage and cooked noodles, and stir gently together. Serve at once or keep warm in oven in covered casserole. Serves 6 to 8.

CAULIFLOWER POLONAISE

1 medium cauliflower, separated into small flowerettes
⅔ cup stock
1 cup butter
1 teaspoon monosodium glutamate
½ teaspoon sugar
5 slices of white bread, crusts removed and cut into tiny cubes about the size of peas
3 hard-cooked eggs, diced
½ cup chopped parsley
salt and coarsely ground pepper

Place cauliflower in a large saucepan or skillet which can be covered later. Add stock, ⅓ cup butter, monosodium glutamate and sugar. Cover pan tightly and cook over medium heat until the cauliflower is almost tender. Remove cover and continue to cook cauliflower over higher heat so that any liquid cooks away completely and cauliflower just begins to brown in fat remaining in the pan. Turn cauliflower pieces frequently.

While cauliflower is cooking, sauté bread cubes in remaining butter in a separate skillet. Turn cubes frequently to prevent them from burning. When they are evenly browned, set them aside till needed.

When cauliflower is cooked and lightly browned all over, transfer it to a serving dish. Combine the sautéed bread cubes, diced hard-cooked egg and chopped parsley, and season this mixture well with salt and pepper. Sprinkle evenly on top of cauliflower and serve at once. Serves 4 to 6.

CELERY HEARTS, PORTUGUESE STYLE

3 scallions, minced
1 clove garlic, minced
3 tablespoons olive oil

3 *cups celery hearts, cut in 1" pieces*
⅓ *cup chicken stock*
salt and pepper
1 *teaspoon monosodium glutamate*
3 *egg yolks*
¼ *cup Madeira*
1 *tablespoon chopped parsley*

Sauté scallions and garlic in olive oil until soft. Stir in celery hearts. Add chicken stock, cover, and simmer about 15 minutes, or until celery is tender. Season with salt, pepper and monosodium glutamate.

Stir egg yolks and Madeira together, then add some of hot pan liquid to yolk mixture. Now, stir yolk mixture into celery. Continue to cook over a low heat, stirring constantly, but gently, until sauce thickens. Sprinkle with chopped parsley. Serves 6.

GREEN BEANS WITH POTATOES AND BACON

2 *pounds green beans, cut in 1" pieces (or 2 packages frozen beans)*
2 *potatoes, peeled and cut into medium-small pieces*
6 *slices bacon, diced*
3 *cloves garlic, minced*
1 *onion, chopped*
¼ *cup butter*
⅓ *cup stock (¼ if frozen beans are used)*
salt and pepper
1 *teaspoon monosodium glutamate*
½ *cup chopped parsley*

Combine all ingredients except parsley in a heavy pot. Cover pot tightly, and cook over low to medium heat until liquid has cooked away and beans and potatoes are tender. Serve hot, sprinkled with chopped parsley. Serves 6.

GREEN BEANS CATALAN

4 *cups green beans, cut into 1" pieces*
¼ *cup olive oil*
1 *onion, minced*
4 *cloves garlic, minced*
1 *large tomato, peeled and chopped*
1 *small green pepper, minced*
½ *cup chopped celery and celery leaves*
¼ *cup white wine*
½ *teaspoon sugar*
1 *teaspoon monosodium glutamate*
salt and pepper
2 *tablespoons chopped parsley*
1 *hard-cooked egg, cut into eighths*
½ *cup black olives*
1 *tablespoon capers*

Place green beans in a heavy saucepan. Add olive oil, onion, garlic, tomato, green pepper, celery and wine. Season with sugar and monosodium glutamate, cover saucepan tightly and cook over medium heat until green beans are tender and very little liquid is left in pan. Add salt, pepper and chopped parsley. Transfer to hot serving plate. Garnish with hard-cooked egg wedges, olives and capers. This is also delicious cold. Serves 6.

LIMA BEANS IN LIMA CREAM

4 *cups shelled baby lima beans (or 2 packages frozen baby lima beans)*
⅔ *cup chicken stock*
¼ *cup butter*
1 *teaspoon monosodium glutamate*
1 *teaspoon celery seed*

½ teaspoon sugar
⅔ cup cream
salt and pepper to taste
2 tablespoons chopped parsley

If frozen limas are used, allow them to thaw slightly. Then proceed with recipe.

Place lima beans in a heavy pot. Add chicken stock, butter, monosodium glutamate, celery seed and sugar, and cook over medium heat until beans are tender. If there is a great deal of liquid left in pan, turn up heat at the last minute and cook uncovered until most of the liquid has evaporated. (Be careful not to scorch the beans.)

Drain beans well and keep them warm. Place any remaining liquid in blender bowl. Add a quarter of the beans, as well as the cream, to the blender. Turn on blender and mix into a fine purée. Season well with salt and pepper, and pour purée over remaining lima beans, tossing gently to distribute purée evenly. Sprinkle with chopped parsley and serve. Serves 6.

MUSHROOMS POLONAISE

1½ pounds sliced mushrooms
½ cup butter
1 onion, chopped
2 tablespoons flour
1 cup sour cream
1 cup heavy sweet cream
½ teaspoon nutmeg
salt and pepper to taste
¼ cup chopped parsley
¼ cup fresh white bread crumbs, lightly sautéed in ¼ cup melted butter

Place sliced mushrooms and onion in a heavy skillet without any fat. Cover skillet and allow vegetables to steam in their own juices until they almost stick to the pan. Add butter. When it has melted, stir in

(*continued on the next page*)

flour. Cook, stirring, for about 5 minutes, over very low heat. Blend in sour cream and sweet cream. Season with nutmeg, salt and pepper. Continue to cook, uncovered, until mixture has thickened. Stir in parsley.

Pour into a buttered, shallow casserole. Sprinkle top with bread crumbs. Bake in a 350 degree oven until mixture has set and bread crumbs have browned a little more. Serves 6.

MUSHROOMS PROVENCALE

2 *pounds mushrooms*
8 *cloves garlic, minced*
⅓ *cup chopped shallots*
¼ *cup sweet butter*
¼ *cup olive oil*
salt and pepper
1 *teaspoon monosodium glutamate*
1 *cup chopped parsley*

If mushrooms are small, trim off stems and leave them whole. If they are large, trim off stems and cut into thick slices.

Place mushrooms, garlic and shallots in a large, heavy skillet. Do not add any fat or liquid. Cover skillet and allow vegetables to steam in their own liquid until they almost stick to the pan. Stir in butter and olive oil, and season with salt, pepper and monosodium glutamate. Stir well. Stir in chopped parsley and serve at once. Serves 6.

MUSHROOMS IN MADEIRA

2 *pounds mushrooms*
½ *cup chopped shallots*
8 *cloves garlic, minced*
⅓ *cup butter*
2 *tablespoons olive oil*

½ cup Madeira
⅔ cup heavy cream, or 3 tablespoons Preserved Cream (page 29)
salt and pepper
1 teaspoon monosodium glutamate
½ cup chopped parsley

If mushrooms are small, simply trim off the stems and leave whole. If they are large, trim off stems and slice them ¼ inch thick.

Place mushrooms, shallots and garlic in a heavy skillet without any fat. Cover skillet and allow vegetables to steam in their own juices until they almost stick to the pan. Add butter and oil, and stir. Pour all but 2 tablespoons Madeira into skillet; add cream. Cook over high heat until the liquid in the pan has reduced to the consistency of a medium cream sauce.

Season with salt, pepper and monosodium glutamate, then stir in remaining Madeira and chopped parsley, and serve at once. Serves 6.

MADEIRA ONION RINGS

These are particularly good with broiled foods—especially steak.

6 large Spanish onions, sliced ¼″ thick and separated into rings
1 cup butter
1¼ cups Madeira
½ cup chopped parsley
1 teaspoon monosodium glutamate
salt and pepper to taste

Place onions in a heavy skillet without any fat or liquid. Cover skillet and let onions steam in their juices until they are dry and almost stick to the pan. Add butter and continue to sauté about 10 more minutes, uncovered. Add 1 cup Madeira. Raise heat and cook onions over a high flame until the Madeira is no more than a glaze in the pan. Stir in the rest of the Madeira, the parsley, and seasonings. Serves 6.

PEAS IN MADEIRA CREAM

4 cups very small, young peas (or 2 packages frozen petit pois, partially thawed)
1 small onion, chopped
1 cup chopped Boston lettuce
¼ cup chicken stock
1 teaspoon monosodium glutamate
¼ cup Madeira
1 cup heavy cream (or ½ cup Preserved Cream page 29)
salt and pepper
½ cup chopped parsley

Place peas in a heavy saucepan. Add onion, lettuce, chicken stock and monosodium glutamate. Cover tightly and cook over a medium heat until peas are barely tender.

Remove cover and cook over high heat until liquid has almost completely evaporated. Be careful not to scorch peas. Stir in Madeira.

While peas are cooking, boil cream in a very deep saucepan until it has reduced to ½ cup. (If you are using Preserved Cream, you do not need to boil again.) Stir thickened cream into peas and Madeira. Season with salt and pepper, stir in chopped parsley, and serve.

Serves 6.

ANGELE'S PARISIAN SPINACH

2 pounds fresh spinach (or 2 packages frozen chopped spinach)
½ cup butter
1 teaspoon monosodium glutamate
1 teaspoon salt
1 teaspoon coarsely ground pepper
4 hard-cooked eggs, sliced

Wash fresh spinach thoroughly, and place in a saucepan with just the water clinging to the leaves. Turn heat up high and cook, uncovered, tossing spinach frequently, until it is wilted. (This will take only a few minutes.)

Remove spinach from heat, place in a strainer and press out every bit of water. Then chop spinach with a sharp knife.

(If frozen chopped spinach is used, allow it to thaw slightly. Cook briefly in its own liquid and drain in the same way as for fresh spinach.)

Melt butter in a saucepan, and add chopped spinach, monosodium glutamate, salt and pepper. Stir well, then add sliced eggs. Stir gently and serve. Serves 6.

SPINACH PANCAKES

2 *packages frozen, chopped spinach, cooked until thawed out, and then very well drained*
1 *raw egg*
2 *tablespoons dry bread crumbs (approximately)*
salt and coarsely ground pepper to taste
½ *teaspoon nutmeg*
¾ *cup butter*
1 *teaspoon monosodium glutamate*
4 *hard-cooked eggs, sliced*

Mix cooked spinach with raw egg, bread crumbs, salt and pepper, nutmeg, ¼ cup of the butter (melted) and monosodium glutamate. If necessary, add more bread crumbs so the mixture may be handled easily.

Wet your hands with cold water. Taking about 2 tablespoons of the spinach mixture, shape it into a plump pancake, enclosing a slice of hard-cooked egg in the center. (This may be done ahead of time and chilled.)

To serve, melt remaining butter in a large skillet. Sauté the spinach pancakes gently on both sides until they are heated through. Serve with any butter remaining in skillet. Serves 6.

SPINACH, ORIENTAL STYLE

This dish goes especially well with grilled foods or with Oriental entrées such as Korean Meat.

2 packages frozen chopped spinach
3 tablespoons sesame seeds
2 tablespoons sesame oil (or peanut oil)
2 cloves garlic, minced
juice of ½ lemon
½ teaspoon coarsely ground pepper
½ teaspoon sugar
3 tablespoons Japanese soy sauce

Thaw spinach partially, then cook in its own liquid until it is completely thawed out. Drain very well, pressing out all the water.

While spinach is cooking, toast sesame seeds in a dry skillet, stirring frequently, until they are golden and fragrant. Remove from heat and grind up the seeds, either in a blender or in a mortar and pestle, till they are almost a powder.

Reserving about a teaspoon of sesame seed powder as a garnish, combine all ingredients. Serve at room temperature.

BRAISED TURNIPS IN MUSTARD SAUCE

½ cup butter
5 cups peeled turnips cut into 1" dice
1 cup stock
½ teaspoon sugar
salt and pepper
1 teaspoon monosodium glutamate
1 teaspoon cornstarch

3 *tablespoons Dijon mustard (approximately)*
2 *tablespoons chopped parsley*

Melt butter in a heavy pot, and when butter is hot, add raw turnips and toss. When turnips begin to sizzle, add stock, sugar, salt, pepper and monosodium glutamate. Cover, and simmer over medium heat until turnips are tender.

Remove from heat; drain turnips thoroughly and keep hot, reserving cooking liquid. Add additional salt and pepper to cooking liquid. Stir cornstarch into mustard, and stir mustard mixture into cooking liquid. This should make a creamy sauce. Stir in half of chopped parsley, and pour sauce over turnips. Toss gently, and sprinkle with remaining chopped parsley. Serves 6.

ZUCCHINI IN LEMON BUTTER

3 *pounds zucchini, cut into ½″ slices*
⅔ *cup butter*
2 *tablespoons stock*
grated rind and juice of 2 lemons
1 *teaspoon monosodium glutamate*
½ *teaspoon sugar*
salt and pepper to taste
chopped parsley

Place zucchini in a heavy pot, and add butter, stock, lemon juice and rind. Season with monosodium glutamate, sugar, salt and pepper. Cook over medium heat, covered, till steam comes from pot. Remove lid, and raise heat. Stir zucchini gently, and cook over high heat until just tender, stirring gently once or twice more to prevent sticking. There should be practically no liquid remaining in pot. Taste for seasoning and correct if necessary. Sprinkle with plenty of chopped parsley. Serve at once. Serves 6.

ZUCCHINI WITH HAM

½ cup olive oil
2½ pounds zucchini, sliced ½" thick
½ pound ham, finely diced
3 cloves garlic, minced
coarsely ground pepper
1 teaspoon monosodium glutamate
salt to taste
½ cup chopped parsley

Heat olive oil in a skillet. Add zucchini, and sauté over high heat, stirring occasionally until the zucchini begins to brown. Add ham and continue to sauté. Stir in minced garlic, lower heat, and cook mixture until zucchini are just tender but not mushy. Season with pepper, monosodium glutamate and salt. Toss gently; sprinkle with chopped parsley, and serve. Serves 6.

BAKED ZUCCHINI, ITALIAN STYLE

6 cups sliced zucchini
1 large onion, chopped
6 cloves garlic, minced
1 No. 2 can tomatoes, well drained and chopped
salt and pepper
2 teaspoons monosodium glutamate
½ teaspoon sugar
1 cup chopped parsley
1 teaspoon oregano
1 teaspoon basil
⅔ cup olive oil

Combine zucchini, onion, garlic, tomatoes, salt, pepper, monosodium glutamate, sugar, parsley, oregano and basil. Arrange in a broad, not too deep casserole, and pour olive oil over the top. Bake in a 400 degree oven about 50 minutes, or until oil is bubbling around the zucchini. Serve hot, or at room temperature. Serves 6.

SAUTEED ZUCCHINI

This recipe may be used also with halved Italian frying peppers. If there are leftover sautéed vegetables, add a bit of wine vinegar to them and serve at room temperature a day or 2 later.

- ¾ *cup olive oil (approximately)*
- 2½ *pounds zucchini, sliced ¼" thick*
- ½ *teaspoon sugar*
- 1 *onion, chopped*
- 5 *cloves garlic, minced*
- *salt and coarsely ground pepper*
- 1 *teaspoon monosodium glutamate*
- ⅔ *cup chopped parsley*

Heat olive oil in a heavy skillet, and add sliced zucchini. Sprinkle with sugar, then sauté over very high heat, turning zucchini frequently until all the slices are nicely browned.

Lower heat, add onion and garlic, and sauté over low heat until they become soft. Season with salt, pepper and monosodium glutamate. Stir in half of chopped parsley, and sprinkle with remaining chopped parsley before serving. Serves 6.

SAUTEED SWEET POTATOES AND APPLES

3 *large sweet potatoes, peeled and cut into small dice*
6 *tart, hard apples, peeled, cored and chopped*
¾ *cup butter (approximately)*
1 *teaspoon grated lemon rind*
1 *teaspoon sugar*

Sauté sweet potatoes and apples separately in large skillets, using approximately half of the butter for each. (More or less butter may be needed.) Sprinkle the apples with lemon rind and sugar. They will need less time than the sweet potatoes, so you can start them later.

Sauté sweet potatoes until they are crisp and tender all over. Sauté apples until they are lightly browned all over, but not mushy. To serve, either toss gently together or make a ring of sautéed apples around a platter and arrange sweet potatoes in a mound in the center.

Serves 6.

FAVORITE MASHED POTATOES

6 *large potatoes, peeled and diced*
salt
½ *cup soft sweet butter*
½ *cup sour cream*
white pepper

In a deep pot, cover potatoes with water. Add some salt, and bring to a boil. Lower heat and cook until potatoes are completely soft. Then pour potatoes into a colander or strainer and drain very well. Return potatoes to pan, and shake over low heat for a few moments to be sure they are completely dry.

Place potatoes in bowl of mixer or in an ordinary bowl. In mixer, beat with high speed, adding butter, sour cream, some salt and white pepper. Or, mash and beat by hand until potatoes are very fluffy. If these are not to be served at once, place in a casserole, and drop a lump of butter in the center. Cover casserole and keep in a warm oven. Do not try to keep for longer than ½ hour or so. Serves 6.

SAUTEED POTATOES, HOME STYLE

½ cup butter
2 tablespoons olive oil
6 potatoes, peeled and diced
2 onions, chopped
1 large green pepper, diced
3 cloves garlic, minced
salt and pepper
1 teaspoon monosodium glutamate
⅔ cup chopped parsley

Melt butter and olive oil together in a large, heavy skillet. When fat is hot, add the potatoes, and sauté over low heat until the potatoes are tender and lightly crisp all over. Stir in onions, green pepper and garlic. Continue to sauté over medium heat until these are soft and the potatoes are cooked a little more. Season with salt, pepper and monosodium glutamate, stir in chopped parsley, and serve while potatoes are still crisp. Serves 6.

POTATOES ANNA

This is an easy way to make Potatoes Anna: Use a large, heavy black skillet. Allow at least 1 large peeled potato per person. Slice the potatoes thin. Then, for 6 potatoes, melt ⅔ cup of butter, and pour a little

(*continued on the next page*)

of the butter in the skillet. Stack the potatoes in the skillet—and don't worry too much about the arrangement; after they are golden they will look beautiful, no matter how you have arranged them.

Pour remaining melted butter evenly over the top. Place the skillet on the lowest rack in a 450 degree oven, and bake about 1¼ hours, or a little longer at a reduced heat if you wish. When the butter bubbles around the potatoes and they begin to look golden brown on top, loosen them around the sides and bottom with a spatula. (This may not even be necessary if your skillet is well-aged.)

To serve, invert a serving plate over the skillet. Then, over the sink, flip the skillet over so that it is on top of the serving plate. The potatoes will drop onto the plate, and the excess butter can be poured off. (This may be kept and used again for sautéing, if you like.) If necessary, you may place the serving plate in a warm oven to keep hot. The potatoes will retain their crispness.

FRENCH SCALLOPED POTATOES

This can be a one-dish meal if slices of sausage (such as Polish kolbasa or knockwurst) are placed between the layers of potatoes.

3 *pounds potatoes, peeled and sliced less than ¼" thick*
salt and pepper
monosodium glutamate
nutmeg
light cream
butter

The proportions for this recipe are almost impossible to give, as so much depends on the size of the casserole, the starchiness of the potatoes, etc.

Butter a baking dish that isn't too deep. Arrange the peeled, sliced potatoes in the dish, sprinkling each layer with salt, pepper, monosodium glutamate and nutmeg, until the dish is three quarters full.

Add enough light cream to come just to the top layer, but not over it. Dot the top generously with butter.

Bake uncovered in a 250 degree oven about 1 ½ hours, or until cream has been absorbed into the potatoes and the top is golden brown. Serves 6.

FLUFFY, STEAMED RICE

Everyone seems to have a favorite method for cooking rice. I consider my own method quite perfect, since it has never failed.

For 1 cup of long-grain rice, bring to a boil, in a deep pot which may be covered later on, at least 1 ½ quarts of water well-salted with at least 1 tablespoon of salt. When water is boiling rapidly, sprinkle in the rice. Keeping the heat high, stir rice occasionally until water begins to boil again. When the water is again boiling rapidly, it will not be necessary to stir any more. After about 8 minutes, taste a grain of rice. If it is still slightly firm, but more than half cooked, remove pot from stove.

Pour rice into a colander, and rinse rice with hot water. Let water drain off, then return rice to the pot, sprinkling it in lightly so that it doesn't pack down.

Cover the pot tightly and return pot to very low heat, or place in a 300 degree oven. Rice will steam tender in the moisture surrounding it. This will take about 20 to 35 minutes (longer in the oven than on top of the stove). The very bottom layer of rice will stick to the pan, but the rest of the rice will be very light and fluffy.

One cup of raw rice makes about three cups of cooked rice, or approximately three to four servings.

PERSIAN RICE I

To make delicious Persian Rice, follow the above recipe for Fluffy, Steamed Rice to the point of rinsing and draining the rice. While rice is draining, place in the bottom of the pot rice was cooked in 2 raw, peeled potatoes, cut into thin slices, and a chopped onion. Sprinkle rice on top of potato and onion, then pour 1 cup of melted butter over rice. The butter will drip down into the onion and potatoes.

Cover pot with a clean, folded cloth, then with the lid, tightly. Place pot over low heat on top of the stove for at least an hour. The potatoes and onions will form a crisp layer in the bottom of the pot and the rice will steam tender.

Fifteen minutes before this dish is completed, you may add some blanched, sliced almonds which have been sautéed till golden in a little extra butter, as well as some yellow raisins. Uncover pot and sprinkle this mixture over the rice. Do not stir in until last minute, and then do it very gently, adding salt as well, and being careful not to disturb the bottom layer of onions and potatoes.

To serve, scoop up rice, and add a little of the crisp bottom layer. This dish is a true delicacy.

PERSIAN RICE II

You can make Persian rice without the onion and potato. Simply follow the preceding recipe, but omit the potato and onion. The bottom layer of the rice itself will become crisp and a little should be added to each serving.

MEXICAN-STYLE RICE

4 *tablespoons lard*
1 *cup long-grain rice*
1 *teaspoon ground cumin seed*
½ *green pepper, diced*
2 *cloves garlic, minced*
1 *small onion, chopped*
2 *teaspoons salt*
1 *tomato, chopped*
2 *cups stock*

Heat lard in a heavy pot which may be covered tightly. Add rice and sauté over low heat, stirring occasionally, for about 5 minutes. Stir in cumin seed, green pepper, garlic, onion and salt, and continue to sauté until the vegetables are tender, then stir in chopped tomato. As soon as tomato appears wilted, pour in stock, all at once.

Cover pot, and place in a 350 degree oven for about 20 minutes. Uncover pot. Most of the liquid will have been absorbed. Reduce oven heat to 300 and allow rice to remain in oven about 15 minutes longer. At this point, the liquid will be entirely absorbed and the rice quite dry. Toss rice lightly with a fork. Serves 4 to 5.

RICE PANCAKES

These pancakes should be made with leftover rice. They are excellent served for breakfast with bacon and syrup. Or you can add bits of meat to the recipe and make them into a main course or side dish.

For each cup of cooked rice, use a medium-size egg. Beat egg lightly and stir into rice. Season as you please—a bit of curry powder is good occasionally, or chili, or bits of sausage. Be sure to add salt and pepper.

Heat bacon fat to a depth of ¼ inch in a large skillet. Drop spoon-

(*continued on the next page*)

fuls of the rice batter into the fat, leaving a little space between spoonfuls. Flatten the spoonfuls of rice batter. Fry, on both sides, until the pancakes are crisp and a nice golden brown. Serve at once.

VEGETABLE RISOTTO

4 *tablespoons butter*
4 *slices bacon, diced*
2 *tablespoons olive oil*
1 *onion, chopped*
3 *cloves garlic, minced*
2 *potatoes, peeled and diced*
2 *carrots, scraped and diced*
3 *zucchini, sliced*
2 *cups shredded cabbage*
1 *package frozen cut green beans, thawed and drained*
2 *cups long-grain rice*
3½ *to* 4 *cups stock, or a mixture of stock and tomato juice*
2 *teaspoons monosodium glutamate*
½ *teaspoon sugar*
salt and pepper
¼ *cup grated Parmesan cheese*

Combine butter, bacon and olive oil in a deep, heavy pot. When they are hot, and the bacon is sizzling, add the onion, garlic, and all the vegetables. Sauté over high heat about 10 minutes, stirring occasionally. When vegetables have wilted, stir in the dry rice. Continue to sauté for a few minutes longer. Then add 3 cups of liquid (stock, tomato juice, or any combination), along with the monosodium glutamate, sugar and a good amount of salt and pepper.

Place in a 350 degree oven, uncovered, and allow to simmer until liquid is almost absorbed. Add a little more liquid, and continue to cook, uncovered, until rice and vegetables are tender. A bit more, or less, liquid may be needed.

Before serving, sprinkle with Parmesan cheese. Serves 6 to 8.

BLACK BEANS IN GARLIC SAUCE

2 *cups black beans*
1 *to* 2 *heads of garlic, separated into cloves, peeled and minced*
⅓ *pound bacon, minced*
1 *teaspoon cumin*
1 *tablespoon salt*
1 *teaspoon monosodium glutamate*
coarsely ground pepper

Wash beans, and soak overnight in water to cover. In the morning, place in a deep pot, and add enough additional water to cover beans. Add a little of the garlic. Bring to a boil, lower heat and simmer until beans are completely tender. Drain beans, reserving some of liquid for later use. Keep beans warm.

Cook bacon in a skillet over low heat until it is just crisp. Remove bacon, crumble and reserve. Add remaining garlic to bacon fat and sauté, over low heat, until it is soft.

Place beans in a casserole. Stir in crisp bacon, sautéed garlic, remaining bacon fat, cumin, salt, monosodium glutamate and pepper. Add about ¾ cup of the liquid from the beans, and place in a 325 degree oven. Bake, covered, about 1 hour. Serve hot. Serves 6.

WHITE BEANS
(To Serve with Roast Leg of Lamb)

½ *cup diced lamb fat* (*trimmed from leg of lamb*)
1 *onion, diced*
4 *cloves garlic, minced*
2 *No.* 2 *cans white beans drained and rinsed with hot water in a colander*
3 *tablespoons tomato purée*
⅔ *cup stock* (*preferably unthickened lamb sauce, page* 52)

(*continued on the next page*)

½ teaspoon monosodium glutamate
salt and pepper
½ cup chopped parsley

Place diced fat in a heavy saucepan over a low flame. Cook till the bits of fat are crisp, then add diced onion and garlic. Sauté until onion and garlic are soft.

Drain beans into a colander and rinse with hot water until all of the packing liquid has been drained away. Drain beans well and add to saucepan.

Add tomato purée, stock, monosodium glutamate, salt and pepper to taste. Simmer over low heat about 15 minutes, adding more stock if necessary. The bean mixture should not be thick.

Stir in chopped parsley, and serve with roast leg of lamb. Serves 6.

REFRIED BEANS

This is the perfect accompaniment to any Mexican dish.

3 *No. 2 cans pinto or kidney beans*
⅔ cup lard or bacon fat (approximately)
2 *tablespoons chili powder*
salt and pepper
1 *teaspoon monosodium glutamate*
grated Parmesan cheese
1 *small onion, chopped*

Empty cans into a strainer, and run hot water over beans until all the packing liquid has been rinsed away. Drain beans well.

Heat half of the fat in a large skillet. Add beans. When they are hot, begin to mash and stir them in the fat until they almost form a purée. Season with chili powder, salt, pepper and monosodium glutamate, and continue to cook over low heat, adding a little more fat from time to time. The longer the beans cook, the more fat they will need. Mash and stir as beans cook.

Just before serving, sprinkle with grated Parmesan cheese and chopped raw onion. Serves 6.

REFRIED BEAN CAKES

1 *recipe Refried Beans (above)*
½ *cup grated Parmesan cheese*
1 *cup finely chopped onions*
6 *pieces Jack or mozzarella cheese, each* 1″ *x* 1″ *x* ½″
¾ *cup dry bread crumbs*
lard for sautéing

Add grated cheese and chopped onions to Refried Beans. Refrigerate till cold. Then divide mixture into 6 parts. Shape each part into a patty, pushing a piece of cheese into the center of each. Roll each bean cake in dry bread crumbs, then refrigerate 1 hour or more.

Heat enough lard to cover the bottom of a skillet to a depth of ¼ inch. Sauté bean cakes in hot lard, turning to brown both sides and heat through. Serves 6.

9. MARINATED VEGETABLES AND SALADS

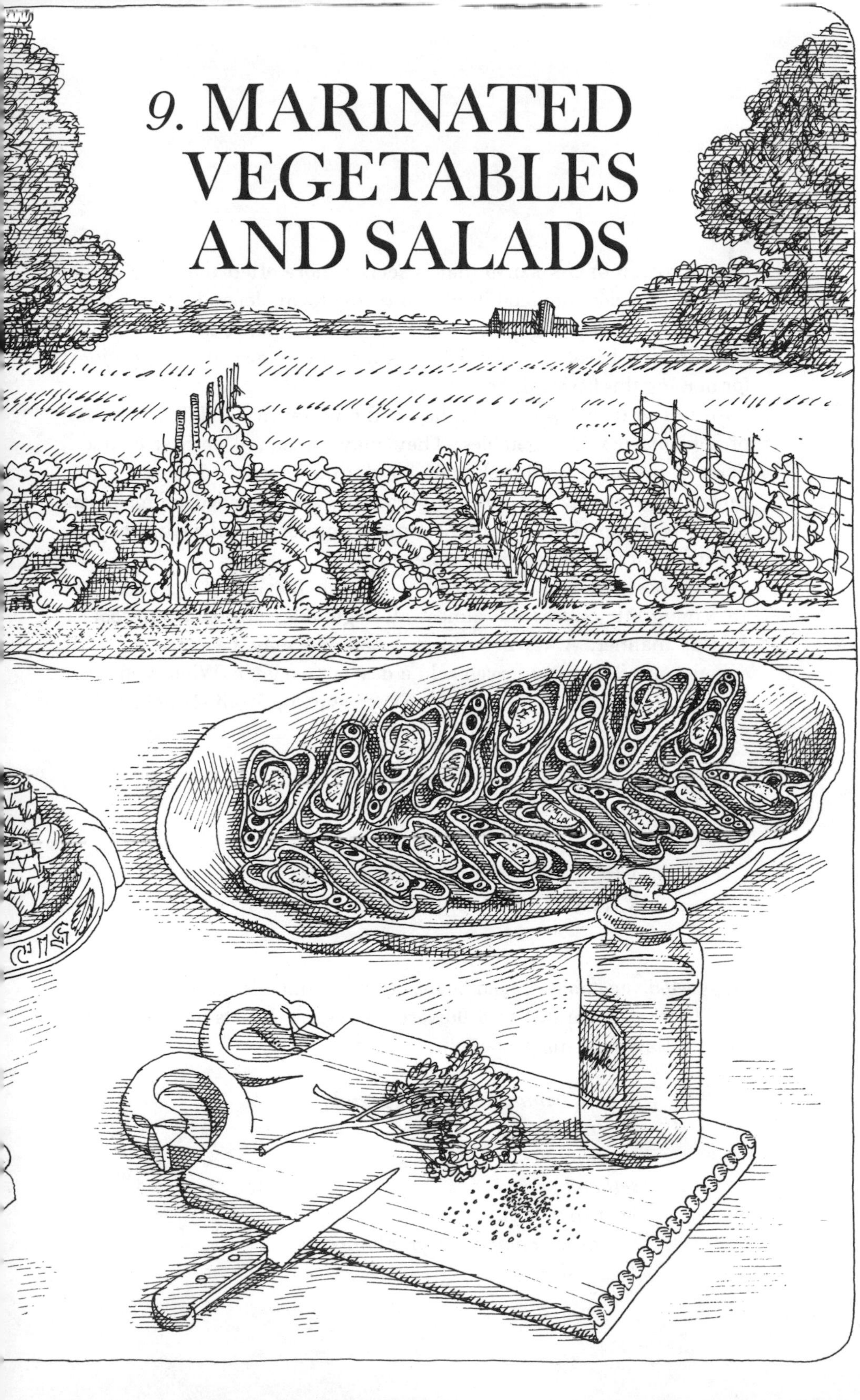

THE TOSSED GREEN SALAD that is served more often than any other type of salad does not lend itself to a recipe form, depending as it does on the availability of greens and the cook's imagination. It is a subject about which I feel strongly. I have stated my views and suggestions for making this basic salad on page 24.

In this chapter I wish to emphasize the versatility and deliciousness of cold marinated vegetables. They may be served as first courses, Some of the salads in this chapter, combining marinated cooked vegetables with greens and other ingredients, are intended as meals in themselves, especially in summertime. Many of the salads in Chapter 2, First Courses, can serve the same purpose.

The most common method of preparing marinated vegetables is in Vinaigrette Sauce, and almost all vegetables are delicious cooked in this manner. A warm leftover vegetable may be seasoned with Vinaigrette Sauce and served cold a day or two later. When you wish to cook a vegetable in Vinaigrette Sauce starting from scratch, follow this basic recipe:

VEGETABLES COOKED IN VINAIGRETTE SAUCE

Suggested vegetables: green beans cut into 1-inch lengths; cauliflower and broccoli separated into flowerettes; celery hearts or root celery, cut up; Italian frying peppers cut in strips.

3 *cups trimmed, cut-up vegetable*
⅔ *cup olive oil*
⅓ *cup stock*
salt and pepper
½ *teaspoon sugar*
1 *teaspoon monosodium glutamate*

1 *small onion, chopped*
3 *cloves garlic, minced*
4 *to* 6 *tablespoons wine vinegar*
1 *cup chopped parsley*

Combine all ingredients except vinegar and parsley in a heavy pot. Cover pot tightly, and cook over high heat, stirring and checking frequently until the vegetable is just tender, and the stock has cooked away, leaving only the oil as liquid. Remove from heat, and add vinegar and half of parsley, stirring in gently. Cool. Sprinkle with remaining parsley before serving. Serves 6.

I like to make a salad of frozen small, whole green beans, cooked in Vinaigrette Sauce, and I complement this with a fresh tomato salad, flavored with basil. At serving time, I mound the beans in the center of a platter and arrange the fresh tomato salad as a border, interspersing a few wedges of hard-cooked egg among the tomatoes. I like to sprinkle all with capers, a few anchovies, and plenty of parsley. This platter looks and tastes very good.

Sliced raw mushroom salad is excellent. If the mushrooms are tossed in dressing just before serving, they maintain a sort of nuttiness and crispness which I like. If they are allowed to stand in the dressing, they wilt and acquire a cooked quality which some people prefer. Cooked seafood is delicious when added to mushroom salads.

Belgian endive is a versatile vegetable. It may be left raw and broken into pieces, then mixed with vinaigrette. It is good when eaten immediately, or if it is allowed to stand a day or 2, it will soften and almost seem cooked. I like a truly cooked endive salad: I poach the endive, whole, in boiling salted water until it is completely tender, then drain well, and pour a vinaigrette dressing over the endive while it is still hot. When this cools, I have a most delicious salad. A good garnish is plenty of chopped, hard-coooked egg mixed with parsley, and sprinkled on top.

Carrots are delicious in vinaigrette. They need a touch of sugar and they should be sprinkled with dill rather than parsley to bring out their best flavor.

Some people like the flavor of Roquefort cheese in their salads. Simply add 2 or 3 tablespoons of finely crumbled Roquefort or blue cheese to a Vinaigrette Sauce.

AIXOISE SALAD

2 pounds fresh green beans, cut into 1" pieces
½ cup stock
1½ cups olive oil (approximately)
3 cloves garlic, minced
¼ teaspoon sugar
½ teaspoon monosodium glutamate
salt and freshly ground pepper
3 large, waxy potatoes, cooked, cooled, peeled and diced
¼ cup wine vinegar (approximately)
1 cup chopped parsley
1 cup ripe pitted olives
14 artichoke hearts, cooked and quartered
6 hard-cooked eggs, quartered
2 large green peppers, seeded and cut into strips
5 tomatoes, thinly sliced
½ teaspoon dried basil
6 filets of anchovies, cut into thirds
½ cup capers
1 large onion, peeled, sliced and separated into rings

Place green beans and stock in a heavy saucepan. Add ⅔ cup olive oil, garlic, sugar, monosodium glutamate, salt and pepper. Cook over medium heat, covered, until beans are barely tender. Remove cover, raise heat and cook a few minutes longer.

While beans are still hot, add diced potatoes, a little wine vinegar, half of parsley and pitted olives. Allow to cool and place in refrigerator until needed.

At serving time, line a large platter with greens. In the center of the platter, make a mound of the green bean-potato mixture. Around this mound arrange a circle of artichoke hearts, hard-cooked egg quarters and green pepper strips, alternating them. Now, make an outer circle of overlapping sliced tomatoes. Drizzle a little olive oil over the tomatoes and sprinkle with salt, pepper and basil. Place a bit of anchovy on each tomato, then a few capers and finally a little parsley. Sprinkle center mound with remaining parsley and toss onion rings all over platter. Serves 6.

This salad is really lovely to look at and delicious as well.

IBERIAN PEPPERS

8 *Italian frying peppers*
2 *medium-size tomatoes, cut into halves and sliced thin*
2 *medium-size onions, sliced thin*
3 *cloves garlic, sliced*
4 *anchovies*
monosodium glutamate
1 *teaspoon oregano*
1 *teaspoon basil*
salt and pepper
1 *cup olive oil (approximately)*
½ *cup chopped parsley*

Cut frying peppers in half, lengthwise. Remove stem and seeds, and place side by side, hollow sides up, on a flat baking sheet. Into each pepper place a slice of tomato, a slice of onion, several slices of garlic, and on top of all ½ strip of anchovy. Sprinkle with monosodium glutamate, oregano, basil, pepper, and very lightly with salt. Spoon a little olive oil on top. Bake in a 400 degree oven for 30 to 40 minutes, or until peppers look wrinkled and the other vegetables are lightly browned and soft. Serve at room temperature. Sprinkle with chopped parsley before serving. Serves 6.

ZUCCHINI, SOUTHERN ITALIAN STYLE

2 *cups olive oil*
2 *pounds unpeeled zucchini, sliced ⅛″ thick*
14 *anchovies*
¼ *cup lemon juice*
1 *teaspoon freshly ground pepper*
3 *cups chopped parsley*

In a skillet heat 1 cup of olive oil until it is almost smoking, and add enough zucchini slices to cover bottom of pan. Turn zucchini so that

(*continued on the next page*)

it browns slightly on both sides. Drain on a paper towel. Repeat until all zucchini slices are cooked.

Place remaining olive oil in blender (or use a mortar and pestle), and add anchovies and lemon juice. Blend until all are reduced to a fine anchovy sauce, then add pepper.

Spoon a little of this anchovy sauce into an attractive serving casserole—it doesn't need to be heat-proof. Sprinkle some parsley on top of the sauce. Arrange a layer of cooked zucchini on top. Spoon a little more sauce on top of the zucchini. Follow with a generous covering of parsley. Continue to make alternate layers of zucchini, anchovy sauce and parsley until all the zucchini has been used. Allow this to mellow in the refrigerator at least 24 hours before using (it will keep at least a week). Serve at room temperature. Serves 6.

TURKISH ARTICHOKES

8 *small artichokes*
16 *small white onions, peeled*
1 *cup olive oil*
juice of 2 lemons
½ *cup water*
1 *teaspoon sugar*
2 *teaspoons salt*
pepper to taste
1 *tablespoon chopped dill*
lemon wedges

Prepare artichokes by breaking off 2 or 3 lower rows of petals (these are always woody) and then cutting off the stems. Then slice off about 1 inch from the top of the artichokes. With a small spoon, dig into each artichoke to remove the hairy choke. (This step may be eliminated if time is a factor; however, artichokes are much more pleasant to eat if they have been prepared in this manner.)

As each artichoke is completed, drop it into a bowl of salty water. When all the artichokes have been prepared, remove them from the water and arrange in a heavy saucepan which may be tightly covered.

Fill the spaces in between the artichokes with the little onions, and add all remaining ingredients. Cover pan and cook over medium heat for 30 to 45 minutes, or until artichokes are completely tender. Serve at room temperature, garnished with additional chopped dill and wedges of lemon. Serves 6 to 8.

POTATO SALAD

Really good potato salad, combined with a slice or 2 of ham and some olives, can provide a delicious summer luncheon. The best potato salad is made with new potatoes rather than the winter variety. New potatoes are waxy and less apt to crumble when they are sliced. However, if you use the method given below, you can make a salad with any kind of potatoes.

2 *pounds potatoes*
½ *cup strong chicken stock*
⅔ *cup olive oil*
3 *tablespoons wine vinegar*
salt and pepper to taste
1 *onion, minced*
1 *small green pepper, minced*
⅔ *cup chopped parsley*

Wash potatoes; place in a deep pot. Cover potatoes with water, and bring to a boil. Lower heat and simmer until potatoes are tender when pierced with a fork. Drain, cool, and refrigerate until they are cold. (Potatoes are easier to peel and slice when they are cold.)

Peel the potatoes, then slice and place in an oven-proof dish. Add chicken stock, olive oil and vinegar, and season with salt and pepper. Place in a 350 degree oven for about ½ hour, or until the potatoes are hot and the liquid is simmering. Remove potatoes from oven, and allow them to stand until lukewarm. Add minced onion, green pepper and half of chopped parsley; toss gently. Chill slightly, then serve sprinkled with remaining chopped parsley. Serves 6.

HOT POTATO SALAD

Follow the preceding recipe. Do not add any vinegar, and serve the salad hot.

BAKED ONIONS AND TOMATOES

2 large Spanish onions
salt and pepper
⅔ cup olive oil
2 large tomatoes
½ teaspoon sugar
½ teaspoon basil
2 hard-cooked eggs, sliced
12 anchovies
1 tablespoon capers
2 tablespoons chopped parsley

Peel onions, and slice them ¼ inch thick. Using only the large center slices, you should have about 6 slices. Place onion slices in a baking dish, and season with salt and pepper. Drizzle a little olive oil over each slice.

Cut tomatoes into slices, and place a slice of tomato on each slice of onion. Season with salt, pepper, sugar and basil. Drizzle some more olive oil on tomatoes.

Place vegetables in a 375 degree oven and bake about 45 minutes, or until the onions are tender and the tomatoes wrinkled. Baste occasionally with additional oil.

Remove from oven, and place a round of hard-cooked egg on top of tomatoes. Place 2 anchovies, crisscrossed, on each egg slice. Garnish with capers, and in the center of each egg slice put a small pinch of chopped parsley. Serve at room temperature. Serves 6.

MARINATED LENTILS

¾ cup lentils
2 cups water
salt and pepper
⅓ cup olive oil
2 tablespoons wine vinegar
2 green onions, finely chopped
¼ cup chopped parsley

Pick over lentils and wash them well. Place in a pot, add water, and bring to a boil. Lower heat and simmer until tender, about 30 to 40 minutes. Drain. Add salt, pepper, oil and vinegar, then cool to room temperature. Add chopped green onions and half of chopped parsley. Garnish with remaining parsley. Serves 4.

MARINATED MUSHROOMS

These are whole, raw mushrooms which are simply marinated in Vinaigrette Sauce long enough to acquire a cooked quality. Use enough Vinaigrette Sauce to cover mushrooms. Large mushrooms need more time to marinate than small ones. Mushrooms should be marinated for several hours before they are served. They will keep in the refrigerator for several days. Use plain as part of a cold first-course plate, or stuff with Tarama, egg salad, or what you have.

BEANS WITH TUNA FISH

2 *No. 2 cans beans (beans should be packed in their own juice; if you like, combine 2 different-colored beans, such as red kidney and small white beans)*
2 *7-ounce cans tuna fish*
1 *cup finely chopped scallions*
1 *clove garlic, minced*
1 *cup Vinaigrette Sauce (page 57)*
1 *cup chopped parsley*

Empty beans into a strainer or colander, and rinse with cold water until beans are completely free of packing liquid. Drain very well. Place beans in a bowl.

Mash tuna fish somewhat coarsely, then add to beans. Add scallions, garlic, Vinaigrette Sauce and half of parsley. Toss gently together. Serve on a bed of crisp greens; garnish with remaining chopped parsley. Serves 6.

MIDDLE EASTERN WHEAT, MINT AND PARSLEY SALAD

1 *cup large-grain burghul (cracked wheat)*
1 *quart water*
1 *cup finely chopped scallions*
1 *cup chopped parsley*
½ *cup finely chopped mint*
¾ *cup olive oil*
½ *cup lemon juice*
salt and pepper to taste
black olives

Rinse burghul, and place in a bowl. Add water and allow to stand at least 2 hours. Drain off water, and press with a towel to remove all water.

Combine burghul with all remaining ingredients except olives, and toss; season to taste. Serve on a bed of crisp greens garnished with black olives. Serves 4.

IMAM BAYELDI

The name of this old Armenian recipe means "the Holy Man fainted"—of shock because the eggplant tasted so good!

2 *large or 4 small eggplants*
1 *cup olive oil (approximately)*
2 *large onions, chopped*
1 *green pepper, chopped*
6 *cloves garlic, chopped*
1 *cup chopped celery*
1 *cup chopped celery leaves*
1 *cup chopped parsley*
½ *cup tomato purée*
¼ *teaspoon crumbled bay leaf*
½ *teaspoon oregano*
1 *teaspoon dried mint*
½ *teaspoon sugar*
salt and pepper to taste

If the eggplants are large, cut them into quarters. If they are small, cut them lengthwise into halves. Salt cut sides generously and let stand for about ½ hour. (This draws out the bitterness from the eggplants.) After ½ hour, rinse eggplants and dry with paper towels. Brush cut sides with some of the olive oil. Place eggplants on a baking sheet, cut sides up, in a 300 degree oven and bake until centers are soft and lightly browned.

While the eggplants are baking, prepare the following stuffing: sauté onions, green pepper, garlic and chopped celery in remaining olive oil until the vegetables are soft but not brown. Add chopped celery leaves and parsley. Stir until leaves are wilted, then add tomato purée

(*continued on the next page*)

and herbs. Add sugar, then salt and pepper to taste. Cook a few more minutes. Set this stuffing aside until needed.

When eggplants are tender, allow them to cool so they may be handled easily. With a small knife, make an incision lengthwise, down the center of the cut side, being careful not to cut all the way through the eggplant. With your fingers, press soft pulp away from incision on the 2 long sides so that a good-size hollow is formed. Fill the hollows with the prepared filling, using a spoon.

Arrange stuffed eggplants in a pan, close together. Sprinkle with additional olive oil if filling looks dry. Bake in a 350 degree oven 45 minutes, basting 2 or 3 times with the oil in the pan. Serve at room temperature. Serves 6.

Note: The stuffed eggplants freeze very well. If time is a factor, this recipe may be speeded up. Instead of stuffing individual eggplant halves, slice the eggplant ½ inch thick and, after it has been baked till tender, place slices of eggplant in a casserole, arranging them alternately with the stuffing. Bake as for individual servings. (This dish doesn't look as handsome as the other version.)

EGGPLANT, PESTO STYLE

Pesto is a deliciously pungent green sauce (see page 59), and it is a kitchen standby in much the same way that a good Vinaigrette Sauce is. Pesto may be used warm to dress noodles or spaghetti, or served cold on such vegetables as eggplant.

1 *cup olive oil (approximately)*
1 *large eggplant, peeled and cut into* 1″ *cubes*
1 *cup basil Pesto at room temperature*

Heat 1 cup olive oil in a skillet until it is hot, then sauté eggplant cubes in the oil, turning them frequently, until they are all golden brown. Drain. Transfer eggplant to casserole, and bake in a 350 degree oven about 45 minutes, or till cubes are all very tender. Cool slightly.

Add 1 cup of Pesto to eggplant and toss very gently so that eggplant cubes are not mashed or broken. Serve at room temperature. Serves 4.

GREEK STUFFED TOMATOES

8 *small tomatoes*
2 *pounds fresh spinach, or* 2 *packages frozen chopped spinach, slightly thawed, cooked and well drained*
1 *small onion, minced*
2 *cloves garlic*
¾ *to* 1 *cup olive oil*
½ *cup pine nuts*
1 *teaspoon chopped capers*
salt and pepper
2 *teaspoons monosodium glutamate*
1 *teaspoon sugar*
2 *hard-cooked eggs, sliced*

Prepare tomatoes by removing a circle from the stem ends, carefully scooping out seeds and pulp, and turning tomatoes upside down on paper towels to drain.

Wash fresh spinach well. Place in a saucepan, cover and allow spinach to steam in its own liquid over a medium heat. As soon as spinach is wilted, drain well and squeeze out water. Chop spinach finely.

Sauté chopped onion and garlic in ½ cup of olive oil. When onion and garlic are soft, add pine nuts and continue to sauté until pine nuts are lightly browned. Add to spinach along with capers and half of remaining olive oil. Toss so that ingredients are evenly distributed. Season with salt and pepper and 1 teaspoon monosodium glutamate.

Sprinkle the inside of each tomato with salt, pepper, and a pinch of sugar and remaining monosodium glutamate. Stuff tomatoes with spinach mixture, packing them firmly, then arrange tomatoes in baking pan. Spoon a little olive oil over each tomato.

Bake in a 375 degree oven for 30 to 40 minutes, or until the skins of the tomatoes are wrinkled. Baste once or twice with pan juices and oil. Serve at room temperature, garnished with slices of hard-cooked egg. Serves 8.

DANISH STUFFED TOMATOES

4 *cucumbers*
2 *tablespoons salt*
2 *tablespoons sugar*
1 *teaspoon pepper*
1 *cup sour cream*
½ *cup mayonnaise*
½ *cup chopped dill*
6 *small tomatoes*
2 *hard-cooked eggs*

Peel cucumbers, and cut in half, lengthwise. With a spoon, scoop out seeds and discard them. Slice cucumbers thin. Place in bowl, sprinkle with salt and place in refrigerator for at least 2 hours. After 2 hours, pour off water which has accumulated and press out any additional water, so that cucumbers are dry. Add sugar and pepper and stir.

Combine sour cream and mayonnaise. Pour over cucumbers and toss lightly, adding half of dill. Place in refrigerator till needed.

Remove a circle from the stem ends of the tomatoes. Carefully scoop out all the seeds and pulp. Turn the tomato shells upside down on paper towels so that any juice may drain.

Stuff each tomato with the cucumber mixture. Sprinkle remaining dill on top of each tomato, and garnish with a slice of hard-cooked egg.

Serves 6.

NEAR EASTERN MELANGE

2 *cups olive oil (approximately)*
1 *cup eggplant (unpeeled) cut into 1″ cubes*
2 *tomatoes, sliced ½″ thick*
1 *cup zucchini cut into ½″ slices*
1 *cup green pepper cut into 1″ squares*
8 *cloves garlic, sliced*

1 *large onion, sliced and separated into rings*
1 *cup celery, cut into 1" slices*
1 *cup shredded cabbage*
1 *cup green beans cut into 1" slices*
1 *cup carrots cut into 1/4" slices*
2 *potatoes, peeled and cut into 1/2" cubes*
1 *cup seedless grapes*
salt, pepper and monosodium glutamate
2 *cups chopped parsley*
1 *teaspoon oregano*
1 *teaspoon basil*
1/2 *teaspoon crumbled bay leaf*
1 *teaspoon sugar*

Take your largest, most attractive baking dish. Pour a little olive oil into it. Make one individual layer each of the vegetables (including a layer of garlic) and grapes, seasoning each layer with salt, pepper, monosodium glutamate, parsley, oregano, basil, bay leaf and a little olive oil. Use just a bit of sugar on the layers of tomato. Make the top layer an assortment of all the vegetables. Bake uncovered in a 350 degree oven for 1 1/2 hours, or till oil is bubbling and vegetables are completely tender. Serve at room temperature. This will keep in the refrigerator for a week. Serves 8.

GUACAMOLE

This is a salad-type dish best served with Mexican foods.

1 *large avocado*
3 *tablespoons Salsa Fria (page* 60)
salt and pepper
tabasco sauce (optional)

Peel and chop the meat of the avocado coarsely. Stir in the Salsa Fria, salt and pepper to taste. If you like your foods hot, add a little more tabasco sauce. (Do not prepare this dish too much more than an hour in advance of serving because it darkens upon standing.) Serves 4 to 6.

SPINACH IN THE STYLE OF ROME

2 *pounds fresh spinach*
⅔ *cup olive oil*
8 *scallions, sliced*
8 *cloves garlic, sliced*
salt and freshly ground pepper
1 *teaspoon monosodium glutamate*
lemon wedges

Wash and trim spinach. Drain and wrap in towels to absorb as much moisture as possible. Place in a saucepan over medium high heat and cook only till spinach wilts. Drain and press out all the water.

In a large, heavy skillet, heat olive oil till it is almost smoking. Add scallions and garlic and sauté until they are tender. Add spinach, and toss. Season with salt and pepper and monosodium glutamate, and toss again lightly. Transfer to a serving dish. Serve at room temperature, with lemon wedges. (Occasionally, hard-cooked egg slices are used to garnish this dish.) Serves 6.

ONION RELISH

This relish is especially good with Indian curries, or with hamburgers. It will keep in a refrigerator for about a week.

finely diced onions
lemon juice
coarsely ground red pepper (*available in stores that specialize in Italian products*)

Place onions in a bowl, and add enough lemon juice to half-cover the onions. Add a good amount of coarse red pepper and toss. Allow to stand, well covered, in the refrigerator for at least an hour before using.

CURRIED MACARONI SALAD

1 *pound elbow macaroni, cooked in boiling salted water till tender, then drained*
1 *cup mayonnaise*
2 *tablespoons curry powder*
⅛ *cup wine vinegar*
1 *cup thinly sliced radishes*
1 *green pepper, diced*
¾ *cup thinly sliced, peeled, seeded cucumber*
1 *cup chopped scallions*
½ *cup finely chopped celery*
1 *cup chopped parsley*
⅔ *cup finely sliced carrots*
½ *cup chopped sweet pickles or chutney*
salt and pepper

Rinse drained macaroni in hot water and keep warm.

Combine mayonnaise, curry powder and wine vinegar in a small bowl, and pour over warm macaroni. Add remaining ingredients; toss gently. Allow to come to room temperature. Serve on crisp greens. Serves 6.

Note: Bits of tuna fish or smoked meat may be added to this dish to make it more substantial.

SALAD NICOISE

There are two ways to go about making a Salad Niçoise, and each method has its advantage. The first method I shall describe has tremendous eye-appeal—the finished salad is like a picture.

A Salad Niçoise must always contain certain basics: tuna fish, tomatoes, beans, olives, green pepper, anchovies, capers, onion rings and, of course, greens. The dressing is always a vinaigrette. Now, to make the picture-type Niçoise, arrange a beautiful bed of crisp greens on a large platter. In the center of the platter, arrange the contents of 2 or 3 cans of tuna fish, right next to each other. Around the tuna fish, place mounds of olives, slices of tomatoes, strips of anchovies, green pepper and onion rings. Generally wedges of hard-cooked egg are included also. Sprinkle capers on top. Just before serving, pour 1½ to 2 cups Vinaigrette Sauce (page 57) over all.

The Salad Niçoise which I like better is one mixed in a large bowl. It doesn't look as pretty, but the flavors come together and taste so good. To make this, mash up the tuna fish in the large bowl. Then add all other ingredients except 3 large tomatoes and 4 cups of greens. The salad is arranged on the greens and the tomatoes are used as a garnish.

Other ingredients for a Niçoise Salad may include cooked green beans, or diced potatoes. Occasionally I like to add bits of feta cheese too. This makes a very ample lunch for 4, or a delicious first course for 6.

RICE SALAD

You can make as little or as much as you like of a rice salad. It can be a traditional salad, or it can be a one-dish meal incorporating cold meats, seafood and vegetables. Here is a fairly basic recipe for the one-dish meal preparation. You can always subtract ingredients and keep the recipe simple.

1 *double recipe Fluffy, Steamed Rice (page* 301)
2 *cups Vinaigrette Sauce (page* 57)
⅔ *cups mayonnaise*
1 *cup chopped scallions*
¾ *cup thinly sliced, peeled, seeded cucumber*
2 *cups chopped parsley*
1 *cup finely sliced radishes*
1 *cup very finely sliced raw carrots*
1 *green pepper, diced*

1 *medium-size can tuna fish, mashed*
3 *cups cooked shrimp cut in half (lengthwise)*
2 *cups finely diced, cooked, smoked ham or tongue*
salt and pepper
½ *cup chopped, sweet pickles*

Transfer rice from pot to a large bowl while rice is still hot; do not pack down. Combine Vinaigrette Sauce with mayonnaise, using a whisk, and pour over rice. Toss gently, adding all remaining ingredients. Cool. Serve on a bed of crisp greens. Serves 8.

AVOCADO AND BACON SALAD

juice of 2 limes
¼ *cup olive oil*
½ *cup sour cream*
¼ *cup mayonnaise*
salt and coarsely ground pepper
2 *cloves garlic, minced*
8 *strips bacon, diced*
1 *large head Boston lettuce, washed and broken into pieces*
2 *small avocados, cubed*

Combine lime juice, olive oil, sour cream, mayonnaise, salt, pepper and garlic.

Place diced bacon in a skillet and cook over low heat until it is crisp. Drain crisp bits and reserve.

Just before serving, combine lettuce, avocado cubes and crisp bacon. Pour lime-juice dressing over salad and toss gently. Serve on additional crisp greens. Serves 4 to 6.

MEXICAN CAULIFLOWER SALAD

3 *cups raw cauliflower, shredded thin, like cabbage*
1½ *cups Vinaigrette Sauce* (*page* 57)
1 *cup Salsa Fria* (*page* 60)
salt and coarsely ground pepper
4 *teaspoons cilantro* (*optional*)

Cover cauliflower with Vinaigrette Sauce and marinate at least 4 hours. Drain off Vinaigrette Sauce. Stir Salsa Fria into cauliflower, along with additional salt and pepper. Serve on crisp greens. Sprinkle with cilantro if available. Serves 6.

MEXICAN RADISH SALAD

2 *cups finely sliced radishes*
½ *cup vinegar*
1 *tablespoon salt*
1 *teaspoon sugar*
1 *teaspoon coarsely ground pepper*

Combine radishes with vinegar, salt and sugar. Allow to marinate for at least 2 hours. Drain vinegar, pressing all the liquid out of the radishes. Add pepper. Toss the radishes lightly and serve. Serves 4.

MONJU OZA'S CARROT AND PEPPER VEGETABLE

This is the innovation of an Indian friend who was my neighbor for a number of years. It is as delicious with simple broiled foods as it is with Indian dishes. (And it keeps very well in the refrigerator.)

⅔ cup peanut oil
2 teaspoons whole mustard seeds
2 teaspoons ground cumin seed
2 tablespoons curry powder
¼ teaspoon cayenne pepper
3 carrots, cut into thin slices
3 green peppers, cut into 1" squares
3 tablespoons brown sugar
salt and fresh pepper
juice of 2 lemons

In a deep saucepan, heat peanut oil until it smokes, then add mustard seeds. Cover saucepan and turn heat up high till mustard seeds pop and look almost black. Turn heat down, and stir in cumin, curry powder and cayenne pepper. Add sliced carrots and green pepper, stirring into spiced mixture. Cook only till vegetables begin to change color; they should not entirely lose their crispness. Stir in brown sugar, salt and pepper to taste. Remove from heat and add lemon juice. Serve at room temperature. Serves 6.

10. DESSERTS

SINCE I HAVE WRITTEN at length about cakes, cookies, tarts and other baked desserts in my *Art of Fine Baking*, I have included here only a few of the basic baked items and have concentrated instead on other areas of dessert-making: fruits, flans and creams.

Compotes

A really good compote can make a wonderful ending for a rich meal. To make a fruit compote which will hold its shape, bake it rather than cook it on top of the stove. When you cook a compote on top of the stove, the bottom tends to get very cooked and mushy, while the top remains rather raw. In the oven, surrounded by even heat, the compote cooks evenly. Make compote of peaches, pears, little Hungarian plums, quince or any firm fruit that strikes your fancy.

The main difference in cooking various compotes lies in the amounts of sugar various fruits require—rhubarb needs a great deal; ripe peaches need little. As for cooking liquid, rhubarb has so much natural liquid that it needs no additional water in cooking. It can stew in its own juice. (For rhubarb, use at least half as much sugar in weight as there is fruit, being sure that the top layer is sugar. Cover the pot tightly, place in a 325 degree oven and bake until tender and juicy.)

Actually, most fruit compotes need little liquid, although the addition of a sweet wine such as Madeira or port adds to their flavor. One of the best fruit compotes is made with the little Hungarian (sometimes called Italian) plums. These need just a little water to start with, but a good amount of sugar since their skins tend to be tart. Their juices are royal purple, and the compote itself is utterly delicious if it has been seasoned with grated lemon rind and a small cinnamon stick.

Apple compote is a nice novelty. It is made slightly differently because a syrup for the apple slices should be made ahead of time. The syrup consists of equal parts of water and sugar. Bring it to a boil, stirring until the sugar dissolves. Then add sliced, cored tart apples and bake in a 325 degree oven until they are tender. Of course a little grated lemon rind improves their flavor; also, you should choose apples which are firm and tart to begin with (such as greenings).

BAKED PEACHES IN PORT

6 *ripe, whole peaches, skinned (immerse peaches briefly in boiling water, then peel)*
1 *cup sugar*
juice and rind of 1 *lemon*
½ *teaspoon mace or nutmeg*
1 *cup port*

Place whole peaches in a baking dish. Combine remaining ingredients and pour over peaches. Cover pan, using aluminum foil, if necessary. Bake in a 400 degree oven, basting peaches occasionally with liquid in the pan, until peaches are soft—from 45 minutes to an hour. Remove cover from pan and cool. Chill before serving. Serves 6.

BAKED PEARS IN MADEIRA

6 *ripe, whole pears, peeled*
⅔ *cup sugar*
1¼ *cups Madeira*
juice and grated rind of 1 *lemon*

Place whole pears in a baking dish. Combine sugar, 1 cup of Madeira, lemon rind and juice, and pour over pears. Cover dish, with aluminum foil, if necessary.

Place in a 375 degree oven until pears are soft, about 45 minutes. Baste pears occasionally with liquid in the dish. When pears are soft, remove from the oven and cool. After they are completely cool, pour over remaining Madeira, and serve. Serves 6.

BAKED PRUNES IN PORT

1 *pound large prunes*
port
½ *cup sugar*
1 *cinnamon stick*
grated rind and juice of 1 *lemon*

Soak prunes overnight in port to cover. In the morning, place in a baking dish. (If necessary, add more port to cover prunes.) Add remaining ingredients. Cover baking dish, with aluminum foil, if necessary, and bake in a 325 degree oven about 1 hour, or until the prunes are tender. Cool, then chill the prunes. Serve with thick sour cream or whipped cream. Serves 6.

PEARS IN ORANGE SAUCE

6 *pears, peeled, cored and quartered*
1 *cup water*
¾ *cup sugar*
grated rind and juice of 1 *orange*
⅔ *cup Cointreau*

Place pears in a pot. Combine water and sugar, and pour over pears. Cover pot and bake in a 350 degree oven until pears are tender. Add grated orange rind and juice. Allow to cool, then pour over Cointreau. Serve chilled. Serves 6.

APRICOT WHIP WITH MADEIRA

½ *pound dried apricots*
¾ *cup sugar*
⅔ *cup Madeira*
2 *egg whites*
1 *cup heavy cream, whipped until stiff*
¼ *cup blanched, sliced, toasted almonds*

Soak apricots overnight in water to cover. In the morning, place them in a saucepan, and add half of sugar and additional water, if necessary. (The water should just about cover the fruit.) Bring to a boil and simmer until apricots are tender. Drain apricots.

Cook any remaining liquid down until it is almost a glaze in the pan. Add to cooked apricots. Cool.

Purée fruit and juice in blender, using ½ cup Madeira for additional liquid.

Beat egg whites until they are stiff. Gradually beat in the remaining sugar, a little at a time. Continue to beat egg whites until sugar is dissolved.

Fold the stiffly beaten egg whites and half of whipped cream into the apricot purée. Pour into a serving dish. Sprinkle with almonds. Chill well before serving.

Beat remaining Madeira into remaining whipped cream, and serve with the apricot whip. Serves 6.

ORANGES WITH STRAWBERRIES

This is a delicious combination. Allow 1 to 1½ peeled, sliced oranges per person, and ½ to ⅔ cup sliced strawberries.

Peel the oranges. Arrange segments of oranges on a large dish.

Hull, slice and sugar the berries lightly. Sprinkle berries, with their juice, over the segmented oranges. Chill slightly and serve.

PINEAPPLE WITH KIRSCH

1 *medium pineapple, peeled and cut into fairly small pieces*
¼ *cup butter*
2 *tablespoons sugar*
2 *ounces kirsch*
¾ *cup heavy cream*

Sauté pineapple pieces in butter over high heat until lightly browned on all sides. Sprinkle with sugar and add kirsch. Continue to cook until liquid is almost evaporated, then stir in heavy cream. Serve warm. Serves 6.

MY HUSBAND'S FAVORITE DESSERT

This dessert is so very simple that it seems almost foolish to include it, yet it is too delicious to omit!

five 7½-*ounce jars junior pears (baby food)*
⅔ *cup pear eau de vie, or cognac or port*
1 *cup sweetened whipped cream*
6 *crystallized violets*

Empty jars of pears into a large bowl, add liqueur of your choice and stir in well. Divide contents of bowl among 6 sherbet glasses. Chill well. Top each glass with a rosette of whipped cream and garnish each rosette with a violet. Serve well chilled. Serves 6.

CARAMEL CUSTARD

½ cup sugar
juice of ½ lemon
8 egg yolks
5 whole eggs
1¼ cup sugar
4¾ cups milk, heated till hot
1 teaspoon vanilla

Combine ½ cup sugar and the lemon juice in a skillet. Heat, stirring, over low heat, until sugar has melted and turned into a caramel-colored liquid. Pour into a 9 x 5 x 3 baking dish, tilting the dish to cover the entire bottom with liquid.

Beat egg yolks, whole eggs and 1¼ cups sugar together; beat in hot milk and vanilla. Pour into prepared baking dish.

Place baking dish in a pan of hot water in a 350 degree oven, for about an hour, or until the custard is just firm. Cool, then chill. Before serving, turn out of baking dish by first loosening edges with a sharp knife and then inverting on a serving dish. Serves 8 to 10.

FROZEN RASPBERRY MOUSSE

1 cup raspberry purée (2 to 3 packages frozen raspberries, drained, puréed and sweetened to taste with a little granulated sugar; seeds discarded)
¼ cup framboise or kirsch
2 egg whites
pinch of salt
2 tablespoons granulated sugar
2 cups heavy cream, whipped

Combine raspberry purée with framboise or kirsch. Beat egg whites with salt till they are stiff. Beat in sugar, a little at a time, and continue beating till whites are very firm. Fold whipped cream and stiffly beaten egg whites together. Fold in raspberry purée. Pour into a bowl which can be placed in freezer, then cover with aluminum foil and freeze in freezer until mixture is firm. Serves 6.

CHOCOLATE MOUSSE

8 *ounces semisweet chocolate*
½ *teaspoon salt*
8 *egg whites*
½ *cup sugar*
3 *tablespoons liqueur (Grand Marnier or cognac)*
1 *teaspoon vanilla*
whipped cream

Melt chocolate over hot water in a double boiler, or in a bowl in the oven (using low heat).

Add salt to egg whites, and beat until egg whites are very stiff. Gradually beat in sugar. Continue to beat until meringue loses its graininess; then beat in liqueur and vanilla.

Fold chocolate into egg white mixture, and pour into a serving dish. Chill for at least an hour before serving. Serve with whipped cream. Serves 6.

FROZEN FRUIT SHERBETS

Sherbets made with frozen fruits (berries or peaches) are very easy to make, and wonderful to have on hand.

¼ *cup heavy cream*
¼ *cup liqueur of your choice*

1 10-*ounce package sweetened, frozen berries, or peaches (cut into 4 or 5 pieces)*

Place a metal loaf pan or bowl into the freezer so that it will be very well chilled.

Add a little of the cream or liqueur to the blender bowl, then add part of the frozen fruit. Using a rubber scraper, move ingredients up and down the sides of the blender to move the fruit down into the blades while the motor is going. As soon as fruit is reduced to a mush, pour it into the chilled metal pan. Do not allow fruit mixture to become too liquid, just mushy.

Repeat with remaining fruit, cream and liqueur until all is used. Replace chilled pan in freezer with fruit mixture each time it is filled. Chill in freezer an hour or 2 before serving. Serves 3 to 4.

ORANGE GELATIN

A delicious fruit dessert can be created using any fruit juice and unflavored gelatin.

1½ *cups fresh orange juice*
1 *package unflavored gelatin*
⅓ *cup sugar (optional)*
¼ *cup lemon juice*

Pour ½ cup fruit juice over gelatin (in a small pan or metal cup). Stir until gelatin is absorbed into liquid. Then place over low heat until the mixture is completely liquid and clear. Stir into remaining fruit juice (including lemon juice). Taste and if necessary, add sugar, and place over low heat until sugar is dissolved. Pour into a serving dish and chill. Serves 4.

RASPBERRIES IN PORT JELLY

1 *package frozen raspberries*
2 *packages unflavored gelatin*
1 *cup port*
1 *cup heavy cream, whipped*

Defrost berries. Drain off all the juice; set berries aside, then sprinkle gelatin into juice. Heat, stirring, until gelatin dissolves and liquid becomes clear. Cool to room temperature, then stir in port.

Place port mixture in the refrigerator to chill. Do not allow it to set completely—it should be the consistency of unbeaten egg white.

Add whipped cream, beating it in with a rotary beater. Do not beat too long or too vigorously: the whipped cream and port mixture should almost be folded together. Place in refrigerator for a few minutes, or until mixture seems nearly set. Then fold in the drained raspberries. Chill for several hours, or until the dessert is completely set. Serve garnished with additional whipped cream. Serves 6.

RICE PUDDING

6 *cups milk (approximately)*
½ *cup long-grain rice*
½ *cup sugar*
grated rind of 1 *orange*
2 *teaspoons vanilla*
3 *egg yolks (optional)*
½ *cup yellow raisins*
¼ *teaspoon each: cinnamon and nutmeg*

Heat milk and keep it warm. Add about 2 cups of the warm milk to rice, in a deep pot. Cook over low heat, stirring frequently. From time to time, add more milk, as rice absorbs it. When the rice is entirely cooked, it should be in a very light creamy sauce.

Stir in sugar, grated orange rind and vanilla. If you wish a thicker sauce, stir in egg yolks and replace over very low heat, stirring constantly until the mixture has thickened a little. It will thicken more when it cools.

Stir in raisins, then pour into a serving dish. Sprinkle the top with a mixture of cinnamon and nutmeg. This dessert is best served at room temperature. Serves 6.

ITALIAN CHEESE DESSERT

1 *pound Italian ricotta cheese*
1/4 *cup confectioners' sugar*
3 *tablespoons liqueur of your choice*
2 *tablespoons instant espresso coffee*
1 *tablespoon unsweetened dark cocoa*

Place cheese in a bowl, and beat in sugar, then liqueur. Divide evenly into 6 dessert plates or sherbet cups. Chill. Just before serving, mix instant espresso and cocoa together; sprinkle a little of this mixture lightly over each portion. Serves 6.

Cakes and Cookies

PRINCESS CAKE

Here is a delicate white cake which is rich and buttery. Fold ⅔ cup grated chocolate into the batter, and you will have a wonderful marble cake.

1 *cup butter*
2⅔ *cups sifted flour*
1 *teaspoon vanilla*
8 *egg whites*
pinch of salt
¼ *teaspoon cream of tartar*
1⅔ *cups sugar*

Set oven at 350 degrees. Grease and dust with flour a deep 10-inch tube pan.

Cream butter with half of flour until light and fluffy. Add vanilla.

Beat egg whites with salt and cream of tartar until they hold soft peaks. Add sugar, a tablespoon at a time, beating well after each addition. Beat whites at least 5 minutes, or until they are very firm.

Fold a quarter of the stiffly beaten egg whites thoroughly into creamed butter-flour mixture. Pour mixture back over remaining egg whites. Fold gently together while sprinkling in remaining flour. Be careful not to overmix.

Pour into prepared pan. Bake about 1 hour, or until the cake is golden brown and pulls away from sides of pan.

FILBERT TORTE

8 *egg whites*
pinch of salt
1 *cup sugar*

12 *egg yolks*
1 *teaspoon vanilla*
2¼ *cups filberts, finely grated*

Set oven at 350 degrees. Grease bottom of one 10-inch tube pan.

Beat egg whites with salt until they hold soft peaks. Gradually add sugar, a tablespoon at a time, beating after each addition. Continue beating 5 more minutes, or until meringue is very stiff.

Stir egg yolks with a fork to break them. Add vanilla to egg yolks, then fold a quarter of the egg whites into yolks. Pour this mixture over remaining stiffly beaten egg whites, sprinkling grated filberts on top at the same time. Fold all together only until there are no lumps of egg white showing. Pour into prepared pan.

Bake 45 to 60 minutes, or until top is springy to the touch. Allow torte to cool before loosening sides and removing from pan.

When cake is completely cool, dust with confectioners' sugar and serve.

MELTING TEA CAKE

This is a delicious cake. It is as light and delicate as a sponge cake, yet rich as a pound cake. Try it and see.

½ *cup whole blanched almonds*
1 *teaspoon vanilla*
1 *teaspoon grated lemon rind*
1 *cup butter, melted (see directions below)*
4 *whole eggs, plus* 4 *egg yolks*
1 *cup sugar*
1½ *cups sifted all-purpose flour*
2 *tablespoons sifted cornstarch*
⅛ *teaspoon mace*

Set oven at 350 degrees. Grease and dust with flour a 9-inch tube or kugelhopf pan. Arrange blanched almonds around bottom of pan.

Melt butter over low heat and cool to lukewarm temperature (do not clarify). Add vanilla and grated lemon rind to butter.

(continued on the next page)

In a large bowl combine whole eggs, egg yolks and sugar. Beat for a minute, then set bowl over a saucepan of hot water, and place saucepan over low heat for about 10 minutes, or until eggs are slightly warmer than lukewarm. (Do not let water boil.) Stir eggs occasionally while they are being heated to prevent them from cooking on the bottom of the bowl.

When eggs are warm, beat until they are cool, thick and tripled in bulk. Sprinkle flour, cornstarch and mace on top. Fold in gently, adding butter mixture at the same time. Continue to fold until there is no trace of butter. Be careful not to overmix.

Pour batter into prepared pan. Bake about 45 minutes, or until cake is golden brown and comes away from sides of pan.

BASIC SPONGE SHEET

4 *eggs*
pinch of salt
¼ *cup sugar*
½ *teaspoon vanilla*
¼ *cup sifted cornstarch*
¼ *cup sifted flour*

Set oven at 400 degrees. Grease an 11 x 16 jelly-roll pan and line with wax paper. Grease and lightly flour the paper.

Separate eggs. Beat whites with salt until they hold soft peaks. Gradually beat in sugar, sprinkling it in a little at a time. Continue beating until whites are very firm, about 5 minutes in all.

Stir yolks with a fork to break them up. Add vanilla. Fold a quarter of the stiffly beaten egg whites thoroughly into egg yolks. Pour egg yolk mixture on top of remaining whites. Sprinkle cornstarch and flour over mixture. Fold all very gently together by hand or with the mixer turned to lowest speed. Fold until no pieces of egg white show. Be careful not to overmix.

Pour into prepared pan, spreading batter evenly. Bake 10 to 12 minutes, or until cake is very lightly browned. Be careful not to overbake. Loosen sides and remove cake from pan at once. Cool on rack before peeling off paper. Cake should be flexible from end to end.

Make a jelly roll with Basic Sponge Sheet, or spread it with Speedy Chocolate Butter Cream before rolling it up. (It can also be cut into strips and layered with any filling of your choice.)

GENOISE

Gênoise is the classic French butter sponge cake. It is very delicate and absolutely delicious, no matter how it is served.

6 *large eggs*
1 *cup sugar*
1 *cup sifted all-purpose flour*
½ *cup sweet butter, melted and clarified*
1 *teaspoon vanilla*

Set your oven at 350 degrees. Grease and lightly flour one of the following:

two 9" *layer cake tins*
three 7" *layer cake tins*
one 11 x 16 *jelly-roll pan*
two shallow 10" *layer cake pans*

Combine eggs and sugar in a large bowl. Beat for a minute, or until they are just combined. Set bowl over a saucepan containing 1 or 2 inches of hot water. Water in pan should not touch bowl; nor should it ever be allowed to boil. Place saucepan containing bowl over low heat for 5 to 10 minutes, or until eggs are lukewarm. (Heating the eggs helps them whip to greater volume.)

While it is not necessary to beat the eggs continuously as they are warming, they should be lightly stirred 3 or 4 times to prevent them from cooking at the bottom of the bowl.

(*continued on the next page*)

When the eggs feel lukewarm to your finger and look like a bright yellow syrup, remove bowl from heat. Begin to beat, preferably with an electric mixer. Beat at high speed for 10 to 15 minutes, scraping sides of bowl with a rubber spatula when necessary, until syrup becomes light, fluffy and cool. It will almost triple in bulk and look much like whipped cream. It is the air beaten into the eggs that gives Gênoise its lightness.

(If you beat by hand with a good rotary beater it will take about 25 minutes.)

Sprinkle flour, a little at a time on top of the whipped eggs. Fold in gently, adding slightly cooled clarified butter and vanilla. Folding can be done with electric mixer turned to lowest speed, or by hand. If you use the hand method, be sure your fingers are spread apart. Bring your hand to the bottom of the bowl and bring its contents to the top. Continue to fold until all ingredients are homogenized.

Be especially careful not to overmix.

Pour batter into prepared pans. Bake in a preheated oven 25 to 30 minutes, or until cakes pull away from the sides of the pans and are golden brown and springy when touched lightly on top.

Remove cakes from pans as soon as possible. Cool on a cake rack.

ANGELE'S RUM SPONGE CAKE

5 *eggs, separated*
pinch of salt
1 *cup sugar*
1 *teaspoon vanilla*
½ *cup potato flour, sifted*

Set oven at 350 degrees. Grease bottom of a 9-inch tube pan.

Beat egg whites with salt until they stand in soft peaks. Gradually add sugar, a little at a time, beating the mixture until it is very stiff.

Add vanilla to egg yolks and stir with a fork to break up yolks. Stir about a quarter of the egg white mixture into the egg yolks, blending well. Pour yolk mixture back on top of remaining egg whites. Sprinkle potato flour on top. Fold all together until there are no lumps of egg white showing: be careful not to overmix.

Pour into prepared pan. Bake in preheated oven about 35 minutes. Cool in pan. When cake is cool, remove it from the pan and pour Rum Syrup (below) over it. Serve with whipped cream, if desired.

Rum Syrup

½ *cup sugar*
½ *cup water*
1 *teaspoon corn syrup*
½ *cup rum*

Combine sugar, water and corn syrup in a saucepan, and stir over low heat until sugar is completely dissolved. Bring to a boil without stirring. Remove from heat. Cool syrup completely before stirring in rum. Gradually spoon syrup over cooled cake until all the syrup has been absorbed in the cake.

LEMON CREAM

This keeps for months in the refrigerator. In England—where it is called Lemon Curd—it is used as a spread for hot breads. It can be a quick tart or cake filling, or the base of a lemon cream dessert. (To make the lemon cream dessert, simply fold together half lemon cream and half whipped cream. Pile into sherbet glasses and serve.)

½ *cup sugar*
juice and grated rind of 2 *large lemons*
¼ *cup sweet butter*
5 *egg yolks* (*or* 3 *whole eggs*)

Combine sugar, lemon juice and rind and sweet butter in a heavy saucepan. Allow butter to melt (over low heat) and sugar to dissolve.

With a small wire whisk, beat yolks or whole eggs together lightly

(*continued on the next page*)

in a heavy saucepan. Pouring in a fine stream, add the butter mixture to the eggs, beating constantly. If the butter mixture is hot enough, the eggs will immediately thicken. If they don't, place the entire mixture over low heat and beat constantly with a wire whisk until mixture has thickened.

SPEEDY CHOCOLATE OR MOCHA BUTTER CREAM

This is an extraordinarily smooth, delicious butter cream which may be used as a filling for a cake, or for tiny cream puffs.

½ *cup soft butter*
6 *ounces semisweet chocolate, melted and* cooled
1 *egg yolk*
½ *teaspoon vanilla*
2 *teaspoons cognac*
1 *teaspoon instant coffee* (*optional*)

Cream butter briefly until it is fluffy. Beat in cooled, melted chocolate, egg yolk, vanilla and cognac. If mocha flavor is desired, add coffee powder. This butter cream can be used immediately, or refrigerated until needed. It will harden in the refrigerator and should be brought to room temperature before being used. This butter cream will keep up to a week in the refrigerator.

Makes about 1 cup.

RICH TART PASTRY

A tart is a European version of pie which has one definite advantage over pie—the crust maintains its crispness. A tart may be baked with a tart fruit filling; or it may be baked unfilled, and some sort of filling may be added later.

If the sugar and lemon rind are omitted from the following recipe, the resulting pastry can be used for making savory appetizers—quiche Lorraine, salt sticks, and many others.

2 *cups sifted flour*
3 *tablespoons sugar*
¾ *cup butter*
½ *teaspoon salt*
2 *teaspoons grated lemon rind*
3 *hard-cooked egg yolks, mashed*
2 *raw egg yolks*

Place flour in a bowl, and make a well in the center. Add all ingredients to well. (The butter should not be ice cold, nor should it be so soft that it is oily.)

With your fingertips, make a paste of center ingredients, gradually incorporating flour to form a smooth, firm ball of dough. Work quickly so that the butter does not become oily. When sides of the bowl are left clean, the pastry is finished. Wrap it in wax paper and chill until dough is firm enough to roll.

Roll pastry between sheets of wax paper. This is enough pastry for one 9-inch flan ring, with some left over for a lattice top, or for approximately 30 tartlet shells.

Note: To make pastry which is less fragile and crisper in texture, substitute 2 egg whites for the raw egg yolks.

TARTLET SHELLS

Use Rich Tart Pastry (above). It should be cold but not so chilled that it cannot be rolled easily.

Arrange at least 12 tartlet tins side by side, touching each other.

Roll pastry a little less than ¼ inch thick between 2 pieces of wax paper. Carefully remove the top sheet of paper. Then flip pastry over tins, very loosely so that the dough can settle into the shells. After it settles, with a rolling pin, roll over dough and tins. The tins will then be lined with dough. Gather up the excess pastry surrounding the tins and re-roll it if you have more tins.

(*continued on the next page*)

With your fingertips, or with a small ball of floured dough, press the dough in the tins down firmly. Chill lined tins well, preferably in the freezer, before baking them.

To bake tartlet shells, place a number of them on a baking sheet. Bake in a 350 degree oven on the second rack from the bottom for about 10 minutes, or until shells are light brown. Prick each shell 2 or 3 times with a fork during first 5 minutes of baking when air bubbles appear. The pastry should not stick; but if it does, gently loosen the edges with the point of a small knife. They should then come free from the tins.

The baked tartlet shells may be filled with any salad mixture and garnish, or, if you are splurging, with caviar and a garnish of finely chopped onion, hard-cooked egg or any other garnish of your choice.

CREAM PUFF PASTRY

This pastry is used for cream puffs and éclairs, and also for tiny puffs which may be filled with egg or shrimp salad, or with any filling of your choice. The filled small puffs are perfect for serving with cocktails.

½ *cup butter*
1 *cup water*
1 *cup sifted flour mixed with* ¼ *teaspoon salt*
4 *large eggs*

Combine butter and water in a saucepan, and cook over medium heat until butter is melted and mixture is boiling.

Turn heat to very low, then add flour-salt mixture, all at once. Stir vigorously until a ball forms in the center of the pan. This takes from 3 to 5 minutes.

Remove from heat. Add 3 eggs, 1 at a time, beating hard after each addition. (This beating can be done in an electric mixer.)

The final egg should be lightly beaten with a fork and added gradually. The paste must be just stiff enough to stand in a peak when a spoon is withdrawn. Therefore, it is sometimes necessary to add slightly less—or even more—egg than specified in the recipe. This depends on the dryness of the flour and the size of the eggs.

Fit a pastry bag with a large, round (No. 9) tube. On a lightly greased baking sheet, press out large—or tiny—mounds of this pastry. Bake pastry in a 375 degree oven. Bake until the pastries are golden brown and no beads of moisture show.

Stick the point of a small knife into the sides of the pastries, and turn oven heat off. Leave small pastries in oven 10 minutes; let larger puffs remain in oven 15 to 20 minutes more to allow the steam inside to evaporate. Yield: approximately 90 small puffs or 25 medium-size puffs.

SALLY DARR'S ALMOND THINS

½ *cup sweet butter*
¾ *cup sugar*
1 *egg, separated*
1 *teaspoon vanilla*
1 *cup sifted flour*
½ *cup finely chopped blanched almonds*
½ *teaspoon cinnamon*

Preheat oven to 400 degrees. Grease a 14 x 18 cooky sheet.

Cream together the butter and ½ cup of the sugar until very light. Beat in the egg yolk and vanilla, and gradually stir in flour.

Using a wet knife or spatula, spread the batter on the greased cooky sheet. Spread batter as thinly as possible.

Beat the egg white until it is just stiff, then brush it all over the dough. Combine almonds, cinnamon and remaining sugar; sprinkle this mixture on top of the pastry.

Bake in preheated oven for 10 to 15 minutes, or until pastry is golden brown. Immediately cut pastry into diamond shapes, and cool.

POLVORONES

This is a recipe for an authentic Spanish cooky which was given to me by my very dear friend Carmen Aldecoa, who came from Spain to escape the Fascist tyranny, and is now a professor of Spanish.

1 *pound lard*
1½ *cups sugar*
grated rind of 1 *lemon*
1 *teaspoon cinnamon*
1 *tablespoon sesame seeds*
½ *cup blanched almonds*
9 *to* 10 *cups flour*
confectioners' sugar

The lard should be at room temperature. Cream it well with the sugar, adding the grated lemon rind and cinnamon.

Place sesame seeds in a small, dry skillet and toast them over low heat, shaking the pan frequently so that they toast evenly. Remove from pan and cool.

Place almonds in a pan in a 350 degree oven until they are golden brown. Pulverize them in a blender, or in a Mouli grater. Add to the first mixture along with sesame seeds.

Add enough flour until the mass is quite brittle and will just hold together. Knead lightly for a few minutes.

Divide dough into 2 portions and roll 1 portion out on floured table, cloth or board until it is just less than ½ inch thick. Cut into ovals with a cutter. Reserve scraps for re-rolling.

Roll the second portion of dough, and handle in the same way. Then re-roll scraps and cut into ovals.

Line a baking sheet (2 may be necessary) with white paper, parchment or paper napkins. Place cookies very close together on the lined baking sheet. Bake in a preheated oven (325 degrees) on the center rack. Bake for 20 to 30 minutes, or until cookies are very light golden in color, but not brown. Remove from oven and cool. When cookies are completely cool, roll them in confectioners' sugar. These keep well. Yield: about 90 cookies.

POLISH MAZURKA

Here is a recipe for a simple bar cooky that goes well with cooked fruit desserts.

1 3/4 *cups butter*
1 3/4 *cups sugar*
8 *hard-cooked egg yolks, mashed*
1 *teaspoon vanilla*
4 *cups sifted all-purpose flour*
1/2 *teaspoon salt*
1 *egg white*
1 *teaspoon water*
2 *cups blanched, sliced almonds*

Lightly grease an 11 x 16 jelly-roll pan.

Cream butter with sugar. Add mashed hard-cooked egg yolks and vanilla. Gently stir in flour mixed with salt. Press dough into prepared pan, and chill until dough is firm.

Set oven at 350 degrees.

Mix egg white lightly with water, then brush mixture over top of dough. Sprinkle with almonds, and bake in preheated oven for 50 to 60 minutes. Cool slightly before slicing into small bars or squares. Yield: approximately 96.

Index